# IN SEARCH OF
# NICE AMERICANS

# IN SEARCH OF NICE AMERICANS

★ ★ ★ ★ ★

## OFF THE GRID, ON THE ROAD AND STATE TO STATE IN TRUMP'S AMERICA

## GEOFF STEWARD

Biteback Publishing

First published in Great Britain in 2017 by
Biteback Publishing Ltd
Westminster Tower
3 Albert Embankment
London SE1 7SP
Copyright © Geoff Steward 2017

ISBN 978-1-78590-263-5

10 9 8 7 6 5 4 3 2 1

A CIP catalogue record for this book is available from the British Library.

‐    Set in Minion Pro

Printed and bound in Great Britain by
CPI Group (UK) Ltd, Croydon CR0 4YY

*For Tom Hanks*

# THE ITINERARY IN A NUTSHELL

**DAY 1: 1 AUGUST**

Fly to Seattle. The Edgewater.

**DAY 2: 2 AUGUST**

Explore Seattle. Evening gig: Hurray for the Riff Raff. The Edgewater.

**DAY 3: 3 AUGUST**

Collect car rental and drive to Olympic National Park. Olympic Lodge Port Angeles.

**DAY 4: 4 AUGUST**

Olympic National Park. Olympic Lodge Port Angeles.

**DAY 5: 5 AUGUST**

Olympic National Park. Lake Quinault Lodge.

**DAY 6: 6 AUGUST**

Drop off car and fly to Juneau to cruise Alaska's Glacier Country. *Wilderness Adventurer* ship.

## DAY 7: 7 AUGUST

Glacier Bay National Park. *Wilderness Adventurer* ship.

## DAY 8: 8 AUGUST

Glacier Bay National Park. *Wilderness Adventurer* ship.

## DAY 9: 9 AUGUST

Icy Strait. *Wilderness Adventurer* ship.

## DAY 10: 10 AUGUST

Chichagof Island/Baranof Island. *Wilderness Adventurer* ship.

## DAY 11: 11 AUGUST

Frederick Sound/Stephens Passage. *Wilderness Adventurer* ship.

## DAY 12: 12 AUGUST

Fords Terror/Endicott Arm. *Wilderness Adventurer* ship.

## DAY 13: 13 AUGUST

Depart Juneau. Fly to Salt Lake City, via Seattle. Drive to Sundance Resort.

## DAYS 14–17: 14–17 AUGUST

At leisure. Sundance Resort.

## DAY 18: 18 AUGUST

Fly from Salt Lake City to San Francisco. Drive to Yosemite. Tin Lizzie Inn.

**DAYS 19–20: 19–20 AUGUST**
Explore Yosemite. Tin Lizzie Inn.

**DAY 21: 21 AUGUST**
Drive to Los Angeles. Hotel Mr C.

**DAY 22: 22 AUGUST**
LA insider tour. Hotel Mr C.

**DAY 23: 23 AUGUST**
Universal Studios Hollywood. Hotel Mr C.

**DAY 24: 24 AUGUST**
Fly to Nashville. Hermitage Hotel.

**DAY 25: 25 AUGUST**
Nashville on foot tour. Hermitage Hotel.

**DAY 26: 26 AUGUST**
Countryside touring. Hermitage Hotel.

**DAY 27: 27 AUGUST**
Nashville at leisure. Evening gig: Opry Behind the Curtain tour.
Hermitage Hotel.

**DAY 28: 28 AUGUST**
Drive to Savannah. Marshall House.

**DAY 29: 29 AUGUST**

Savannah insider tour. Marshall House.

**DAY 30: 30 AUGUST**

Drive to Great Smoky Mountains. Blackberry Farm.

**DAYS 31–32: 31 AUGUST–1 SEPTEMBER**

At leisure. Blackberry Farm.

**DAY 33: 2 SEPTEMBER**

Drive to Atlanta airport. Westin Atlanta Airport Hotel.

**DAY 34: 3 SEPTEMBER**

Fly to Liberia, Costa Rica. Journey to Punta Islita.

**DAYS 35–39: 4–8 SEPTEMBER**

At leisure. Punta Islita.

**DAY 40: 9 SEPTEMBER**

Departure.

**DAY 41: 10 SEPTEMBER**

Arrival in UK. Welcome home!

# CHAPTER ONE

*1992 – Walkman – dinner selfies – every six minutes*
*– David Bowie and Prince – sabbatical*
SOUNDTRACK: PRINCE – 'WHEN DOVES CRY'

I should be upfront with you. This is not quite a travelogue; it is not quite an autobiography; it is not quite a motivational self-help book; it is not quite a mid-life crisis. Frankly, I am not quite sure what it is that I have written or quite why you are reading it. Nonetheless, I have written it and you are reading it. I have had two books published previously: one was a children's novel (which outsold Anthea Turner's autobiography published the same week, as did all other books published that week); and the other was a textbook on brand protection. This should be better than both of them. I'm glad we have got that out of the way. I think we are going to get on just fine.

The reason we are both here is that I have grown restless. Admittedly, it has been a slow growth rate; almost twenty-five years. One of my sperm has grown into a motorist in the time it has taken for my wanderlust to re-emerge. But, in my defence, I have been a bit busy.

You see, I last travelled in 1992. By 'travelled', I don't mean commuting on the 06.29 from Haywards Heath to Blackfriars, or driving on the A303 to Cornwall, or flying to Dubai for ten days of fake plastic holidays. That's not travelling; that's just getting there. Despite regular attempts by Southern Rail to thwart me, I have just been getting there every day since, and sometimes back if the train crew hasn't become oddly diminutive ('Train cancelled due to temporary shortage of train crew'). The travelling I am talking about here is authentic Jack Kerouac travelling; romantic, carefree, cash-free, traveller's cheque (do they still exist?) travelling; chucking some denim shorts, some tie-dye T-shirts and a Swiss army penknife (in case I had to whittle wood in a youth hostel in Sydney) into my green Karrimor backpack (do they still exist?) and hitting the road. Going off to find myself in south-east Asia and fulfil my destiny of becoming a musician, an artist or a writer.

1992. That shouldn't be very long ago. But alas it is. Travelling was very different back then. The backpack space that I saved on iPads, iPods and Kindles (and multiple chargers), I filled with a Filofax (like an iPad but made of paper), a Walkman (like an iPod but boxier), and books (like a Kindle but without backlighting). It was in the dark (or, depending on your age and perspective, enlightened) days when internet was where you kicked a football, when playlists were compilations, and when no one had yet developed the urge to take photographs of their mirrors or their meals to airmail back to their friends to demonstrate their happiness.

Travelling in 1992 involved forgetting (as opposed to blocking) your friends, when having twenty friends was impressive. In Facebook terms, a mere twenty friends would label you a self-harming loser, albeit that the term 'friend' has now been redefined to include someone you have never met. After I left England for my gap year, I didn't communicate with my twenty (well, OK, six) close friends for ten months. I survived. Even they survived. Neither of us seemed to notice the other's absence. When I returned home, they hadn't forgotten what I looked like despite my dearth of mirror photographs. Nor do I recall them asking to view photographs of my dinners, which is a shame as I ate locust in Thailand and snake in China (because it was the cheapest dish on the menu and the numerals were English whereas the characters were Chinese). I think you will agree that would have made for an excellent slideshow, for which I would also have made one of my legendary accompanying mix tapes with a witty, pun-filled title such as 'Low-Cost Meals' or 'The Locust Eaters'.

Now I have decided, twenty-four years later, that it is time to travel again. Time that my days are no longer broken down into chargeable time. Time that time becomes my own again. 'Billable time' are two words I intend to replace with 'time out' or, ideally, 'What time is it?' I want to abandon exactitude, accountability, Oxford commas, and precision. For exactly three months. For, you see, I didn't become a musician, an artist or a writer after all. Instead, when I returned to England in 1993, I truly found myself. And I found that, disappointingly, myself was a lawyer. I hope you will forgive me and read on.

Lawyers generally charge their clients by 'the unit'. A unit is six minutes, so there are ten units in an hour. Units are recorded electronically by 'smart-timers' on our screens using a piece of software called CD Tracker; CD stands for *'carpe diem'* in Latin, or in lawyer-speak 'charge the day'. As soon as we start working on a particular case, we click on the appropriate smart-timer, the meter starts running and the client gets charged for our time. Every lawyer is then assessed by their own utilisation rate: for how many units of six minutes every day have they been recording chargeable time? Non-chargeable time, for example tasks such as giving seminars, writing articles, keeping on top of legal developments, mentoring younger lawyers, visiting clients, networking with other lawyers, having a coffee or lunch, or being sociable with work colleagues, needs to be made up, as it is time not properly utilised. Utilisation rate is assessed against a standard, which varies from firm to firm, of at least six chargeable hours a day. The chargeable unit is institutional and constitutional in the legal profession.

I have been lawyering for twenty-four years. If I assume an average of six chargeable hours a day, which any London lawyer will know is a conservative estimate, over twenty-four years (after deducting holidays and weekends), this equates to over 300,000 units. George Best, Oliver Reed, Pete Doherty and Amy Winehouse combined would have struggled to get through that many units in their prime. As a result, I am no longer in my prime either.

When I was in my prime and began work as a fresh-faced junior solicitor, there were no emails and no smart-timers. I didn't have a computer, either on my desk or at home. I couldn't type. My secretary could, and she had a typewriter and a bottle of Tipp-Ex. In those simpler times, the most stressful part of my day was the post tray. Every morning at 9 a.m. our general office staff would deposit the day's post in a tray in the corridor. That would be the only unexpected interruption to my day, aside from the occasional (but rare) fax of fading ink. My firm's then managing partner used to say that he had had a busy morning if he had not completed *The Times* crossword by 11 a.m. This was only the early 1990s; it's not that long ago. I could control and structure my day with: meetings arranged days in advance; written advice; or drafting or research time, valuable quiet time to devote myself entirely to a planned task, without disturbance. On the whole, the job was more sedate and less stressful.

But client requirements have developed at the same pace as technology: now they expect immediate advice; compliance with tight deadlines (requiring work late at night and over weekends); they seethe in a way that they never used to seethe; and the cause of their seething is generally a failure to respond to their email within the same day (or, often, the same hour). Lawyers are in the service sector; I am in the service sector; I accept that. The partners in my firm pride ourselves on the personal hands-on service and responsiveness we provide to clients, which our clients are entitled to as they pay a lot of money for our time.

They deserve and receive excellent service, but that comes at great personal cost. When you are selling your time, it doesn't leave much spare. I am contactable and responding to emails until midnight every day of the week, over weekends and on holiday. Being on holiday simply means doing conference calls from a more difficult venue, with my kids arguing and smashing things in the background. If I don't provide that service, then my competitors will be only too happy to pick up from where I left off. I recently saw an advertisement on a train from the litigation department of a nationwide law firm who were advertising their services with the following slogan: '*Now, as in today, as in immediately*'. To me, that says it all about the sacrifices now required to attract clients in the modern legal services sector.

It is just the way of the internet-connected world. The genie is out of the bottle, so I don't complain about it because I have evolved to accept it and, more tellingly, my generation is responsible for it. I have made a good career out of the law; it is stimulating work with challenging clients and I have earned good money from it. It is not going to change now; it is too late. But I do need a break from it. It is time for me to go on a diet: I have gorged on emails and they have gorged on me, but now I have decided to remove myself from email and go off the grid for three months. I am taking a sabbatical. For the first time in over twenty years, I won't be accounting for every six minutes of my life and it feels good.

So why now, when my career is going fairly well? Why not take my sabbatical, as many do, shortly before retirement?

I have acted on some interesting trials and disputes involving: Formula One teams fighting over who said Lotus first; brewers fighting over who has the right to use 'Budweiser' – the Czechs who used it first or the Americans who used it most; faked G-force testing of aeroplane seats installed in A330s, A380s and B777s (when I learned that the 'brace, brace' position is not to save you in the event of a plane crash but to ensure that you break your own neck and die quickly); the governing body of cycling, the UCI, and the question of whether they might have been complicit in Lance Armstrong's and the US Postal Service team's sophisticated doping programme when they overlooked a positive test of the sport's most valuable asset; and the mis-sale to thousands of customers by a major bank of interest rate hedging products. I accept that the last one is stretching the definition of 'interesting' to the same extent that Facebook is stretching the definition of 'friends', but on the whole, my cases have been interesting and rewarding and the time has flown.

But then something happened. Something unexpected. Something tragic. Something epiphanous that caused me to re-evaluate my life.

David Bowie and Prince both died.

Each artist had featured on my 'Kangaroo Backpacking' compilation tape in 1992: the avant-garde keyboard-enhanced funkiness (despite there being no bass guitar at all – genius!) of 'When Doves Cry', segueing into the pot-enhanced junkiness of 'Andy Warhol' (as in hole). Admittedly, Bowie was twenty years older than me when he died, and he had no doubt ingested a number of exotic life-reducing substances which I haven't encountered so much during my time as a litigator. But Prince was only ten years older than me when he died in an elevator. I could quite merrily continue suing and being sued for another decade, only to keel over in the office lift without breathing pure Alaskan air or inhaling the honky-tonk mustiness of a Nashville bar. Incidentally, the lifts at my firm in which any keeling would be done are made by a company called Schindler. I would like to think that Steven Spielberg would approve of us having Schindler's lifts, but I don't want that to be my final amusing thought as I draw my terminal breath. And, as I will explain shortly, the bar is pretty high in my extended family for final utterances.

So that is why I have decided to take my sabbatical now. As Bowie and Prince have expired prematurely, I need to shift my focus away from work for a while, before I do the same. I need to break from the law and remove myself from the south-east bubble. I need to surround myself with ordinary people again, people who don't take themselves too seriously and would rather, on a Friday night, watch *Mock the Week* than *The Ten O'Clock News*.

The word 'sabbatical' originates from the Hebrew 'Shabbat', meaning literally 'a ceasing'. Its modern-day meaning is 'an extended absence in the career of an individual in order to achieve something'. I feel the last part of this definition imposes excessive pressure on me: I simply want the luxury of spare time again and to spend three months getting up just in time to watch *Pointless* with the kids. But Wikipedia is didactic and tells me that a true sabbatical taker should write a book or travel extensively. Not wanting to disappoint Wikipedia, I have decided to do both. So that is why we are here, you and me; that is why I am writing and that is what you are reading.

My first, unplanned, travel destination, though, is determined by a non-celebrity death.

# CHAPTER TWO

*Death of an outlaw – divorced dads – new boots*
*– Moby Dick – apparitions – medical negligence*
*– ham sandwiches – blessed fruit*
SOUNDTRACK: JEFF BUCKLEY – 'HALLELUJAH'

'You're not all sleeping with Ann, are you?' I ask apprehensively.

'Ann's not sleeping, she's dead,' jokes Gerry.

This is how the conversation runs between the former partner of one of my current partner's five sisters, and me when he picks me up from Cork airport. Gerry has been estranged from the woman he never married, but with whom he still very successfully brings up two kids as a hands-on father, for around five years. His mother-outlaw (if he was never married to her daughter, she can't be his in-law) has just died. Ann is (now was) also my mother-outlaw, as I am also not married to one of her other divorced daughters, Jackie. It's a modern family.

Divorce doesn't fuss the Irish, who don't bother with social stigmas. Being a divorced man myself, I find their total indifference towards divorce to be surprisingly refreshing. 'Surprisingly' because, contrary to what you might think, the Irish are readily able to distinguish between their strict Catholic beliefs and the fiction of some marriages with the sniffy dismissal of a 'so what' or a 'cop yourself on'. 'Refreshing' because I live in the south-east of England, where the social ostracising meted out to divorced dads – particularly by wives on the school run, anxious that their own husbands stick around long enough to pay for their next piece of cosmetic surgery and a Kennel Club-bred French bulldog (or whichever trophy dog is in vogue at the time of print) – has a puritanical quality normally reserved for those with sixteenth-century beliefs rather than those with 16-valve Range Rover Evoques. The Irish way is better.

When I first met Jackie's father, in the pub (naturally), he didn't know his daughter was back in Youghal, nor did he know she had a new man. In egg terms, his reaction was sunny side up rather than over easy. He turned on his bar stool, smiled at me, and said: ''Ave ye gat a nu pair o' boots der, Jacqueline?' To be fair, his observational skills couldn't be faulted. She was indeed wearing a new pair of Uggs. The fact she was also wearing a new partner did not require comment. I liked that.

The Irish way of death is also better, as I am about to learn. Jackie's mother may have lacked the worldwide celebrity of David Bowie or Prince, but in Youghal she was a megastar.

Youghal is a historic, walled seaport community on the coastline of east Cork. One of its claims to fame, perhaps its only claim to fame (apart from having a lighthouse, which I have always felt was an ambitious attempt to impress tourists), is *Moby Dick*. Many of the outdoor scenes of the now irrelevant 1956 Gregory Peck film set in New Bedford, Massachusetts, were in fact filmed by director John Huston in Youghal. A pub in the town, overlooking the Atlantic coast, is named after the film. Youghal has a population of 8,000. Most of them have drunk in Moby Dick's with Ann Foley. Ann had no way of knowing that her liver was not best placed for being a local at Moby Dick's.

You see, Ann had the misfortune of having a rhesus negative blood type, but giving birth to rhesus positive babies. This was viewed as a bad thing in the 1970s, as some of the rhesus positive blood could have passed through the bloodstream into her placenta and she might have developed antibodies to it. Such dangerous antibodies, if left in her system, could seriously damage or kill the foetus in a future pregnancy. During the 1970s and 1980s, Ann's approach to reproduction was one year on, one year off, so the likelihood of future pregnancy was high in her case. The development of anti-D immunoglobulin, a product made from donated blood, should have been a positive development to obviate any risk to future babies. For her first four children, it was.

But in 1977, the year her fifth child was born, a batch of blood was contaminated because one donor, whose plasma had been used to make the anti-D, had jaundice and hepatitis but this had been missed due to a sloppy screening process by the Irish Blood Transfusion Service Board (the BTSB). Ann received the contaminated blood, as did Anita Roddick of the Body Shop. To compound the negligence, despite three BTSB employees realising the mistake, no alarm was raised and no action was taken to trace the women who received doses from that batch. But that wasn't the final mistake made. In 1994, the alarm was finally raised and a national screening exercise for hepatitis C took place in Ireland. Ann was part of that programme and, staggeringly, the BTSB missed the virus in her again.

Ann was oblivious to the state-injected death sentence until she was diagnosed with liver cancer three years ago, found to have been caused by the anti-D immunoglobulin blood products contaminated with hepatitis C administered to her following the birth of her fifth child in 1977. Ann didn't pander to the social stigma of the 'C-word'. Instead, she thought 'so what', copped herself on, and simply told everyone she was 'here for a good time, not for a long time'. With the damages award she received from the Hepatitis C Compensation Tribunal, she took herself off to Medjugorje.

I had never heard of Medjugorje. Until 1981, neither had most people outside of Bosnia and Herzegovina. But then six local schoolchildren, merrily playing in the impoverished former Yugoslav town, witnessed a Marian apparition and well and truly put their hometown on the map. Now, I was also a schoolchild in 1981. I often used to play with my friends in the back fields between Hartlepool and Elwick. There were things I saw which I would tell my parents about, such as sticklebacks, puffballs, an escaped parakeet and even on one occasion a local weirdo who went on to achieve notoriety by also escaping… from a police station before going on to commit a triple murder. There were things I saw which I would not tell my parents about, like a dumped stash of pornographic magazines which Glen Beamson and I found in a plastic bag by the beck, and the breasts of Alison Waters. I feel I should probably explain the latter. One summer's evening, after nightfall, Jonny Alcock and I had climbed a tree to watch Alison, four years ahead of us at school, and indisputably the best-looking girl in West Park – and most probably in the northern hemisphere, or so it felt to us at a time when we had never seen a topless girl before – taking off her bra in her bedroom overlooking the fields, little knowing that she too was being overlooked.

But I am fairly sure I wouldn't have come home from playing in the fields to tell my parents I had seen a vision of the Virgin Mary. If I had, I would have had the back of my leg slapped for lying and been sent to bed without any tea.

Fair fucks (as they say in Ireland) to the Bosnian school-children, though. They were braver than me; and their parents, apparently, believed them. The children are still alive today; and the apparition is still appearing to some of them, in their adult form. The Virgin Mary believes in punctuality, appearing to one of the schoolchildren, who grew up to become a full-time visionary (my careers adviser never gave me this as an option), on the 25th of each month, while one of the other school-children receives her 'messages' (to my regret, my research has been unable to verify that Mary has modernised and is sending text messages of herself in front of mirrors, or of her dinner) on the 2nd of each month.

Although I should not let my own faithlessness and appari-tion-envy influence you, it seems I am in good company. The Catholic Church has declared the apparitions *'non constat'*, which means that it cannot confirm the supernatural status without more evidence, but will not stand in the way of allow-ing the impoverished town of Medjugorje to sell fridge magnets to eager pilgrims. In 1996, a Vatican press office spokesman per-mitted Catholics to continue to undertake pilgrimages there, albeit with an undertone of thinly veiled cynicism: 'You cannot say people cannot go there until it has been proven false. This has not been said, so anyone can go… if they want.' For such an official communiqué, I am full of admiration for the petulant shrug at the end. (On the subject of religious shrugs, outside St Paul's Cathedral at lunchtime, I once saw a guy wearing a sandwich board saying 'Free Shrugs', and whenever he saw anyone reading it, he would forlornly shrug his shoulders at them.)

Despite my and the Vatican's views, what cannot be doubted is the faith that over a million Catholics a year still have in the messages attributed to Your Lady (don't include me in this) of Medjugorje. It is estimated that thirty million pilgrims have visited the town since 1981. Some have reported visual phenomena including the sun spinning in the sky; others have reported visual complaints including damage to their retina. One such visitor was Ann Foley, and seemingly it did the trick. Having been given mere months to live, she defied all medical opinion and lived another three years, during which she certainly had a good time, thanks to the improbable Lady of Medjugorje. Even her own doctors concluded that there could be no medical explanation for the terminal tumours on her liver changing shape and concluded that Ann's own explanation that the Lady had performed a miracle upon her was as plausible as any they could offer. It seems that the '*non constat*' shrug is contagious, passing from the clerical to the medical.

Ann's good times, prolonged by those three miraculous years, have now ended two weeks before my sabbatical is due to start, so Jackie and I add to our travel itinerary an unscheduled trip to Youghal for the funeral. Typically for the Irish, there is no languishing morbidity or introspective grieving; this is going to be a celebration of a life well lived, and Gerry is already cracking corpse jokes after I have been in the car for a few minutes. I say 'the car' rather than 'his car' because as we walked towards the only car parked in the cross-hatched no-parking area immediately outside the entrance to Cork airport, I asked (fairly,

I thought), 'Is this your car?', to which he urgently replied, 'No, it's stolen, get in quick.' I think, or at least hope, he was joking.

The start of this chapter feels a long time ago, but my question to Gerry had been raised because I am apprehensive about seeing Ann again. Alive, she hadn't scared me (well, not much), but I know she is now dead and lying in the living room, in an open coffin. I also know that she has a very close-knit family, and that Jackie and her seven brothers and sisters had not only been taking it in turns to sleep with Ann during her final moments when she was sent back home for palliative care, but they also now have a roster for sleeping with her cadaver in the lounge until she is buried (at least I hope that's when it stops). I am English. I am not used to this fearless embracing of death. The cowardly English tend to hide from death and, ostrich-like, hope that if they don't see it, it won't see them. In Ireland, they touch it, crack jokes in front of it and eat ham sandwiches around it.

I wasn't there when Ann died, but the incident that all family members proudly felt had shown her at her courageous and humorous best was when the priest came round to administer the last rites. She hadn't spoken for hours, her breathing had slowed and she seemed to be on her way out. As the priest was doing his mortal duty, she opened her eyes, looked at him and her family with defiant eyes and said, 'I'm not going anywhere.' Those were her final words. I think that is braver and funnier than the epitaph on Spike Milligan's tombstone, which he no doubt had years to prepare as his final quip, and which reads: 'I told you I was ill.' Predictably, Milligan too was Irish.

When we get to the house, sure enough there she is, lying in the middle of the sitting room, wearing her Michael Kors glasses and favourite maroon leather jacket. Aside from a slightly waxy sheen to her complexion to mask the jaundice, she looks better than the last time I saw her. Her thirteen grandchildren are all taking it in their stride, playing on their iPads in the same room and occasionally peering into the coffin to stroke their nanny's face or hands, and to slip a bottle of Coors Light and twenty Silk Cut Purple into the coffin for her to take with her, a gesture she would have appreciated.

As I admitted in the opening chapter, I probably have six genuine (rather than virtual) close friends. I would like to hope that with family, friends, work colleagues and pre-divorce couple-friends who would rather see me dead than alive, I might get around fifty people to trouble themselves to turn up at the crematorium after my sudden demise in a Schindler's lift. (In fact, the main reason I had four children was to boost the capacity at my funeral: I figure that if each of them marries, stays married and has two kids, then I have secured two full pews of funeral attendees). Whereas Ann has fifty people pass down the line alongside her coffin, expressing their sorrow for your trouble, within only the first ten minutes of the official opening time of the rosary (advertised in the local newspaper for 5–8 p.m.). It is a closely choreographed event, with crowd control and even hastily erected road signs directing mourners to the house.

I will not pretend to understand what is going on during the rosary. It seems that it was another Marian apparition which kicked the whole tradition off in 1214 when she appeared to Saint Dominic. No doubt Our Lady is present again in Youghal this evening, but try as I might, I can't see her and am beginning to feel excluded. My social exclusion then magnifies as everyone follows a drill for which I am singularly undrilled. A genial, gin-pickled giant of a priest arrives, fiddles with some beads and mumbles lots of monotonous, metronomous words through a microphone, which are slavishly repeated without intonation or inflection by the hundreds of people gathered outside the house. I thought the Irish wit was quick until I hear the speed with which they recite and clutter the Hail Mary. Despite them recounting it a hundred times (it certainly felt like that many), not once do I manage to discern with any accuracy what they are all saying. Something to do with being a blessed woman (which I interpret in its non-insulting form for Ann's sake) and having a blessed fruit in her womb (which I take to mean Jesus rather than a holy lemon). As I can't hear what they are saying, I just keep mumbling 'blessed are the cheesemakers'; if Our Lady hears me, she keeps quiet. She also forgives the live football commentary of England v. Slovakia which inexplicably goes off in my jacket pocket when I haven't been able to get a signal all evening. Miracles really do happen, albeit England still don't win.

As the throng dies down, I go to have a look at the Book of Condolences. In doing so, I pass Auntie Jo. I don't know Auntie Jo, but she is obviously impressed by me, as she asks Gerry if I am a doctor on account of the fact that I am wearing a jacket and look posh.

'Jeez, it's a bit late now for a doctor, Auntie Jo. Ann's dead.'

The Book of Condolences is signed by over five hundred people who pass by the coffin to pay their respects, join in the ritualistic murmuring and take a ham sandwich. The next day I estimate that around eight hundred people attend the church service and the burial. If David Bowie or Prince had died in Youghal, I doubt they would have got more than Ann Foley.

All this sad but oddly uplifting ritual reminds me of my

childhood in Hartlepool, where families remain for generations (my mother is in her seventies and is still remembered by some as the little girl from the sweetshop), and makes me realise how important community still is in some places. Places other than the south-east, where I now live. My next-door neighbour died in his eighties a few months ago. I had never met him. I am not a bad neighbour – or at least no worse than him: he had never met me either. To be fair, I have been busy. The Irish way is better, though. I am hoping that some time off work will restore my humanity, even towards Americans. As a first step, I resolve to take round some ham sandwiches to my neighbour's widow, while she is still alive.

# CHAPTER THREE

*American lawyers – travelogues – a list*
SOUNDTRACK: BRUCE SPRINGSTEEN – 'AMERICAN LAND'

Once I liked Americans. I liked them very much, in fact. But working with them has, over the years, eroded my partiality. 'My way or the highway' is an American idiom (even though, ironically, they have unilaterally decided that freeway is a better word than highway). Most American lawyers either can't understand or can't believe that lawyers from one of the oldest and best-respected legal systems in the world might know comparatively more English law than they do.

In 1995, the first year that law firms such as mine started communicating externally using emails, I received a viral email which I still have pinned to my office notice board, as it perfectly summarises the attitude of American lawyers when communicating with English lawyers who are courteously and patiently trying to give them the correct advice. It purported to be an actual transcript of a shipping radio conversation and it went like this:

Americans: Please divert your course fifteen degrees to the north to avoid a collision.

Canadians: Recommend you divert YOUR course fifteen degrees to the south to avoid a collision.

Americans: This is the captain of a US Navy ship. I say again, divert YOUR course.

Canadians: No, I say again, you divert YOUR course.

Americans: THIS IS THE AIRCRAFT CARRIER USS *ABRAHAM LINCOLN*, THE SECOND LARGEST SHIP IN THE UNITED STATES' ATLANTIC FLEET. WE ARE ACCOMPANIED BY THREE DESTROYERS, THREE CRUISERS AND NUMEROUS SUPPORT VESSELS. I DEMAND THAT YOU CHANGE YOUR COURSE FIFTEEN DEGREES NORTH, THAT'S ONE-FIVE DEGREES NORTH, OR COUNTER-MEASURES WILL BE UNDERTAKEN TO ENSURE THE SAFETY OF THIS SHIP.

Canadians: This is a lighthouse. Your call.

In addition to their steadfast belligerence, most American lawyers much prefer talking to reading. They exercise their First Amendment right to freedom of speech, and speak freely (for a handsome fee) and at length. As a result, Americans take longer at everything, such as conference calls or joining the Second World War. I would never question the presentational skills of Americans. Their education system encourages confident public speaking. Public speaking is what they are good at. What they never learn, however, is public listening. Rather than reviewing and carefully thinking about concise, logical, well-written legal reasoning, they prefer to demand written advice (usually within the hour), not read it properly and then painfully draw out the exact same advice, with incessant interruption, over hour-long conference calls, which must only ever be held in Eastern Standard Time. The skill deployed by English lawyers is to steer the conversation in such a way as to allow the American lawyers to believe that they have saved the day and come up with the solution themselves. At the conclusion of the call they will then ask you to amend your previous advice; so you wait an hour and then obediently send them your previous advice, unchanged.

But there was a time, predating my legal career, when I really liked Americans; so much so that my first destination in my gap year was the US, at a time when the road more travelled by backpackers was south-east Asia. Growing up in the defunct north-east of Thatcherite Britain, America was unaffordable. My family holidayed in Blackpool, caravanned in Brittany and, latterly, self-catered in Menorca. As a child, New York and Disneyland were magical but unattainable. But after leaving university, and using my law degree to great effect by working in a dog food cannery in Wisbech, I had saved up enough money to buy a Delta air pass, which was like inter-railing on planes. My air pass entitled me to turn up at any airport unannounced and be on stand-by for any US destination of my choosing: as long as there was a seat left, I could travel. It was *On the Road* on planes.

During the rest of my travels that year, I lived and worked in Sydney and backpacked around Fiji, New Zealand, Australia, Malaysia, Thailand, Singapore, Hong Kong and China, yet the place that has always drawn me back is the States. I found the people warm, welcoming and hospitable, the cities dynamic and exciting, but it was the diverse scenery, the wide open spaces and the big skies that truly got under my skin.

I have been there since on lawyering business, to New York, Boston, Chicago, St Louis, Portland and San Francisco, but touring hotel foyers, conference rooms, and attorneys' offices has not quite captured my imagination in the same way as the National Parks once did. When I obtained approval from my partners to take my sabbatical, there was really only one destination for my travels and the subject of this book. I want to rekindle my love of America and its people and, to keep Wikipedia happy, I want to do it in the medium of an autobiographical travelogue. I want to leave the attorneys behind and go in search of nice Americans.

My favourite author, Evelyn Waugh, described *The Diary of a Nobody*, by George and Weedon Grossmith, as 'the funniest book in the world'. The Nobody in question, a fictional clerk called Charles Pooter, begins by saying: 'Everybody who was Anybody was publishing diaries, so why shouldn't a Nobody?' I have decided to take the same approach as Pooter. Autobiographies of illiterate D-listers, churned out by kop-out cash-in publishers, litter the shelves of Waterstones and WHSmith. Why shouldn't I, an unknown, write my own autobiographical travelogue and the second funniest book in the world?

I write myself an action plan of ten things I would like to achieve while travelling in America:

1. Find some nice Americans (there must be some; after all, Tom Hanks is American)
2. Write a book
3. Go for a run every day
4. Give up Red Bull
5. Give up my BlackBerry
6. See a bear
7. Photograph a hummingbird

8. Meet someone called Jedidiah (I have always enjoyed Westerns and there is always someone called Jedidiah)

9. Derail Donald Trump's presidential election campaign (every little helps)

10. Stop writing myself action plans and do something spontaneous.

# CHAPTER FOUR

*Wigs – corporate lawyers – confusing the Americans*
*– Jesus Christ and Doctor Who – perfect calmness*
*– two spare-children – surviving without Charmaine*
SOUNDTRACK: THE EDWIN HAWKINS SINGERS
*– 'OH HAPPY DAY'*

I don't wear a wig. Jackie and my mother don't know I don't wear a wig, my children don't know, and most of my friends don't know. I don't like to disappoint them. You see, I am not desirous of male pattern baldness, but rather I am not a barrister. I am a solicitor. Solicitors don't wear wigs, at least not wigs especially designed for court.

Telling people that I am a litigator automatically causes their TV-brainwashed brains to conclude that I am the one who stands up in court. I am not. I am the one who sits down in court, crouching behind the one who stands up. I am not in the judge's direct line of sight, but if something goes wrong at trial (the trial bundles are inadequate, the shorthand writer doesn't turn up, or the witnesses perjure themselves) then both the judge and my own gallant barrister will turn to angrily stare at me, at which point I give them a little wave.

As a solicitor, it is my client who is either bringing or

defending the High Court claim. I have to find the client by networking with potential litigants and fellow professionals, which involves attending conferences, seminars, receptions and dinners, usually two or three nights a week. Once I have found a client in possession of a good fortune but in want of a lawyer (generally as a result of extreme schmoozing such as taking them on track days to Goodwood Motor Circuit to aid them with their decision as to which law firm to instruct) and who wants to sue or be sued, then it is my job to advise them on the merits of their case and to guide them through the litigation process, regularly writing to their opponent's solicitors to tell them how wrong they are.

It is also my job to gather in and prepare all of the evidence. Again, contrary to the understanding of my family, I am not a detective searching for smoking guns to send people to prison. I am a civil not a criminal lawyer. Gathering evidence for me involves project managing a team of paralegals and junior lawyers as they trawl through hundreds of thousands of client emails and electronic documents, labelling them as relevant or not relevant. Once this 'disclosure' phase is complete, it is then my job to prepare my client's written witness statements. Based upon lengthy 'proofing' interviews with witnesses, I then draft their witness statements by writing up their evidence for them, improving their grammar along the way.

Barristers, on the other hand, are trial advocates. At the risk of mixing my bird metaphors, a barrister will swan in and out of the case like a peacock. He or she will prepare the pleadings and might comment briefly on the evidence as it is prepared, but as a rule he or she will pay the case no particular attention until it is coming to trial and they are 'under brief', which means that the barrister has set aside however many weeks in which to exclusively cram for trial in return for a handsome fee. Barristers' brief fees can be eye-watering and some of the top QCs can command fees of over £1 million for a big trial. Why? Because they are geniuses and when on their feet, in the heat of trial, can outwit the judge, the witness, their opponent and usually their own instructing solicitors.

The trial itself is pure theatre.

At trial, I will wear my favourite suit (dark), black – never brown – shoes (polished), an un-pocketed shirt (white and ironed) and a tie (flamboyant), whereas a barrister gets to indulge his or her uniform fetish. A male barrister will wear a long, flowing gown over an elaborate buttoned jacket with a white tunic court shirt with attachable wing collar and starched, double-tabbed linen bands (white flappy things instead of a tie); and a female barrister will also wear a gown over a dark suit but with a court bib over a white top or a white tunic with a ladies' collar. To complete the look is the *pièce de résistance*, the exclusive tie-wig made of horsehair which covers half the head with a silly rat's tail at the back. They are hot and uncomfortable but confer gravitas and solemnity on court proceedings. If a barrister is not wearing his or her wig at trial, the judge (who wears Captain Jean-Luc Picard's *Star Trek: The Next Generation* uniform) will refuse to hear them, no matter how loudly they are talking.

Although the wig is what everyone is interested in, as an instructing solicitor sitting behind a barrister at trial, it is actually the flowing gown that is of more use to me. I like to wait until my barrister is on his or her hind legs, engaged in a particularly challenging piece of advocacy, taking heavy flak from the judge or cross-examining an awkward witness, before scribbling an inspired piece of thinking onto an index card in handwriting of which any overworked NHS doctor would be proud, and then tugging on the billowing cloth in front of me until a resigned hand reaches blindly backwards to grasp my index card. I then expect the QC to decipher, understand and seamlessly incorporate my trial-winning point into his or her submissions. On reflection, perhaps this is why barristers are paid so much money.

The relationship between barristers and their instructing solicitors is best summed up by the following incident from a trial. The QC was in the middle of his submissions when a note was passed forward from his instructing solicitor, in a manner not dissimilar to that which I have described. The QC glanced impatiently at it, looked again, paused in surprise, and said: 'My Lord, I am going to make a further point. It comes from behind me, but is *actually* correct.'

Having established that I am not clever enough to be a barrister, I should perhaps explain now how firms of solicitors operate. Law firms comprise four basic hierarchical positions: partners, associates, trainees and secretaries. The latter are the most important.

Partners are senior solicitors who are part owners of their firm (in the same way that fleas are part owners of their dog). They like attending as many meetings as possible, but don't like reading any papers for them or writing attendance notes of them. They like strategising and devising action plans, for associates to then implement for them while they take important clients out for 'supper' or 'dinner' (but definitely not 'tea', which is eaten by my native north-easterners but never by southern lawyers). They like posh venues for their tea but most of all they like PEP (profit per equity partner), or money to you and me.

Associates are younger solicitors and therefore don't require sleep or social lives; they prefer to work at weekends. Associates used to be called assistants, but this term confused American clients who thought that they were paying for secretaries. So the English legal market, pandering to the inferior vocabularies of our US counterparts, rebranded assistants as associates. They were too busy to notice the change to their nomenclature. The *raison d'être* of associates, or so one of my misguided fellow partners once told me in all seriousness, is to make partners look good.

Trainees leave university with law degrees, join a law firm and then undertake intense common-sense training. For two years they have to learn how to listen and pour coffee in meetings; how to count and spell; and how to carry important documents. Crucially, trainees must learn never to speak in meetings in case they inadvertently give advice to clients. Once they have mastered those skills, they qualify as associates and are entitled to command a salary of four times as much as a junior doctor.

For those who think I am being unfair on trainees, I offer up one true story by way of support. A hapless and feckless former trainee of my firm was asked by one of my corporate partners, Charles, to attend a meeting with a very important new client – Charles needed a note-taker, you see. Charles had stressed to the trainee the importance of making a good impression at this first meeting. Upon entering the client's office, Charles gave a confident handshake and introduced himself as Charles Meek. The trainee, nervous and confused in equal measure, followed Charles in, also shook the client's hand firmly, but then also introduced himself as Charles Meek. The client, to his credit, replied: 'One of you is lying.'

Secretaries, with whom partners share very few of their secrets (because knowledge is power, or so partners like to believe, including those who have no power and even less knowledge), seized upon the newly vacated and grammatically more accurate title of 'assistant' for themselves. A good PA is the nerve centre of a good, or even an average, lawyer. The most important role of a PA is to fill a partner's diary, preferably with overlapping meetings as partners feel more important when they are needed in two or more places (or countries) at the same time. Crucially, they need to ensure their partners' diaries are much fuller than their associates', to justify partners delegating most of the hard work to the associates.

My personal assistant is a joyful, indispensable Caribbean lady from Dominica called Charmaine. She is most definitely not from the Dominican Republic. She is from the Commonwealth of Dominica. They are both in the West Indies but they are completely different countries. Confuse them around Charmaine at your peril. I had no idea Dominica existed before I met her. Most people have never heard of it. There is a reason for this. It is one of the smallest countries on earth and has only around seventy thousand inhabitants, compared with the Dominican Republic's population of roughly ten million. But we Brits really should know Dominica as it was once a British crown colony and the official language is English. The Dominican Republic, on the other hand, is part of the Greater Antilles, near Haiti, and its official language is Spanish. I am informed by Charmaine that Dominica is vastly superior. So, to be clear, in case you ever meet her, Charmaine is not a Republican. I am hoping that I will meet lots of Americans who are also not Republicans.

Charmaine's surname is James, which confuses American clients into thinking she is a man; a state of mind that is difficult for them to dispel even when they have heard her unmistakably feminine tones on the telephone. Americans like to reverse things, like history, how to write dates and, seemingly, the order of names. Charmaine is not alone in having a confusing name for Americans; mine always confuses them, presumably due to its uniqueness, and their emails to me often begin with the impolite salutation 'Dear Steward'. This demonstrates formidable ineptitude on two counts: first, that they don't realise that first names are the names that come first in an email sign-off; and second, that whilst Stewart or Stuart might both be established first names for Brits, Steward remains only a surname or a bibbed job at a football ground. To get my own back, I like to take the same approach by opening my correspondence to them with 'Dear The Third'.

Unlike me, though, Charmaine is never angered by the mangling of the order of her name by Americans. She loves Jesus Christ and Custard Creams. These two saccharine pleasures give her fulfilment and make her the happiest and most unflappable person in EC4 (for any American readers, that is a zip code, not a person's name or a Star Wars droid). Her faith is unwavering, in Jesus not in me. She prays for me every night, probably for good reason, because she claims I am the first atheist she has ever met. I doubt this is true: most corporate lawyers don't believe in any God but themselves (and in turn believe that all other non-corporate lawyers duly worship them); but I accept that I am probably the first person to have brazenly told her that I don't believe that Noah lived to 950 years old and travelled in an ark. Everybody knows that only one person has ever lived that long and travelled in an improbable vessel and that is Doctor Who. More on him shortly.

Her faith does, however, give her a profitable life outside of the law. 'Profitable' because one lady in her church keeps giving Charmaine stuff: a fifty-pound note; a microwave oven; a new dress. 'Outside of the law' because whereas Charmaine believes she has received indirect gifts from God, I believe she has received stolen goods.

I am envious of Charmaine's faith. It gives her a perfect calmness, which is very conducive to working for a hyperactive lawyer fuelled on Red Bull and Revels. I test her good nature every day, but she always passes. For seven years I have been trying unsuccessfully to provoke her into using a swear word. Even her skin glows with a pious cleanliness. But what I am truly, truly envious of is her effortless ability to organise my life without getting what my children calmly call 'stressy'.

I will be on my own, though, for the next three months, without Charmaine. I will be typing this book myself, without Charmaine. All the best travelogues are well researched. This therefore will not be one of the best travelogues as I will also be doing all my own research, without the aid of a trainee. True to form as a partner, I will be winging it, providing you with occasional discourse and sharing thoughts, experiences and people I meet along the way.

The hardest part of having a sabbatical, aside from switching off my BlackBerry, is going to be having to run my own life and those of my four children and two spare-children (because Jackie and I aren't married, I am not permitted to call her children my stepchildren, so I prefer to call Jamie and Shauna my spare-children – in case anything should puncture my own).

I have never tried delegating to any of my offspring and if I did, it wouldn't end well. Being on sabbatical is going to involve doing everything for myself, from checking in for flights online to deciding where to go and then locating it. The only thing my children are good at locating is the nearest Wi-Fi. On the whole, they are like trainees, but without the qualifications. So the prospect of three months without Charmaine is daunting. But I have resolved to make a clean break from work and the support network that I enjoy there: no more safety net. I am going off the grid, on the road, state to state. I did it before; I can do it again. Here goes.

# CHAPTER FIVE

*Some introductions – a posh travel agent – a plastic figurine*
*– a collection of children and spare-children*
SOUNDTRACK: FAMILY OF THE YEAR – 'HERO'

If I am going to write a travelogue, I am going to have to be
honest with you. It is not entirely accurate to say that I will be
going on sabbatical without assistance. True, I won't have Charmaine to organise my life, but there are two other important
people to whom you need to be introduced before I leave: one
is a professional traveller; the other is a time traveller.

For an adventurous explorer, who turned his back on a life
of briefcasing in favour of a life of backpacking, Steve must be
as disappointed with his parents as I am with mine over their
choice of name. Steve is my 'sabbatical designer', which is a
posher, more exclusive job title for a travel agent. To be fair to
Steve, describing him as a travel agent would be like describing
me as the boss of Charmaine. He has been integral to the planning of the entire trip, recommending destinations, timings,
transport, tours, accommodation and even what to wear and
what to carry it in.

Steve is in his mid-thirties and resembles a more intelligent,
more likeable version of Jamie Oliver. Since deciding he was

more interested in the world than the world of finance, he has been on permanent sabbatical, building a network of relations with hotels and tour operators across North America, Latin America, China, India and south-east Asia. He focuses his business on self-important, egotistical professionals who consider themselves too busy and important to arrange their own trips. Law firm partners and bankers are therefore some of his most lucrative clients.

Steve is the opposite of his clients. He is diffident, down-to-earth and unpretentious. He is son-in-law material and had Jackie from 'hello'. We have had five meetings with Steve and countless email and telephone exchanges to build a bespoke trip designed around our interests. In essence, his brief is wildlife, music and film. In particular, we want to spend as much time as possible in 'America's Best Idea', the National Parks.

Steve has certainly delivered. I am holding in my hand a beautiful blue travel wallet, which contains flight and event tickets, hotel details, packing list and a spiral-bound day-by-day itinerary... with photographs. We will be taking in three of the fifteen most-visited National Parks: Olympic, Yosemite and the Great Smoky Mountains; as well as the more remote Glacier Bay National Park in Alaska. For music, we will be visiting Seattle (home of grunge) and Nashville (home of country); and for film, Utah (home of the Western) and LA (home of Hollywood). Somewhere out there must be some nice, normal Americans and I am going to find them. The only part of the itinerary which doesn't excite me is 'Day 41: Welcome Home'. That has the threatening ring of eternity and commuting about it.

In addition to Steve the professional traveller, I need to

introduce you to my time-travelling companion. Not Jackie: she is my life companion and she can't time-travel. I am talking now about my five-inch plastic poseable figurine of David Tennant as the Tenth Doctor, in an orange spacesuit. He will be accompanying me throughout. 'Why?' would be a fair question.

I do have one set of neighbours, who live opposite me (on the dark side of the street, in the shade of my oak tree), whom I do know. They are my close friends and carers, David and Shelagh. I am not sure how I reciprocate for them, but David fixes my house and my car, and when Jackie is away, Shelagh gives me lifts to the train station (Shelagh's Wheels) and cooks for me (Shelagh's Meals). She bakes a lovely courgette muffin and also cooks Christmas lunch for Jackie, my spare-children and me.

You may have already gathered from their generosity that they, like Charmaine, are good Christians (I seem to attract salvation). Last Christmas, I tested how devout their faith was. Each year they religiously lay out a wooden nativity set on a table in their hallway, so on Christmas Day, as we sat down for lunch, I sneaked off and replaced one of the wise men with the orange spacesuited Tenth Doctor and waited to see how long it would take them to notice. It wasn't until twelfth night, when they were packing up their cherished nativity set for another year, that they discovered their time-travelling intruder; hence proving my point that religious faith, especially at Christmas, is all just for show. I thought I had won and that that was the end of the joke. But David is very competitive and he kidnapped the Tenth Doctor.

In mid-January, despite David still being only across the road, I began receiving photographs by text from him of the Tenth Doctor outside of a Walmart in the States, at the Arlington

Cemetery in Washington DC, and even a flight tracker screen-grab of him flying back home across the Atlantic. David and Shelagh's daughter had become an air hostess.

So the Tenth Doctor, in addition to witnessing the birth of Jesus Christ, will also now be returning to the States to accompany me on my travels. Rather than publishing gloating holiday photographs of Jackie and me designed to induce envy, I will be posting imaginative photographs of the Tenth Doctor on Facebook to inform friends of my whereabouts. I am expecting him to go viral and to challenge James Corden's Carpool Karaoke with Adele.

As I have introduced my sabbatical designer, my neighbours and my plastic Doctor Who figurine, I should probably now also introduce you to my collection of children and spare-children, who are important cast members and may well feature in this narrative from time to time.

Teachers eulogise about children these days in a way that I am sure prevents most parents from recognising their own offspring. I won't be taking that approach. I am northern and prefer to be direct, objective and impartial. My English teacher, Mr Thompson, was an eccentric thespian who used to like to hold his lessons 'in the round' with him seated in the middle, legs crossed, elbow on his knee and hand gripping his temples, like an exaggerated Rodin sculpture. One time, he had picked on me to read a passage from Conrad's *The Secret Agent*. When I had finished, he asked me whether I liked Conrad.

'Not really, sir. He uses too many words.'

I got a laugh from the other boys. Thompson craned his neck to look me in the eye, swept back his hair, paused for dramatic effect, and said: 'Steward, I don't think I like you.'

He got a much bigger laugh from the boys than I did, but he wasn't smiling.

He was consistent, because at prize-giving on my last day at the school, I reminded him of that incident and he told me that the reason I had not won the English prize was because he still didn't like me. But he told me that he would always remember me, and that was flattery from George Thompson. The truth was he didn't care for dull pupils; he wanted pupils to contribute, to challenge him and to provoke a reaction in him. He was the best teacher I ever had.

Fortunately, I don't dislike any of my children or spare-children (although, like all parents, there are some I like more than others), but my approach to describing them will be more George Thompson than modern-day eulogising school reports. I will take them in the order in which they came out of my ex-wife or Jackie, not in order of importance.

Meggie (eighteen) is a great disappointment to me. She was not appointed as head girl. Other than that, her personal statement reads very well. She is popular and playful, with a slapstick sense of humour, and despite sounding like a southerner (speaking too quickly and too loudly) has evolved into a rather nice young lady. She is now proving more useful to me than she was during her previous seventeen years, as she can not only drive me to the pub but also buy me a pint of ale. She has a photographic memory which she uses to take photos of song lyrics rather than anything remotely academic. The best way of contacting Meggie is to share a new playlist with her on Spotify. Her ambition has always been to be famous for doing nothing (her role model is Paris Hilton); it is my prediction that she will achieve half of her goals.

It is difficult writing about my own children in a way that I find amusing without for ever alienating or mentally scarring them. I have therefore checked that Meggie is happy with the above description. She didn't ask for any amendments other than for me to ensure that she 'sounds better than Mimi, cos I am. And you can quote me on that.'

Mimi (sixteen) is not her real name. Emily is a pretty, feminine name, which is why Mimi didn't want to use it. Don't get me wrong, Mimi is pretty, but she is not feminine. As Meggie was too lazy to learn how to say Emily when she was learning to speak, she used to call her new sister Mimi. Her name is one of the only things that Meggie and Mimi have agreed upon since. Mimi shares far too many of my genes, which is why she is constantly locking horns with her mother and other horned beasts. She is a fiercely competitive, determined, self-motivated girl, who doesn't suffer fools gladly, and therefore doesn't suffer her youngest sister, Mary, at all. I am very close to Mimi; it is safer that way. She is hard-working and ambitious and wants to be a lawyer; I am hoping this book will put her off. In truth, I fear she is a born litigator.

Jamie (sixteen), my spare-son, is very floppy. His long, skinny limbs are floppy, his hair is floppy; both are unruly. But Jamie's personality is very disciplined. He is diligent, courteous, malleable and keeps his bedroom tidy. He looks like a surfer, until he gets on (and falls off) a surfboard. He has no criminal instinct, evidenced by regularly leaving teeth marks in chocolate stolen from the fridge. If you are going to steal a chocolate bar, at least finish it. If he wasn't my spare-son, I would want him as my son-in-law and I would certainly want him in the trenches alongside me, not least because he is a lot taller than me and an easier target. Jamie will go far in media, probably BBC Radio Shetland.

Shauna (fifteen), my spare-daughter, is full of hair, skin and attitude. She has a dark, full mane of curls that throws off different colours like a prism in sunlight. Her skin is that unique Irish pigment, a whiter shade of pale. Her attitude is that unique Irish combination of tempest, and calm before the tempest. She breaks horses but needs breaking herself. Her bedroom looks like it has been hit by one of her own tempests and she thinks her shower is a place to store clothes, with her bathroom floor serving as overflow. The best way to contact Shauna is through her constantly monitored social media; posting embarrassing photographs of her on Facebook tends to provoke the fastest response. She is immune to alarm clocks and the advisable method of waking her is to poke her with a big stick and run away. If I encounter a bear on sabbatical, I won't be afraid as I now know how to handle them. Shauna will either end up working for a conservation project caring for orphaned dolphins or be involved in an international incident, depending on what mood she is in.

My only boy, Joe (eleven), outshines the morning sun. He will not be a sportsman, unless chess or playing FIFA on the Xbox are counted as sports (he beats me at both). He is an affectionate, considerate lad with a lovely, gentle nature and is always keen to please. He displeases me with his indecision: he is at the age where he craves constant paternal endorsement, and he needs my input on every move – 'Um, Daddy, should I eat with my fork or my knife?' If he does not grow up to be a mathematician, he will be a diplomat: he is tactful and sensitive and has achieved the remarkable status of favourite sibling with all three of his sisters. It can't be easy sharing a house with two older sisters and a Mary. He is looking forward to getting my watch when I die but is nonetheless my favourite son.

Mary (ten), my youngest and prettiest child, lives in Maryland. Not the mid-Atlantic state, but a utopian, disconnected state of mind where she doesn't need to absorb any facts or have any comprehension of the world surrounding her. It is a very pleasant land where she only has to focus on the present moment and can jettison from her head any historic or future events that have happened or are planned. That is why, despite going to the Christmas markets in Berlin and Munich, she still doesn't know which country they are in, or even that they are not English cities. Contrary to this healthy therapeutic psychological state, she is also a very dominant, strong-willed personality, with occasional melodrama. She takes no nonsense or prisoners, doesn't mince her words and will always robustly defend herself. Mary is one to watch, and will grow up to surprise everyone.

The alert reader will have noticed that I named my final children Joseph and Mary. None of my offspring is a performer so this was my transparent attempt to secure my youngest two the lead roles in the school nativity play. Their teachers did not, however, fall for it. Joe was a sheep and Mary was an angel.

With the introductions out of the way, it is time to get going. Time to go travelling. You must be as eager as I am. The Tenth Doctor is packed in my hand luggage. I have eaten my farewell muffins from Shelagh. I have switched off my BlackBerry (but packed my laptop just in case). Day 41 feels reassuringly far away, but before I even enter Steve's itinerary I am taking my children and my mother for a week in New York. I am not taking my spare-children as I do not love them as much. I am not taking Jackie, because my mother and her would make it too one-sided.

# CHAPTER SIX

*The Protector – Nazareth – breaking ice – Joe le Taxi*
*– a high-profile murderess – titanium – Wi-Fi*
Soundtrack: Ryan Adams – 'New York, New York'

'**D**on't worry,' she answers with her usual calm assurance, 'I applied for your ESTA authorisations months ago. They are all in your pack. And your taxi arrives in fifty minutes.'

I have had to ring Charmaine on the first day of the first leg. It is not the most independent of starts, but I do not want to fall out with US Customs and Border Protection. As a nation, my fellow Brits have last week inexplicably and shockingly voted to alienate ourselves from the European Union (I think they did it deliberately to increase the cost of my sabbatical with the consequential currency collapse), so I feel I had better quickly familiarise myself with the need for visas, an hour before we are due to leave the house. Admittedly, for nostalgic reasons I prefer the old blue passport (in the same way that I prefer my Cola Cubes to be served as a quarter of a pound) but that felt like a somewhat petulant reason for leaving the EU, albeit it was a central plank to Nigel Farage's jacket pocket manifesto. I voted to remain burgundy. I was in the minority.

As I now nervously hold my inferior EU passport and wait

in line, the severe reputation of the US Customs and Border Protection Protectors coming into view precedes them, and my eldest two daughters (Meggie and Mimi, for those who haven't been paying attention) both warn me not to make any unwise cracks when seeking admission via JFK.

'Where are you staying, Steward?' asks the expressionless Protector.

That's fine. This Protector can order my name howsoever he sees fit. Nonplussed but composed, I consider it only polite to compliment him on his own name instead, and at the same time I congratulate myself on having avoided enquiring as to whether his first name might be Jesus-of.

'Nazareth, that's a great name.'

I feel Meggie's and Mimi's eyes boring into the back of my skull. They no doubt fear that I will shortly be facing at best detention, and at worst crucifixion. Nazareth proves tricky to convert to warm dialogue.

'Where are you staying, Steward?' he repeats, impatiently. It dawns on me that he might have worked out that Steward is my surname and that he is simply being assertive. Either that or he is a simple being.

'Inn New York City.'

'Which hotel?'

Before this descends into an Abbott and Costello sketch, I spare his blushes by explaining that my hotel is confusingly (I am trying to be generous to him) called Inn New York City. I sense I still haven't quite broken the ice.

'Right hand, four fingers... Right hand, thumb.'

I raise my pickaxe and hammer it home. 'So is Donald Trump really going to be your next President?'

'Left hand, four fingers... Left hand, thumb.'

Abandoning my hopeless ice-breaking metaphor, I duly oblige and allow the Protector to collect my fingerprints without further frosty dialogue. It is nearly midnight and he no doubt wants to get home to enjoy his own reflection in uniform whilst fantasising that he is NYPD. It is a small victory but I press a lot harder with my index and middle finger for Nazareth's photograph, as I feel they are the two fingers he most deserves.

Our driver, Joe le Taxi, is a much warmer, more loquacious individual. The metaphor returns and I melt the ice with my opening question.

'Donald Trump is de maaaaan. He's a New Yoiker. He's going to Make America Great Again. We've had enough of O-bama. And Hillary makes Bill look like a choirboy. She's corrupt. She's a murderer. It's time for change. We've had enough of all these immigrants. Not every Muslim is a terrorist, but every terrorist is a Muslim.'

This hasn't gone quite as planned and I am taken aback by the revelation that the Secretary of State and Democratic presidential candidate is in fact a killer. I must have missed that episode of *House of Cards*. I am also conscious that I am pausing a little too long with my response as I mentally try to list to myself all of the other creeds, beside Muslims, which have in recent history committed atrocities, from the Catholic Christians of the IRA to the revolutionary socialists of the Basque Separatists.

I decide to swiftly change tack to less controversial territory.

'Have you always lived in New York?'

'No sir, originally from the Caribbean, St Lucia; moved here aged seven and lived here ever since.'

It seems his violent objection to immigrants has developed later in life, post-green card acquisition.

Lit by atmospheric streetlights of sodium orange, we pass a pile-up on the other side of the road (trivial compared with the potential pile-up if Trump does get into power).

'Cool,' says Meggie, temporarily contributing from her introspective Spotify bubble, 'NYPD in action.' She doesn't hang around to hear the response, reinserting her earphones and withdrawing once again from social interaction.

'I was NYPD for fifteen years,' says Joe, unexpectedly. 'Retired out with invalidity benefit after 9/11.'

I am praying (as only true atheists can pray) that Joe or Mary in the back of the car don't ask if 9/11 is a 7-11 after a lie-in. I would imagine that New Yorkers expect all generations to have an appreciation of 9/11, but my own expectations of my youngest two are a lot lower. Fortunately, they aren't listening as they are too distracted by their ongoing and futile search for Wi-Fi in the car.

Joe le Taxi's apparent dislike of Muslims is now put into context when he explains that he was one of the first on the scene and rushed into the North Tower after the first plane hit, to help get people out, and was crushed in the exiting stampede. He was already in hospital by the time the South Tower collapsed, having titanium plates inserted into his spine.

I ask him to perform another act of heroism tomorrow and pick my mother up from Newark airport, when she joins us for our week in New York.

We arrive at the hotel after midnight, which is gone 5 a.m. in the UK. We are too fatigued to unpack or fully appreciate the magnificence of our red-brick 1890s Manhattan apartment hotel, and have time for nothing other than the priority task of getting my son logged onto Wi-Fi so that he can virtually sleep online.

Mary asks what time it is in England. I am impressed that she realises she has left England.

'Five a.m.'

'That's the latest I've ever stayed up. Cool.'

# CHAPTER SEVEN

*Mr Benn – as if by magic – Charles Lindbergh's propeller*
*– Citizen Kane's sled – Thomas Edison's lamp – book spines –*
*Castro to Deodar – the wrong sister – diary of a New York attorney*
SOUNDTRACK: SNEAKER PIMPS – '6 UNDERGROUND'

When I was a child (as Charles Lamb once said, 'Lawyers, I suppose, were children once'), one of my favourite television programmes was *Mr Benn*. This was a surreal, semi-animated staccato LSD trip of a kids' programme with a very simple but strangely addictive formula. In each episode Mr Benn, wearing a commuter's black suit and bowler hat, would leave the drudgery of his house at 52 Festive Road and walk to his nearby fancy-dress shop, where the fez-wearing shopkeeper would appear, 'as if by magic', and invite him to try on a new outfit from the shop full of mysterious items. In the 1970s, commuters must have been invited to fancy-dress parties most weeks, which would explain the need for a costume shop in a suburban neighbourhood. Part of the excitement as a child was hoping that Mr Benn would select a particular costume that caught your eye on one of the many mannequins, and even if he didn't you knew it was a potential spoiler for a future episode. I remember wanting him to go for the pirate's or the convict's costume, although secretly the baker's costume intrigued me. When he had selected his outfit, the somewhat sinister shopkeeper (never trust a man with a Hitler moustache who suddenly materialises) would then magically reappear; Mr Benn would find himself wearing the costume he had chosen; and the shopkeeper would then usher Mr Benn to the magic door at the back of the shop, where his adventure would begin as he entered a world relevant to his new attire. It was like a low-budget version of Narnia, with red knights (still my favourite episode), clowns and cowboys in place of lions, witches and wardrobes.

Our hotel in Manhattan, on Amsterdam and 71 Upper West, feels like the costume shop in Mr Benn. It is an unassuming townhouse in a quiet, tree-lined block, but the magic lies within. On ascending the outside steps and unlocking the entrance and porch doors, an agreeable waft of antiquity greets the nostrils. The female hotelier, a welcoming one-eyed New Yorker who has lived in the basement of the building like a house-elf for twenty-five years, 'as if by magic' obligingly appears from beneath a trap door (or so it seems). There are only four rooms and we have booked two of them: the Library and the Opera Suite. Both have old-world charm and feel like they could and should appear in an episode in which Mr Benn wears a velvet smoking jacket.

Joe, Mary and I have chosen the Library Suite for three reasons: first, I love books; second, it is the nicer of the two rooms; and third, I am the wallet bearer and this place is expensive so I want the best room for myself (as my teenage daughters and mother are not as stylish and won't appreciate it as much as I will).

It contains a cornucopia of curiosities from a bygone, Phileas

Fogg era. On the brown brick wall facing the entrance door is an enormous wooden propeller which must have once belonged to a pioneering aviator whom I optimistically hope to be Charles Lindbergh. Beneath is an open fire dramatically curtained with copper mesh to protect the black and red Paisley carpet, to be enjoyed from the reclining comfort of a judge-red leather Chesterfield. The high ceiling's centrepiece is a dramatic, back-lit, stained glass window of swirling reds, greens and blues, originating on the Portobello Road in London, tucked in at bedtime by a horizontal Roman blind on a primitive pulley which it is a joy to hoist like a ship's sail every night. Matching the colours of the overhead stained glass is a Tiffany lamp on a mahogany desk with sunken brass inkwells, sitting alongside canvas hat boxes, with a vintage sled propped up behind the desk (called 'Franklin 2' but it might just as well be named 'Rosebud'). To enhance the enjoyment of the room's glassware is a wooden telescopic kaleidoscope on a stand on the mantelpiece. Unlike modern hotel rooms, where working out the counter-intuitive light switch system is nothing but a tiresome irritation, learning each lamp's and lantern's quirks and foibles (and a brass cherubic light is the most mischievous one) is an altogether more fulfilling pursuit, often with pull-cords and double bulbs that Edison himself might once have operated. When illuminated, they cast a dim light over other oddities hiding in crevices and corners, such as brass scales, a stone bust of a New England farmhand, and a wooden bar skittles game.

But it's the books upon books that draw me in and draw the room together. They rise poetically from the floor to the ceiling, stacked in piles, decked on furniture surfaces, racked on lean-to ladders, and insulating the walls on the built-in open bookcases and shelving. Everywhere you look there are enticing spine titles.

Spine titles played an unusual part in my teenage years, as it was the spine title for the *Encyclopaedia Britannica* C–D volume which led to the obscure name of my first band, Castro to Deodar, which to my knowledge is still the only band ever to be named after a Cuban revolutionary leader and an evergreen cedar tree. After I left the band for university, they abandoned the name for the catchier Sneaker Pimps and had a modicum of success in the States with their single about grave burial depth, *6 Underground*. The spine titles in the Library Suite are also a combination of the obscure and the catchy: *The Unique World of Mitsumasa Anno, The Decorative Arts of the '40s and '50s, Simons' List Book 1977, The Basic Writings of Sigmund Freud, Loser Takes All: The Comic Art of Woody Allen*, one intriguingly entitled *How Old Was Lolita?, The Collected Short Stories of W. Somerset Maugham*, Chaucer's *Canterbury Tales*, a 1948 illustrated edition of *A Tale of Two Cities* and last and least, John Grisham's *The Client*, presumably to fuel the open fire. Were my children not in tow, I would be at risk of spending all day reading and seeing nothing of New York.

Although we really should be leaving the room shortly for an introductory stroll through Central Park and down Fifth Avenue (to the New York Public Library, where no books are on offer, as it turns out), I can't resist beginning the day by running my finger along a row of splendidly weathered hardbacks atop a sideboard and it lands on a volume intriguingly entitled *1974 New York Lawyer's Diary & Manual: The Bar Directory of the State of New York*. I left work less than two weeks ago (and, I am sorry to report, have still been opening my emails each day), so the lawyer in me has not yet been laid to rest and I open the diary. Unexpectedly, it is not a desk diary of appointments, but rather a self-penned journal.

If you have never read someone else's personal diary, then you are a better and stronger-willed person than me. You are also missing out, as it happens. I have done it twice before, many years ago. It is a lot more interesting than Facebook, as diaries are of course not designed to be seen and do not contain photographs of mirrors and meals.

The first time was at university, when my housemate (a geographer with a permed mullet, out of fashion even in the late 1980s) and I abused the trust of a close female friend who foolishly left us alone in her room and her diary by her bedside. I hit gold with the page that it fell open upon. My mulleted friend happened to have a crush on her so was disappointed and visibly deflated at her most intimate confession that she was keen on (I believe she said in love with, but I might have embellished that over time) another friend of ours. I did wrestle with my conscience afterwards, but my conscience conceded. My guilt at reading her most personal thoughts was outweighed by being able to mercilessly mock my housemate for the rest of the term, until, that is, he started dating (and eventually married) the diary-keeper. To this day, I don't know if he ever confessed to his wife that we read a few pages of her diary that night, although the fact that I wasn't invited to their wedding might be telling. They are both Facebook friends of mine so, in case she doesn't know, perhaps I should post this news on her wall, alongside the photographs of meals their children have made.

The second time was also when I was at university (it must have been a phase I was going through). This occasion was even more morally reprehensible, as I abused not the hospitality of a female friend in her halls of residence but rather the hospitality of my then girlfriend's mother, who kindly put me up in her other daughter's bedroom during the summer holidays. Looking for some drawer space in which to put my clothes (I was a fastidiously tidy undergraduate), fate smiled upon me and presented another diary. Having read only a few months' worth of recent entries, I realised to my regret that I was going out with the wrong sister. The relationship did not last much longer, which is just as well as it could have been a little awkward after I knew what I learned that night from the sister's rather racy diary entries.

In the Library Suite today, faced with a 1974 diary, I am not going to turn down the prospect of some journalistic voyeurism, so start at a random early entry. It appears that life as a New York attorney was more sedate in those days, when I was aged only three.

1st Friday, February 1, 1974
Sunny & Cold. Vince did not show. Had a quiet Friday mailing. Was taken out for lunch. There might be agitation in the wind.

The last line is lyrical, sinister and magnificent. I want it printed on a T-shirt. 'There might be agitation in the wind.' Is he observing the weather or is this a portent of impending doom? My appetite is whetted. I read on.

I check the name and address section at the front of the

journal but there is no clue as to the identity of the writer. I flick forward a few pages from where I was.

2nd Thursday, February 14, 1974
Mild day – very peaceful. Looking forward to a million-dollar week.

Again, the last line is worthy of being transcribed onto a T-shirt. The author is a walking sound bite. It seems, however, that his optimism was misplaced.

3rd Friday, February 15, 1974
Cold & Cloudy. Shaping up for a lousy week. [Whilst I feel sorry for the shape of his week, I am delighted that he has used the word lousy, and hope that he says it in a stereo-typically Jewish Brooklyn accent.] Changed mind about a million-dollar week – looks like complete disaster. A million-dollar week? Was completely fooled.

I watch helplessly as he (it was 1974, he was an attorney, he used the word 'lousy', he is a drama queen; he is definitely male and single) becomes more fragile before my prying eyes, and his diary fills with doubt and anxiety.

3rd Wednesday, February 20, 1974
Beautiful day. It seems my lifestyle is one where I am inter-ested in living in peace. I cannot cope with excitement of any kind.

I turn again to look for clues as to his identity and notice an embossed name on the front cover of the journal which I initially took to be the company name of the publisher of the diary: Kalman Kaplan. It was 1974, he was an attorney, he would be the type of person to have his name embossed on the front of a leather diary; he was the type of person to be called Kalman Kaplan. It is decided: his name is Kalman Kaplan and I am getting worried about his precarious and fragile state of mind.

2nd Wednesday, March 13, 1974
Very cold. Nothing eventful happened. Was a very peaceful day. It was completed by getting rid of a CANCER in the office.

This man is now also a walking contradiction; he may even be schizophrenic. How can it be a peaceful, uneventful day if he got rid of a CANCER (written in capitals) in the office? And what does he mean by 'getting rid of'? It was 1974, he used the word lousy; was he a Mafioso? This is rapidly turning into a John Grisham novel before my very eyes (and yes, I will now have to confess that I have read more than one, despite wanting to recycle them as fuel). I have to read on.

But that's it. There are no more entries for the rest of the year. What happened next? Was his million-dollar week so bleak that he jumped off Brooklyn Bridge? Having got rid of the CANCER in the office, was he himself then whacked or imprisoned? Or, like most people, did he get bored of writing a diary which he thought only he would ever read?

I have to put Kalman Kaplan on hold because Mary, my youngest, pops up as if by magic. 'Daddy, stop reading. It's our first day in New York. Let's go.' I step back through the magic door, out of Kalman Kaplan's troubled life and back into the Library Suite, where I change out of the red knight costume, into my new T-shirt, for a day of sightseeing, looking back longingly at the journal I have left behind. Kalman Kaplan, I will find you, but for now you will have to wait while I introduce my pesky kids to your city.

# CHAPTER EIGHT

*Narcissism – Betamax video recorder – Enchanted*
*– Tom Hanks lets me down – static movie extras*
*– a misunderstanding about Nazism*
SOUNDTRACK: OKKERVIL RIVER
*– 'OUR LIFE IS NOT A MOVIE OR MAYBE'*

**'D**addy, you're a narcissist,' Mimi informs me.
This cutting accusation is levelled at me by my second, and once favourite, daughter on account of my fretting about whether my new T-shirt is too tight as we walk down the steps of our hotel into a vivid, cloudless New York morning. I have never troubled weights benches or been troubled by my upper body strength and have watched with satisfaction over the years whilst those who have, the likes of Russell Crowe and Leonardo DiCaprio (to pick two obvious equivalents), have slowly allowed their bodies to collapse like a trifle cut from the middle and left in the fridge for a week. I have, however, always looked passable in T-shirts until the past year or so, when my torso has become walrus-like, with grey hairs and new lumps sprouting up whenever I turn sideways in the mirror for a more honest reflection. I no longer enjoy my sideways reflection. I don't enjoy being lumpy. Perhaps Mimi is right. Perhaps I am a

narcissist. Or perhaps the Red Bull and Revels are catching up with me. I vow (again) to give up the Red Bull for my sabbatical (the Revels are staying – I need some intrigue in my life). I prefer Meggie's more tactful suggestion that I do have 'more flattering tops' and duly turn back to the hotel to change into a linen shirt whilst simultaneously changing my favourite daughter.

Mimi is the first to receive a fine in New York. In Cornwall every summer holiday, it is our family tradition to have a daily Best Behaviour Prize, where I decide, the next morning, who was best behaved the day before and reward them with a packet of sweets on the bread-run into Tintagel. It is an excellent parenting technique of encouraging bribery and sugar consumption amongst the next generation. For New York, I have modified the rules. As every other person in Central Park is running, I have made a concession to reduce not only my Red Bull intake but also my children's sugar intake. Instead, we will be having a penalty point system. There will be a cash prize of fifty dollars at the end of the week for the child with the fewest penalty points. Mimi receives a twenty-point fine for calling me a narcissist.

To be a truly great father, I always thought ice cream was all it took. I learn today that I was wrong. To be a truly great father, you don't need to be wise, nor do you need to demonstrate that wisdom by doing your children's English homework; you don't need to be successful, nor do you need to demonstrate that success by taking them on holiday to New York; you don't need to support them in adversity, nor do you need to demonstrate that support by handing over 40 per cent of your income each month to their mother in alimony payments; you don't need to learn from your mistakes, nor do you need to demonstrate that learning by ensuring they don't make the same ones as you

('Promise me, son, not to do the things I've done', as Kenny Rogers more succinctly put it); you don't need to be right all the time, nor do you need to buy them ice creams whenever you are proved wrong. It turns out that to be a truly great father all you actually need to do is blag them into a scene of a blockbuster movie.

When I was growing up (albeit I stopped at five foot eight), scenes from movies were less ingrained in my mind. I only had one chance to digest a film in the cinema and then had to settle for acting out scenes in the playground and waiting a year or two until it featured in the Christmas schedule of BBC or ITV (in which case it would get triple circled, in red, in the bumper edition of the *Radio* or *TV Times*). The James Bond, Steve McQueen and Robert Redford/Paul Newman films were the only ones generally worthy of this treatment, until of course the game-changer, *Star Wars*. Video recorders only featured later in my teens, when my grandmother won a Sanyo Betamax video recorder in a Hartlepool United FC raffle and gave it to my sister and me, which was the equivalent of winning the EuroMillions to a fourteen-year-old boy in the early 1980s.

My children (and spare-children), on the other hand, live and breathe movies and television shows, which are omnipresent on their phones, iPads and, if they are in a retro mood, televisions. They are currently in the right city, as New York is a living, breathing movie set. We begin the day with a stroll from Upper West through Central Park to Upper East.

'*Mr Popper's Penguins*,' says Meggie excitedly, as she points to Tavern on the Green. I remember it more from the original *Ghostbusters* but Meggie is indeed correct. I take a look at the menu prices and inform my children that I don't think the food is suitable for them (a reliable euphemism for frugality which they never question), but that they should take some photographs as they are always free (unless they include people dressed as Pixar characters in Times Square, as we are warned by a helpful old New York lady passing by).

When we cross Bow Bridge, the lake view reveals a cityscape including my favourite building in New York, the San Remo two-tower cooperative apartment building, located a few blocks up from where we are staying. Its imperious twin towers have a Renaissance charm and, overlooking Central Park, it offers one of the greatest views of the city. If it is good enough for rock legends Bono and Barry Manilow, it is good enough for me.

A few years ago, for our compulsory fortnight of summer 'skiff and drizzle' in north Cornwall, I purchased the box set of *Friends*. It was an inspired choice, as it is something which all of my children and spare-children can enjoy together, regardless of age, for hours and hours of unsupervised, harmonious time. Parenting is of course trial and error. What is true of *Friends* and Tom Hanks films is not necessarily true of the remake of *The Texas Chainsaw Massacre*, as I discovered to my cost last summer when Mimi had the worst nightmares she'd had since I showed her *The Lovely Bones* when she was ten. Joe still can't look at a gorilla in a zoo and has been permanently scarred (and scared) by Caesar out of the remake of *Planet of the Apes*. All that scares Mary, on the other hand, is the thought of a worldwide shortage of cocoa beans, and locking herself inside public toilets. The former is unlikely to happen on this trip; but it will be a Miracle on 34th Street if she can get through New York without doing the latter.

'Is that the building in *Friends*?' asks Mary, pointing to the San Remo.

'Yes, Mary, it is.'

'Epic.'

It isn't, of course, but I want this trip to be as memorable as possible and a little parental misinformation never hurt anyone. For example, I went from believing in Father Christmas, to not believing in Father Christmas, to being Father Christmas; the same has not been true of God, although identical logic should apply really.

I freely admit that my youngest two children lead a rarefied Disney existence; for my eldest two it is Warner Brothers, as their school resembles Hogwarts. (There is nothing wrong with a sheltered upbringing as long as I regularly remind them of the importance of hard work and that I will cut them off without a penny once they each reach their 18th birthday and my alimony obligations end.) It is therefore entirely appropriate that the Central Park site which provokes the most excitement is the Merchant's Gate Fountain around which Amy Adams danced as a cartoon princess converted into a human in the surprisingly good *Enchanted*. In the film, the archetypal Disney princess is forced out of her idyllic animated world into the live-action, harsh, cynical city; much as my children will be when I stop paying for their schooling.

As we leave the Central Park of princesses and penguins, for my first time as a parent Tom Hanks lets me down. FAO Schwarz, the toy shop from *Big* where Tom and Robert Loggia danced on the giant floor piano, which we have all been looking forward to visiting, has been closed down. To add insult to injury, nothing yet stands in its place; just a cadaver of a store which once gave so much joy. To be fair, I probably shouldn't blame Tom for this. Even if it was his fault, I can forgive him anything, even the Dan Brown movies. I google it to check I have got the right building. Sadly, I have, and it was indeed closed down in July 2015, due to rising rental costs, by its owner, Toys R (No Longer) Us. The movie scene-destroying pricks!

Appropriately, we next pass Trump Tower, a big black phallus of a building. I comment to Mimi that The Donald is the true narcissist, which is why he built a building out of mirrors. I hope the kids don't notice my hypocritical glance at my own profile reflection in his building, which is altogether more flattering in my linen shirt.

'Is he going to be the next President?' asks Mary.

'I doubt it,' I reply, quietly, in case Joe le Taxi's support is shared by his fellow New Yorkers on Fifth Avenue.

'Why not?' challenges Mary. 'He has already obliterated sixteen rivals, some of whom are rising Republican stars, on the way to winning thirty-seven states in the primaries, and has built a coalition broad enough to range from secular moderates in Massachusetts to evangelicals in Mississippi. I think he will win.'

Coming from a ten-year-old, Mary's political knowledge throws me. We received a free copy of the *New York Times* this morning in our hotel room and Mary woke up earlier than me, so I put it down to that. Strange, as I had always thought she was the dimmest of my children. I decide to regain control.

'Who would like an ice cream?'

Next stop is New York Library, principal location of *The Day After Tomorrow*. I resolve to show the kids all of these movies when we are in Cornwall for two weeks straight after this (I never said my sabbatical was going to be hard). But as we are walking down Fifth Avenue towards 42nd Street, we get distracted by a row of immaculate muscle cars parked up on a side street: a red

1960s Corvette Stingray; a black and gold 1960s Plymouth Hemi GTX; a new silver and black speed-striped Mercedes-AMG GT; a white and red striped Bentley Continental; and a pimped-up Hummer camouflaged in what looks like grey and black space invaders. On the other side of the road is a black Plymouth Barracuda GTX with a camera mounted on the drivers' side.

'Mary,' I say, spotting an opportunity to excite a gullible ten-year-old, 'it looks like they are filming a new episode of *Friends*. Which one do you think is Phoebe's car?'

'Dadddddyyyyyy...' replies Mary knowingly, without missing a beat. 'Phoebe drives a yellow cab.'

As she is still holding the same ice cream from last proving me wrong, I shift the focus this time by pushing her into the road beside the celebrity cars.

We take the mandatory tourist photos, shoving New Yorkers, cast and crew members aside so that Joe can do thumbs-up selfies in front of the cars to send to his school friends. Unperturbed by our English colonial effrontery, one of the kindly crew (everyone in New York seems a patient and kindly human being, until they sit behind the wheel of a car and become a psychotic horn-honker) informs us that they are going to be shooting a scene for *Fast & Furious 8* and that the best place from which to view it will be on the steps of the library (the same steps up which the protagonist son of the meteorologist in *The Day After Tomorrow* runs to escape the tsunami, which, like the original Daleks, can't get up stairs).

*Doctor Who* has helped me in so many real-life situations. And here is another one. As we walk down to the library and are about to cross the road to stand on the steps, I recall the opening scenes of *Doctor Who* spin-off *Torchwood*'s 'Children of Earth', in which none of the adults notice that all of the children in the world have simultaneously stopped moving. The same is true now, except I do notice. There are some suspiciously representative street walkers who have all stopped walking: two young women in dresses at a shop entrance; a white guy in a suit holding a briefcase (it's Saturday lunchtime and thirty degrees, so his disguise doesn't fool me); a handsome and well-dressed black guy pretending to look at his mobile phone; and now a middle-aged English guy in a fresh linen shirt and hiking shorts with his four kids trailing behind.

'Come on, Daddy,' nags Mimi, 'we need to get across to the steps to get the best view.'

'Sssh,' I snap, paternally. 'Stand very still.'

In Meggie's case, this is easy as being static is her natural state, but the others are more actively resistant and the usual questioning and doubting follows. I explain.

'I am pretty sure those people standing still are movie extras. If we stay put, they will think we are extras too and we could get in the actual movie.'

'Are you in shot?' asks a crew member carrying a walkie-talkie. The two women with shopping bags nod.

'OK everyone else, we are going to start shooting, can you please keep moving and clear this area.'

She walks towards us, holding her walkie-talkie threateningly.

'We're in shaaat,' I reply confidently, in my best Brooklyn accent. I want to use the word 'lousy' as well but it doesn't seem appropriate. She looks suspicious but not in the mood for an argument in front of four children. She smiles like Mona Lisa and moves on to clear the non-acting riff-raff off the sidewalk.

This is Saturday afternoon at the height of the tourist season;

the obvious time to close one of the busiest streets in New York. An eerie silence descends as the traffic is stopped and Fifth Avenue is rendered motionless. I am expecting a high-speed car chase to roar past at any moment, but instead, eight police cars, a stretch limo, the space invader Hummer and the Plymouth Barracuda (driven by a big bald guy who is most definitely not Vin Diesel) amble past, barely threatening the speed limit for a built-up area, with a swooping camera crane following them at a considerably greater speed.

Then it's all over. Admittedly, it is not one of the great cinematic extra moments: it isn't quite like appearing as an unwelcoming alien species in the cantina scene in *Star Wars*, or in the tribal spear- and sword-waving throng to whom Mel Gibson gives his freedom speech in *Braveheart*, but nonetheless, we are now genuine movie extras, as unpaid and unknown as White Guy in Suit.

'Daddy, that was amazing,' is what Mimi actually says, her permanently fixed teenage scowl temporarily transformed into a transient, retainer-wearing smile.

'Daddy, you are amazing,' is what I hear Mimi say. See, not a narcissist at all.

We get back to the hotel during a lovely evening of long shadows to await the arrival of my mother. Mimi and I go for a dusk walk around the neighbourhood in the hope that she will arrive while we are out. We find a health food store which sells healthy choc mint smoothies. I have committed to Mimi that I will go all week without a Red Bull. She is scared of its effect on my health. I am scared of her. The choc mint smoothie seems like a safe alternative. She lets me have one.

We time our return badly, arriving just as Joe le Taxi deposits Mum with us. She has spent the past three weeks on her own mini-sabbatical, travelling across Canada on the Rocky Mountaineer train, something I had wanted to do on my sabbatical but which Steve wouldn't let me: I am allowed to do Alaska or the Rocky Mountaineer, but not both. Joe le Taxi tells me all about my mum's trip, updates me on how Angela and Len are (the cousin and husband with whom she stayed on Vancouver Island, about whom Joe le Taxi can now talk authoritatively), and in particular that she has not seen any bears. I increase his tip on the basis that I will no longer need to spend her first evening listening to stories of her trip.

'What are we doing tomorrow?' is Mum's opening line, right before hello. She likes to have an itinerary and she likes to ask what it is. This might explain Joe.

'Let's just play it by ear, Mum,' I say. 'You need to get into a New York state of mind. This is not a tour.'

There is no reply. (Without Charmaine or Steve, there is also no itinerary.)

'Isn't yours a fabulous room?' I ask.

There is hesitation.

'It's a bit dark.'

I issue her with a 1,000-point fine for being a day late, and leave Meggie and Mimi to reacquaint themselves with their grandma in the Opera Suite, and to the inevitable game of charades. I go to bed.

Joe is delighted with the text responses from his friends about being in *Fast & Furious*. I caution him to ensure that movie stardom doesn't change him. When I kiss Mary goodnight and tuck her into her sofa bed in the lesser of the two rooms in the Library, she asks me why Mimi had called me a Nazi this morning. It seems I was right about Mary all along.

# CHAPTER NINE

*Banana bread – Grandma Elaine – bedside wrappers – John Lennon – a famous footballer called Patrick – fingering Impressionists – a miracle on my back – two episodes in the toilet*
SOUNDTRACK: JOHN LENNON – 'NOBODY TOLD ME'

'You've got banana bread. We didn't get any banana bread. I like banana bread. Oooh, this is a much nicer room. It's got more light.'

I love my mum, obviously. I am her son; I have to. But I haven't lived with her for almost thirty years. It has flown by. Living with her for a week, in a New York apartment, is going to be considerably slower. In my gap year, she gave me some extra money for my trip on condition that I rang home (from a public call box) every Sunday evening. It is a tradition that has continued ever since (although I am no longer paid for it and there are no longer public call boxes). Ten minutes on the phone, once a week, is, traditionally speaking, enough time to interact with one's mother; plus personal appearances at birthdays and Christmases. Rather ambitiously, though, I offered to bring her on a leg of my sabbatical (the shortest leg). It is payback for all the childhood holidays at the Dalmeny Hotel in Lytham St Annes, although I don't recall the Dalmeny serving banana bread. I do, however, recall a rather lovely waitress called Wendy.

Grandma Elaine (as she is known to the kids) is well-read and knowledgeable, but fills the gaps in her knowledge by making stuff up. I am going to have to be wary about the invented New York facts she will be espousing to the kids. She is enthusiastic, light-hearted, high-spirited and sprightly; entertaining her can be more tiring than responding to Joe's questions. Since my dad died eighteen years ago, she hasn't sat down much. I am hoping that the heatwave in New York will slow her down a little and, if I am lucky, melt her.

She is the only person who still calls me Geoffrey. I think she is also the only person I know who likes the name Geoffrey.

After Mum's morning inspection of my room and my breakfast, she decides we should go to the Metropolitan Museum of Art 'for the kids'. I am feeling slim and handsome today so brave a tight T-shirt. First, I take her past the Dakota Building, which is only a few blocks from our hotel.

I had never heard of John Lennon in 1980. I was ten years old and my parents tended to play more Kenny Rogers (whom I used to like because he always sang like he had a sore throat) and Barbra Streisand than The Beatles. But I do remember when he was murdered, by a not-so-nice American. That was the first I had heard of him. I was at an age when it was just about acceptable to still get into my parents' bed in the morning. I have probably merged the two incidents I remember from getting into their bed, but my unreliable recollection is that both of them happened on the same occasion.

I had found an unusually robust wrapper on my dad's bedside table and asked him what it was. He had told me that it was a game that he and Mum played at night; I pictured individually wrapped chess pieces. My dad no doubt welcomed the interruption to this awkward conversation when there was a news flash on BBC Radio 2 (Terry Wogan was all they ever listened to) to announce that John Lennon had been shot dead outside the Dakota Building.

'Are you sure that's it?' asks Mum. 'I thought he was shot on the steps to the Dakota Building. It doesn't even have any steps.'

No banana bread and no steps. This is an inadequate start to New York for my mother. Hopefully the Met will have both.

As I am lining everyone up for a photograph on the steps of the white Beaux-Arts façade of the Met (in height order with my mum in the middle next to eleven-year-old Joe), Patrick Vieira and his daughter walk past us. Patrick Vieira was a sublime Arsenal midfielder and one of the invincible team that won the Premiership in the 2003/04 season without having suffered a single defeat. He currently manages New York City FC, which would explain his presence alongside us.

I wait until he has passed before alerting the kids to his footballing fame, not least because Joe is wearing his Manchester United away kit and Patrick Vieira and Roy Keane did not get on particularly well.

'Is he on FIFA '16?' asks Joe, presumably because otherwise Joe won't accept him as a bona fide footballer.

'Why didn't you tell me, and I would have got a photo with him?' complains Meggie, ever drawn to celebrity.

'He used to play for Man United,' espouses Mum, wrongly.

As we queue for our Met tickets, Wi-Fi is available in the lobby. Meggie gets straight onto Snapchat to inform her friends that she met 'a famous footballer called Patrick something who footballed for Arsenal'.

There is an art to getting four children and a grandmother around a museum. It is not dissimilar to conducting an art heist. Get in; find the best stuff; get out before any of them set off the alarms. Mary has form here, having reached to try to pick off some petals from van Gogh's *Sunflowers* at the Rijksmuseum in Amsterdam, aged six. But it is my mother who commits the first offence at the Met. I have opted for the European paintings, a snack (hopefully banana bread) at the American Art Café overlooking Central Park, and some quick Egyptians at the Temple of Dendur room (because it sounds a bit like Temple of Doom).

I have been to the Met before, so escort my caravan of family members straight to one of my favourite paintings there, Jules Bastien-Lepage's *Joan of Arc*. It is a huge oil painting, filling the high-ceilinged corridor wall, of three saints (Michael, Margaret and Catherine) appearing to Joan in her parents' garden, rousing her to fight against the filthy English invaders in the Hundred Years War. The saints subtly merge with the farmhouse and the trees and while I am distracted by challenging Joe and Mary to find the four faces in the painting, Mum decides to get a closer impression, oblivious to the red line. Fortunately, the usher is more alert than my mother and orders her to 'Step back from the painting, ma'am'. It is a firm but polite admonishment, but is met by my mother with: 'Well, it doesn't say you can't cross the red line.'

I call an emergency family huddle and we all agree that from now on no one will try to finger any of the Impressionists in the next room. I fine Mum another thousand points for crossing the line.

We manage to navigate the remainder of the European paintings without groping or prodding Rousseau, Corot, Seurat, Gauguin, Monet, Manet, Renoir, Cézanne, Degas, Toulouse-Lautrec or even, in Mary's case, van Gogh. As a reward, I buy my mum a slice of cake (still no banana bread, but she seems to be appeased) at the café and reload the kids with sugar as I sense that the art and culture is sapping their energy levels.

The Temple of Dendur doesn't take very long. It is housed in the most beautiful room in the Met, framed by floor-to-ceiling glass, with its own moat, but let's face it, Ancient Egyptians are boring: they have been dead for too long. Sadly, I think that is the kids' view of John Lennon as well, as they didn't seem very impressed by the Dakota Building. Meggie and Mimi take some selfies in front of sphinxes and sarcophagi. They also ask me to join them for a photograph in front of the moat; when I see the result I realise that I should have stuck to linen shirts and petulantly decide that it is time to leave before I grow moobs.

Crossing Central Park at noon, in the middle of July, wearing a small but heavy backpack and my dark cotton T-shirt, a miracle occurs. When I take off my backpack to rehydrate, an image of Jesus of Nazareth appears on my back. I quickly put my backpack back on: I don't want any New Yorkers to witness my miracle for fear of being compelled to become the leader of a religious cult. I don't have time for any of that.

The American Museum of Natural History is one of the largest museums in the world. Sticking to my art heist model, we visit the African room and the dinosaurs, try but fail to find the model of Theodore Roosevelt from *Night at the Museum*, buy Mary a tutti-frutti ice-cream larger than her brain, and are out within forty minutes.

We have tea (definitely not supper, as I can be northern again now) a few blocks up from our apartment in Manhattan, in an Italian restaurant on Amsterdam Avenue run by a Hungarian lady who seems to think that my mum is my wife and that she is too good for me. My children exact revenge upon her for this slight when Joe, suffering from mild sunstroke (I must remember to apply sun cream to his skin tomorrow), vomits all over (rather than in) the male toilet, and Mary (predictably) locks herself inside the female toilet. To test my parenting skills, the two events occur simultaneously. I am now well versed in releasing my hysterical youngest daughter from toilets so I heroically step in and tell the Hungarian restaurateur that she can cancel the Fire Department. I am less well versed in vomit clean-up, so smear it around the toilet seat with hand towels and tell Joe to improve his aim in the future. In his defence, he aimed his mouth in the toilet bowl but made no allowance for the river of puke finding a tributary through his nostrils.

Energised by my double parenting triumph, when I return to my room I am drawn back to the dark world of Kalman Kaplan. I type his name as a search term into Google.

Google is a marvellous thing. If I were a real author or journalist twenty years ago I would have had to spend weeks in the British Library trying to track him down. But now, from the comfort of my Victorian bed on holiday, I find him (or at least someone with his name) instantly. I was wrong about him being a lawyer. He must have been given a desk diary in 1974 by a friendly New York lawyer (if such people existed in those days). The Kalman Kaplan that Google offers up was born in 1941. That fits. He would have been thirty-three when he was writing his diary in 1974, and he will now be seventy-four. I am delighted (for him and for me) to see that he is still alive.

But then it gets very interesting. He is a professor of psychology at the University of Illinois and a published author of numerous books with titles such as *Living with Schizophrenia, A Psychology of Hope: A Biblical Response to Tragedy and Suicide, Biblical Stories for Psychotherapy and Counselling,* and *The Seven Habits of the Good Life.* The disturbed diarist whose own psychological state in 1974 was causing me concern went on to become one of the leading biblical psychological experts on suicide, spirituality and mental health. I even find an online interview with him where he is commenting on narcissism, defending Narcissus, whom he says 'goes back and forth between being self-involved and absorbed in others'. He cites the example of giving a gift that is expressive of yourself and your personality, which he says 'breaks the dualism between egoism and altruism'. That sounds exactly like me: I am always buying books that I like as gifts for others. I may well have gifted you this very book. I like Kalman Kaplan. I want him to be my Facebook friend. This feels like destiny. I am on fire and track down his email address online.

I can't be certain whether his first name is Kalman or Kaplan; let's face it, he is American and they invent first names, so it could be either. I don't want to cause the same offence that American lawyers cause me when consistently plumping for the wrong one. So my email to him reads as follows:

Dear Mr Kalman Kaplan

Good news! I think I might have found your diary from 1974, in New York.

Are you the same Kalman Kaplan who would have used lyrically magnificent phrases such as:

- 'There might be agitation in the wind'
- 'Looking forward to a million-dollar week'

- 'Was a very peaceful day, completed by getting rid of a CANCER in the office'?

If so, please can I have your permission to reproduce the first two on a T-shirt? More importantly, if you would like to be reunited with your diary, I can let you know where in Manhattan it now resides. I would be very interested to hear how the rest of 1974 panned out as I was getting worried about you. Congratulations on all of the books that you have written since.

Apologies for the intrusion.
Geoff

PS You will be featuring in my own book which I am currently writing, so if we do speak, we can decide who might play the part of you in the movie.
PPS Hope you have a million-dollar week.

# CHAPTER TEN

*Cardigan – wizards – statues and smallpox – imbecile test –*
*building kitchens and skyscrapers – Ken Dodd's hair*
SOUNDTRACK: THE REPUBLIC TIGERS
*– 'BUILDINGS AND MOUNTAINS'*

Meggie: Daddy, can you put my cardigan in your bag?
Me: It's the hottest day so far. Why do you even have a cardigan?
Meggie: Because I don't want to not have a cardigan.

We are walking around Greenwich Village. Walt Whitman once walked around Greenwich Village. He also once said: 'Simplicity is the glory of expression.' I can't compete with the simplicity of Meggie's expression: she is a simpleton. I end up carrying her cardigan because… that's what dads do.

A street sign causes unexpected excitement amongst Meggie and Mimi, and more selfies and Snapchatting. The street in question is Waverly Place. The cause of the enthusiasm is a Disney Channel comedy programme that they grew up with called *Wizards of Waverly Place*, which made someone called Selena Gomez very famous, apparently.

To sustain Joe's and Mary's interest and sugar levels, I have promised to take them to Stieber's Sweet Shoppe. It is a foolhardy promise. It is over thirty degrees; I am carrying Meggie's cardigan in my bag and my mother on my back like Yoda. We traipse all over the side streets of Greenwich in search of old-fashioned candies and freshly made fudge. We arrive at the correct address, despite my children and mother suggesting that my Time Out city guide might be mistaken. There is no Stieber's Sweet Shoppe. It has gone the way of Tom Hanks's toy shop. New York is a living, evolving organism, and even the current guidebooks can't match its pace of change. Now I have two overheating, stroppy, sugar-free, sun cream-free younger children to contend with, convinced that it was me who closed down the sweet shop. I push them into the Washington Square fountain to help them cool down.

I have booked us on the ferry from Battery Park to Liberty Island and Ellis Island. The pride that I had in booking it online this morning to avoid the queues was soon subsumed by the realisation that I couldn't print off the bloody tickets. I had to draft in Mimi and the house-elf downstairs to rescue the situation, but not without getting a little 'stressy', according to Mimi.

Before taking the ferry, I want to avoid any future embarrassments with former NYPD heroes by teaching Joe and Mary about the 9/11 terrorist attack, so we are calling in at Ground Zero on our way to Battery Park. The memorial, entitled 'Reflecting Absence', is magnificent in its simplicity: the footprint of the destroyed towers is now two giant water features, with a seemingly infinite waterfall channelled from the centre of each down a well. In a city of skyscrapers, two holes plummeting into the ground is inspired. I ask Mary if she understands what it symbolises.

'What does symbolise mean?'

My heart sinks with the type of reverse pride that I experienced in Berlin when I took them to the Memorial to the Murdered Jews of Europe, where Joe and Mary had a giant game of hide 'n' seek whilst Mimi held her finger as a moustache for the family video.

I don't deserve my children and they don't deserve history lessons. We move on.

Even Mary knows that the Statue of Liberty symbolises New York. It is the only thing she does know about New York, as she is, I'm sure you will agree by now, the dimmest of my daughters. It is the one place that she has asked to visit and as she is also the prettiest of my daughters I am happy to oblige. She will look cute in the photographs in front of the statue. After a short ferry ride and a long hot dog for Joe, we are on Liberty Island and there she is, the back of her iconic copper-green crowned head poking out behind the ICE CREAMS * SNACKS bar. I had always thought that she carried a flaming torch but from here it could easily be a Cornetto.

During the siege of Fort Pitt in 1763, one of our brave, gentlemanly British militia captains, William Trent, recorded in his journal an incident when delegates from the Delaware Native American tribe came to warn the British of 'great numbers of Indians' coming to attack the fort, and pleaded with them to flee in order to avoid bloodshed. The British refused to leave and, as a token of their gratitude for the warning, gave the Delaware dignitaries two blankets and a handkerchief fresh from the smallpox hospital. It was an early form of biological warfare deliberately designed to convey the disease to the Native Americans. It worked. The French, on the other hand, gave America a sculpture known as *Liberty Enlightening the World*, intended as a gift for America's 100th birthday in 1876. Perhaps unsurprisingly for the French, it was ten years late; nonetheless, it was a better gift than smallpox. We Brits had backed the wrong horse: we should have given the Americans a statue and the French a disease. After all, the Americans went on to become slightly more important on the world stage than the French.

There is little else to do on Liberty Island than to take photographs with the Statue of Liberty looming behind us like a giant weeping angel. Unfortunately, with her pedestal she is over 300 feet tall, which means that the best camera angle to get both us and her in shot is from beneath the chin, pointing upward. I say 'chin' singular, but in my case I have started a collection. No matter which angle we try, several creases swell in the gap that once existed between my neck and chin, like a gathered curtain. I decide just to photograph my children instead, with their taut juvenile jawlines. I focus mainly on Mary as she is the prettiest.

From Liberty Island it is a small ferry hop across to Ellis Island National Museum of Immigration, a journey which allows Joe just enough time to consume his second hot dog (he is starting work on his own chin collection). Between 1892 and 1954, over twelve million immigrants from Ireland, the UK, Germany, Italy, Russia, Poland and Austria-Hungary entered the USA, but before doing so they had to pass through a giant sieve designed to weed out undesirable immigrants. That sieve was inspection at Ellis Island. There are a few undesirables on our ferry who I hope will be sieved out.

The undesirables back then who were denied access to the New World included: those with loathsome or contagious diseases such as typhus fever and cholera (if bad skin is not permitted today, an entire party of rowdy American teenagers nearby are out of luck); the Chinese (who were excluded in their entirety by the Chinese Exclusion Act, until the Union Pacific Railroad needed cheap labour); anyone with favus (a contagious fungal scalp condition, which again will hopefully exclude the American teenage party) or trachoma (a contagious disease of the eye); single women (they were not allowed to leave Ellis Island unless accompanied by a male relative or under the care of an immigrant aid society, for fear of them falling prey to native con artists and pimps); masturbators (in 1899, one male immigrant, overexcited by the prospect of so many single women entering his new country with him, was deported for masturbating); and idiots, imbeciles and the feebleminded (immigrants about whom there were doubts were subjected to an interview to determine their intellectual capacity).

Given the last two categories, it is surprising that the Scottish ancestors of that lunatic wanker Donald Trump ever managed to get into the country. This book won't, if he gets elected and it gets published.

Fortunately, they no longer do admission tests, so my mum and kids all make it into the museum. In the 1890s, had the inspectors heard the following conversation, which we have over a pizza lunch on the island, then my entire family would have had to abandon their American Dream.

Joe: Um… Daddy, would you drink a bacon milkshake?

Me: I would rather drink my own vomit.

Mary: Drinking your own vomit isn't too bad. I sick in my mouth and swallow it all the time.

Joe: It's bad when it comes out of your nose though.

The last sight of the day is the entirety of New York.

In the late eighteenth century, the site we are visiting used to be an idyllic farm with a stream, owned by a Dutch family called van Roosevelt (from whose line came two Presidents – more on them later). A century later it went upmarket and became the Waldorf-Astoria Hotel. In 1930, some serious construction activity began on the site. It took my builders over a year to build my new kitchen and patio area. Between March 1930 and April 1931 it took less time to build the Empire State Building, the world's tallest building for forty years until the topping out of the World Trade Center's North Tower in late 1970.

Despite this, I can't find it anywhere. I am pretty sure that we just need to keep going down 42nd Street past the library, but I was rather banking on being able to see the once tallest building in the world. In a grid of skyscrapers, however, it is not possible to see the top of any other buildings. It is like putting Mary in the middle of a circle of basketball players and asking her to identify the tallest one by his knees.

Lacking faith in my helmsmanship for the second time today, Mum informs a passing pedestrian that her son is a useless navigator and asks where she can find the Empire State Building; he points to a building one block down the street. Only by standing directly beneath it can we see the iconic antenna.

We are going up the Empire State Building for two important reasons. First, Meggie has already started work on her bucket list. Other than Dairy Milk, her favourite thing in the world is sunsets. Watching a sunset from the viewing platform of the Empire State Building is top of her bucket list. Even though she hopefully has approximately seventy years left in which to fulfil her bucket list, as we are here it seems opportune to knock off the top one. The second reason is *Sleepless in Seattle*. If Tom Hanks has visited it, so must we.

Tom ran to the elevator without queuing, was allowed straight up, and had the place to himself, Meg Ryan and a teddy bear called Howard. Our experience is not quite so exclusive. I bought an expensive tripod for just such sunset opportunities but it is confiscated from me as I pass through security, having queued for forty minutes – not because it is a security risk and could be used as a weapon to bludgeon the other photographers out of the way, but because there is barely room for me to hold the camera to my face on the viewing platform. No one stands a chance of seeing their own feet, let alone setting up a tripod. Joe and Mary have the dampest view, as their faces are pressed hard to the Turin Shroud image which has reappeared on my back.

We do, however, have a jaw-inspiring, awe-dropping view of the New York cityscape in the fading light, as I learn from checking my camera display, my camera having survived being shoved through and over the four rows of people between the perimeter and me. Tom Hanks didn't have to put up with this pulsating multitude of shameless selfie-posers. I don't especially like people, so being surrounded by a heaving homogeneous horde of humankind is hell. However, I regard my role as a father to be chief memory (and gene) provider for my children so it is worth ascending to the top of the Empire State Building and sharing the armpits of New York in order to see the width of the smile on Meggie's face as we descend. Meggie will never forget this evening and that makes me joyous, as does Mum's windswept hair, which makes her resemble Ken Dodd.

Before I go to sleep, I tally up the penalty points so far:

Mimi: 20 (calling Daddy a narcissist).

Meggie: 20 (calling Mary a dwarf over lunch); 20 (teasing

Mary about locking herself in the toilet and making her cry on her pizza).

Joe: 80 (texting his mother whilst on holiday, despite never texting me); 20 (fake laughing when issued with his first fine).

Mary: 100 (laughing at Joe's fine).

Grandma Elaine: 1,000 (being a day late); 1,000 (prodding a priceless work of art).

# CHAPTER ELEVEN

*Bloody children – bloody zoos – bloody rush hour*
*SOUNDTRACK: REM – 'LEAVING NEW YORK'*

As soon as I wake up, before even tucking into my much envied banana bread, I check my emails. There is no response from Kalman Kaplan. He has only had a day. There is plenty of time. Not for us, though: it is our last day in New York. I am already looking forward to disposing of my own mother and returning my children to theirs: I didn't keep the receipts but she always accepts them.

There are many downsides to having school-aged children. They sap your energy, your time, your current account and your life. They put wrinkles on your forehead and chins on your chin. They enter your bedroom at inconvenient times, either when John Lennon has died or whilst you are playing chess. They crush your dreams of Lamborghini and Rolls-Royce and replace them with second-hand Land Rover and roof box. Despite you paying their mobile phone bills, they don't ever return your calls or your texts, unless they need money or a lift or a mobile phone upgrade.

They eat a lot. They grow out of clothes and shoes a lot. They get ill a lot. They need to go to the toilet a lot, usually when there is no toilet. When there is one, they usually don't flush it. They are untidy. They are tardy. They lose stuff. They find stuff that they shouldn't. They dash your hopes and aspirations for them by not even playing the guitar or trying to act: they don't ever get the lead roles in the nativity play despite being called Joseph and Mary. And if you are very unlucky, or come from Hartlepool, they give birth whilst still at school and you get to start all over again. If that happens to me, I will insist that my grandson is named Jesus. It is my only hope.

But worse than all this, children like zoos.

Every city I take my kids to – Basel, Amsterdam, Paris, Berlin, Munich – we have to visit the zoo on our last day. I have made many parenting mistakes: balancing Meggie and her best friend on a ledge in the school gym without realising that Meggie has the balance of a new amputee; leaving my sister in charge of Mimi without realising that my sister drops babies onto sink edges; leaving the suction pump on in a holiday villa swimming pool without realising that Joe likes to stick his hand (and arm) up holes; chasing Mary down the landing dressed as a zombie without realising that when she looks behind her, laughing, she can't see the wall in front of her.

These mistakes all resulted in broken bones. But by far my biggest parenting mistake has been to allow zoos to become the tradition for the last day of holidays. And there is one here. In Central Park. Bugger.

I have nothing against zoos per se. I don't want to get into the pros and cons of animals in captivity. Overall, I consider zoos to be a good thing for introducing children to conservation and wildlife. But before this turns into a *Guardian* article, I should declare that for me the real problem with zoos is a different one to the traditional argument. It is simply that they are put in the wrong places. Zoos are always put in great cities. There are much greater things to do in great cities than visit a zoo. Zoos shouldn't be in cities at all. They should be in the middle of nowhere, where there is plenty of nowhere for the animals to have decent-sized enclosures. They should be the only tourist attraction for miles and miles. Zoos should be the only reason for visiting a place. If Hartlepool had a zoo, finally there would be a reason to visit my mum. Visiting a zoo in a great city like New York is like going to Canterbury to visit WHSmith.

Whilst the kids are watching overweight sea lions clapping and bobbing, kissing and fishing, I leave them with my mother, who is also acting like she has never been to a zoo before, and sneak off to down a Red Bull while Mimi is not looking. I very nearly made it all week without, but if the kids are allowed a zoo in New York, then I am allowed an energy drink to get me through it. I re-emerge behind the kids with newfound enthusiasm to visit the aviary, until a parrot shits on my camera lens. Bloody zoos.

Then New York does something unexpected. It starts to rain. It has been in the thirties, stiflingly hot and humid, all week. No one was expecting rain. But it feels right somehow. It feels very cinematic for our last day. I can picture Meg Ryan's pretty face (pre-face lift) smiling cutely (pre-Botox), her button nose (pre-nose job) twitching, as the rain falls all around but barely touching her, and Tom looks on affectionately. As far as I am aware there is no such scene in *Sleepless in Seattle*; there might be one in *You've Got Mail* but I can't face watching it a second time to find out. Filled with movie-like nostalgia for this magnificent city, we retreat to our apartment and for the first time in New York get to rest a little before getting ready to go home.

After a few hours, Joe le Taxi is back with his reliable but extortionate executive taxi service and immediately sends me into turmoil.

'How long until Grandma Elaine's check-in?' he asks.

'Not for two hours,' I casually and confidently respond as we all get into his car.

'Two hours!!! Man, it's rush hour in New York. You need to allow three and a half hours to get to JFK at this time of day.'

Our flight home is four hours after Grandma Elaine's so I hadn't wanted to waste our final afternoon in the airport, but nor had it occurred to me to factor in rush hour. We have been lazing around in our apartment for hours when we should have been depositing Grandma Elaine. I am not Charmaine; how am I supposed to know these things? It is not the prospect of Mum missing her flight that is troubling me; more that I will have to get her a seat on our flight back to Gatwick and put her up at our place for a day or two before the jet lag permits her to return to the north-east. I have served my time and done a full week's community service with her. I need to dispose of her.

This is where Joe le Taxi's NYPD driver credentials come to the fore. He knows every nook and cranny, every side road, and seemingly controls all of the traffic lights to keep them on green. This is going to cost me in tip money but it will be worth it.

'There are some drinks and snacks in the back,' says Joe as he jumps from lane to lane, accelerating past more reasonably paced drivers. He knows this is a tipping journey so we are getting the full service.

'Do you have any banana bread?' asks Mum.

'Joe, she *has* to make this flight,' I plead.

This is the speed at which our scene in *Fast & Furious 8*

should have been shot. Joe le Taxi beats Vin Diesel hands down and speeds us to JFK, zigzagging through the gridlock, with an hour to spare. It is emotional, but it is time to bid farewell to Grandma Elaine and New York.

As the kids are hugging her, I say: 'One more thing, Mum.'

'Yes, dear?'

'A thousand points for leaving early.'

'Geoffrey!'

I wave her into her departure gate, and relax. Now my sabbatical proper can begin. Even better, when I return the kids and swap Mum for Jackie, things should get a lot cheaper.

'Daddy, you owe me fifty dollars for the Best Behaviour Prize,' pipes up Mimi.

# CHAPTER TWELVE

*Seattle – Sheffield – common people – Cleveland badminton*
*team – Jimmy Page – ungrateful daughter*
SOUNDTRACK: LED ZEPPELIN – '*D'YER MAK'ER*'

'**Y**ou know, life is a random process, I think, but you can add a narrative to it.'

Wise words, Jarvis Cocker. I am watching *Pulp: A Film about Life, Death and Supermarkets* on the Delta flight from Heathrow to Seattle. It is Day 1 of Steve's itinerary.

Jarvis is right and that is what I am trying to achieve with this journal: to add a random narrative to the military precision of my Steve-organised sabbatical life. I once wrote a children's novel entitled *The Lost Grandad*, provoked by the death of my father two months before the birth of my first child and his first grandchild. I gave a copy of the book to Jacques, a French divorcé, lothario, gardener and swimming-pool attendant (in that order) in a sleepy, shuttered village in the Midi-Pyrénées called Mansonville. The ability to speak colloquially, yet in a poetic and lyrical way, without conscious thought or self-editing, is something that impresses me. Jarvis can do it, and so could Jacques. Upon receiving a copy of my book, impressed that I had written a book at all (he hadn't read it or he might not have been so impressed), he said: 'Spoken words are like butterflies; they fly away; but written words are fixed for ever.'

No one is going to remember the trials I acted upon as a lawyer. Mindful of my father's and Prince's premature deaths, at an age only ten years older than me (and the growing casualty list of David Bowie and Ann Foley), I want to set some permanent, fixed words of my own in print in case Schindler should exclude me from his list and his lift should get me instead. It also gives me the chance, with the benefit of conscious thought and a lot of self-editing, to sound more poetic and lyrical than what I really am when I speak.

The Pulp documentary makes me cry. This is not unusual. I am at an age where I cry at a lot of films. It is about Pulp re-forming to do a farewell tour in order to be able to say goodbye properly to their hometown, Sheffield, which is the last date of the tour. As Jarvis sings 'Common People' to the common people of Sheffield, I am overcome and my tears begin to flow. Conventional wisdom says we only have five senses, but in my view music is a primeval sixth sense rather than a mere subset of sound. Music is something you sense as well as hear. It connects with the instinctive rhythm of human beings in a way that nothing beautiful, a sunset, a poem or the laughter of an infant, ever can. No other animal relates to music like we do: birds, giraffes and monkeys don't tap their feet or nod their heads in response to the beat of a drum. Philosophers and poets speak of a natural order, but there is a natural rhythm which lives in our souls. For me, nothing is more emotional than watching live music. This is why Jarvis performing his grateful gyrations to his grateful people makes me cry on the plane.

It was Stuart Adamson (add him to the casualty list) who

made me want to play guitar. I was listening to 'In a Big Country' by Big Country in 1985 on my Sanyo (cheaper than Sony) Walkman in a clapped-out blue Bedford van, returning to Cleveland from the British Under-16 County Badminton Championship in Nottingham. It was then that I had my one and only vision: not the Marian apparition of Medjugorje; this was something far more spiritual. I saw myself on stage, playing guitar to a packed arena, and there was dry ice (this was the 1980s). I was too big for Castro to Deodar. I was destined to play in a covers band called LAP (standing for Limited Ability Partnership) with three other lawyers and an IT guy in an investment bank (who is also the same age as Prince and may therefore expire at any moment; but bass players are easy to replace). Coincidentally, it is a band whose repertoire includes 'Disco 2000' by Pulp.

Admittedly, Stuart Adamson is not one of the guitar greats. But I was only fifteen and my music taste was still going through puberty. Big Country was the acne I needed to overcome before I matured into Led Zeppelin.

Led Zeppelin are on my bucket list. I have now taken my children on the trip of a lifetime to New York; I have shown my eldest daughter, Meggie, a sunset from the top of the Empire State Building, thereby ticking off item one on her bucket list. Eighteen is of course too young to be compiling a bucket list. Her generation only discovered what buckets were three years ago – they have never used them to wash a car, for instance – when crowd-funding for the ALS Foundation (which pioneers research into Amyotrophic Lateral Sclerosis, a fatal disease which affects nerve cells in the brain and spinal cord) inspired the thrill-seeking flock of Facebook-land to have buckets of iced water tipped over their heads, with spectacularly successful profile- and fund-raising results (it raised $100 million). But despite Meggie now knowing how to use a bucket and despite the Empire State Building sunset coming off her bucket list, she still refuses to invite Jimmy Page round to my house to jam with me.

'Meggie, I leave for Seattle in the morning, and then on to Alaska,' I said yesterday. 'Like Chris McCandless in *Into the Wild*, I might never return. The number one item on *my* bucket list is to jam with Jimmy. Can you invite him over tonight?'

'No,' she replies, conclusively and somewhat ungratefully, I feel.

By way of background, Meggie and Mimi used to go to a pleasant but modest primary school in West Sussex. It is not an academy of the rich and famous; rather, it educates the children of commuting PR executives, IT consultants, doctors and, yes, the occasional lawyer.

One January, on the first day of the new term, Meggie had sent me a text along the following lines: 'You will be excited about the new boy in my class. His dad is a famous guitarist.' It wouldn't have been that well punctuated or spelled.

'Who????!!!!' I had replied urgently.

'Jimmy someone,' came the casual reply some hours later.

Hendrix was out for obvious reasons; it could be only Page. Uncharacteristically, I made a point of attending every parents' evening, school play and speech day that term, but it wasn't until the following term, at the end-of-year play, that I finally got to meet the man who wrote 'Stairway to Heaven' and, closer to home, whose gold disc I had unexpectedly had to purchase following a charity silent auction. He too is a divorced dad so was ostracised by the mum mafia at school. They had a lot more to disapprove of in him than in me. The Argentinian mother of the boy in my daughter's class is his second divorced wife, but was uncontroversial when compared with the spot of bother he got himself into in the US in the early 1970s when he supposedly dated a fourteen-year-old girl, Lori Maddox; old habits die hard and he is currently dating a woman from Surrey who is a mere forty-six years younger than him.

As a solo dad looking for somewhere to sit for the tea and cake on offer before the school play, Jimmy found the mums were not at their most welcoming, which for once worked to my advantage, as I was typically sitting on my own. He was slimmer than I remembered him, but with the wizened, tanned face, the white hair tied in a ponytail and the slight lugubrious slur of his reedy voice, there was no mistaking that this was an aged rock star, not a PR executive, IT consultant, doctor or lawyer.

I introduced myself as Geoff; he introduced himself as Jimmy; in rock history, it wasn't quite as momentous as The Beatles meeting Elvis Presley, or Johnny Cash meeting Bob Dylan, but in my history it was a monumental meeting of minds. It started well, with me keeping surprisingly calm and telling him that I thought (I knew of course, and had done all I could to encourage it) my daughter and his son were good friends, but then I panicked and admitted that I owned one of his gold discs and played in a covers band. After all, how better to impress the greatest rock guitarist of all time than to reveal that I collect his unwanted possessions and play rhythm guitar in a covers band comprising such rebellious, hell-raising names as Dave, Chris, Tim and John. It was the great philosopher Homer (Simpson) who once said that covers bands offer 'the thrill of live music without the fear of hearing anything new'. I doubted Jimmy would agree with Homer and approve of covers bands. But I was wrong.

We were called into the play before I could embarrass myself further. I thought that was my Jimmy Page Experience done, but to my delight he sought me out at the end of the show, the mums still not wanting to socialise with him (or me). I commented on how confident all of the kids had been on stage and it was then that he uttered the words I want inscribed on my tombstone.

'The kids see you and me on stage, Geoff, rocking out, and we inspire them.'

Wise words, Jimmy Page. Not only had he remembered my name, but he was comparing his performance at Knebworth to a crowd of 200,000 with mine at the Turk's Head to a crowd of 180 colleagues and secretaries. In his eyes, a band is a band; live music is live music; a performance is a performance. In my eyes, we are standing back-to-back on stage, riffing; we are two peas in a pod, Jimmy and me.

Some might be content with sharing Victoria sponge and inspirational live performances with Jimmy Page. But now that we have broken the ice, I want him to come over to my place; I want to show him my Fenders, Gibsons and Gretschs; I want him to like me and jam with me; perhaps have a sleepover in my room, with Turkish delight and Tizer. And, in order to secure this, I have been attempting emotional blackmail and bribery on Meggie ever since, but she continues to deny her father this small wish.

'Right hand, four fingers. Right hand, thumb.'

The Seattle Border Protector is too young and handsome to be this humourless, but he has been well drilled and has had his smile surgically removed. Jackie almost breaks his resolve by continuing to stare into the camera during the whole pointless grilling as to why we are coming to Seattle (like he cares), and with her response as to what her occupation is: 'I do nothing.'

'Well, he didn't tell me when to stop looking into the camera.' It must be the uniform, as she is never that obedient with me.

It has taken over two hours to get through the most inefficient border control in the US (I bet Tom Hanks didn't have to put up with that for *Sleepless in Seattle*), which means that our luggage is impatiently waiting for us on the other side, having outstayed its welcome on the carousel.

We check in at the Edgewater Hotel. It is by the edge of the water, just off the sidewalk where people walk by the side of the road.

'Steward? We don't have a reservation under Steward. Might the reservation be in your surname?'

'Steward is my surname.'

'Oh, I'm sorry, I thought that was your first name. Sure, here it is.'

As we take in the magnificent view from the lounge across the water of Puget Sound, Jimmy's and my paths cross again. It is uncanny, like our destinies are interwoven. A photograph hangs on the lounge wall, of Jimmy staying here at around the time he might have been on the run from the California police department for his underage girlfriend. I text Meggie a photograph of me pointing at Jimmy's framed photograph and looking forlorn, adding, 'Now do you feel guilty?'

'No,' she replies conclusively and, I still feel, ungratefully.

# CHAPTER THIRTEEN

*Geeks, grunge and coffee makers – phasers, Dorothy's dress
and Nazi werewolves – Ron and the FBI – celebrity cartoon
cubbyhole – Tom Hanks – coffee and Brazilian footballers
– Hurray for the Riff Raff*
SOUNDTRACK: PEARL JAM – 'I AM MINE'

It seems that indolence is my natural state. It is Day 2 of Steve's itinerary and neither the excitement nor the jet lag have prevented me from having a full night's sleep. Jackie is motionless beside me; over the years I have learned that it is unwise to waken a sleeping Irishwoman. As I have vowed that I will go for a run every day, I spring out of bed and quietly dress in my virgin running gear, feeling as virtuous as a New Yorker. I go for a dawn jog alongside the Seattle Seawall through the Olympic Sculpture Park. I am neither an Olympian nor a work of art, but that will change soon enough with my now rigorous daily running regime.

Until fairly recently, Seattle was an overcast and overlooked fishing and logging city, heavily reliant upon traditional port industries and one old Tom Hanks movie. It has an NFL team called the Seahawks; they are the equivalent of my football team, Middlesbrough FC, and are not very good. The only excitement in the city would come from the occasional navy warship pulling into the harbour and spilling white-uniformed sailors into the boulevards, bars and brothels. But in the past twenty-five years Seattle has woken up even more resolutely and impressively than I did this morning. A generation of IT geeks, coffee makers and internet entrepreneurs have acted as pathfinders in their respective sectors and revolutionised the world, taking with them the pleasant city of Seattle.

The businesses which have emerged from nowhere, like the nearby Mount Rainier materialising from the mist, and Mr Benn's shopkeeper, are now 'as if by magic' world leaders in their field. A young Seattle programmer called Bill Gates did quite well for himself by writing a rather popular software package called Microsoft Windows; an English teacher called Jerry Baldwin made pretty good coffee in the Pike Place Public Market, trading from a little market stall under the name Starbucks; and a young man called Jeff Bezos had an idea that books didn't need to be purchased on the high street and could instead be sold on the newly emerging world wide web: he called his online book store Amazon. Two of the three richest men on the planet herald from Seattle; the same cannot be said of Middlesbrough. This corporate dynamism was all happening at around the same time a grungy guitarist and vocalist called Kurt was writing some revolutionary songs across the water in the Olympic Peninsula backwater town of Aberdeen. It is fair to say that Seattle has had a productive quarter of a century.

We all know about Bill Gates. He seems to be a good chap and a generous philanthropist. In the centre of Seattle, by the still futuristic Space Needle (built in the 1960s and inspired by the space-age cartoon *The Jetsons*), stands the enormous Gates

Foundation, built fairly recently from the look of it and erected as a public monument to his modest do-gooding. I have no interest in visiting the Gates Foundation: sorry, Bill, but I find you and your building a bit dull. I am more interested in your fellow Windows creator and lesser-known business partner, Paul G. Allen (he presumably added the G to distinguish himself from the 1980s Tottenham Hotspur midfielder), who has built a much more interesting building with his loose change: an abstract, psychedelic, irregular-beaten-panel of a structure called the Experience Music Project (EMP). And that is our first stop after breakfast and a Red Bull (I saw the fridge in a petrol station that we walked past; it is the first day proper of my US trip and Red Bull will stave off jet lag. It's medicinal. I won't tell Mimi).

Within this pop culture museum, Paul G. Allen has housed the type of cool stuff that a billionaire IT geek should by rights collect: such as original *Star Trek* phaser guns; Dr McCoy's medical scanner and hyposptray; Uhura's space micro-dress (who wouldn't want to own that?); Dorothy's dress and the lion costume from *The Wizard of Oz*; the Nazi wolf head from the nightmare sequence in *An American Werewolf in London* (by far the most terrifying and unexpected film scene from my childhood); a Gizmo puppet from *Gremlins*; Kurt Cobain's cardigan from his *MTV Unplugged* session; and a room full of guitars tracing the history of the guitar from Martins to Fenders. That, Mr Gates, is a much better way to spend your money than on philanthropy, although Paul G. Allen should note that the EMP would be even better were he to start collecting *Doctor Who* memorabilia.

I enjoy wandering around the EMP at my leisure, subject to

Jackie repeatedly asking me how many more guitars we need to see (to which the easy answer is always 'just one more'). Jimmy Page continues to stalk me, as one of his live performances is playing on the massive screen inside. I take a photograph of it for Meggie in case she hasn't yet appreciated how significant her friend's father is to me.

I have always enjoyed exploring cities by myself (occasionally I allow Jackie or my children to join me) and have never once signed up to a ghastly umbrella-raising tour guide. However, Steve, my trusty sabbatical planner, persuaded me at a lunchtime meeting on a busy day in the office that I would get more value (and he would get more commission) out of a short stay in Seattle by having a bespoke tour guide. Eager to get back to my desk, I was hoodwinked into agreeing and am now regretting it. For the next five hours we are entrusting ourselves to a stranger who will no doubt address me as Steward.

'Here's the thing, Steward,' says Ron. 'There are two things you have to remember on this tour. The first is my train of thought when I lose it; and the second is that when I say right, I probably mean left.'

It is Ron who is to be our private guide for our afternoon in Seattle. To my surprise, I like him instantly. He is slight, wiry, quirky, intellectual, with school teacher rubber shoes, and very, very Jewish. That this tour is going to be something different to those offered by umbrella wielders is apparent from the outset when I realise, all too late, that Ron hasn't arranged how he will meet us. All I know is that his name is Ron and that he will be at the EMP at noon. It is a big and confusing building. I have no idea what he looks like, and he has no idea what I look like. Neither of us has the other's mobile number. If he had said,

'Look out for a ginger Woody Allen', it would have been easy. Charmaine would never tolerate such flimsy arrangements.

Jackie spots an enormous black Chevrolet Suburban SUV outside the museum, with blacked-out, bulletproof windows and a burly, black-suited, black-tied FBI driver. She has delusions of grandeur and thinks that will be our car; I think if she gets in that car she will be abducted and waterboarded. I am scared of the scary-looking driver so leave her to approach him on her own to establish if we are to be his passengers for the day. Irritatingly, Jackie is right (she usually is both irritating and right): the FBI guy in fact transpires to be a placid Romanian called Sarin, after the chemical weapon. He has lost Ron, who is walking around the circumference of the museum looking for us, equipped only with our names and an intellectual air, but Sarin has an advantage over us and calls him on his cell phone. Soon we are all united.

'You like music, right?' asks Ron, who has obviously been well briefed by Steve. It's a safe ice-breaker. Better than asking about whether Donald Trump will be the next President.

'Sure do,' I reply, getting into my role and going native.

'That's great. I was going to take you to Nirvana's record label, Sub Pop, but I called them up and they admitted that their offices aren't very interesting. They don't even have album covers on the wall. Are you in the music industry?'

'No, I'm a lawyer.'

'Oh dear. Well, we'll see some great music sights anyway,' lies Ron, before we embark upon a tour of famous and beautiful Seattle houses, none of which belongs to a musician; architecture seems to be Ron's passion.

We begin with Queen Anne Hill, an affluent neighbourhood

whose name derives from the architectural style of the mansions. The views from the top of Queen Anne Hill across Lake Union are spectacular. The houses are grand wooden piles, embellished with turrets and stepped porches. Each is beautifully unique. The town planners, until very recently, have insisted that the properties are all 'sole resident', which gives a picture-book character to Seattle. Only in recent years have multi resident buildings (flats to you and me) been emerging to deal with the increasing homeless problem.

The next stop on our house-viewing tour is as quirky as Ron's potential had promised. Ballard is a historic and hip neighbourhood of Seattle, full of some of the best restaurants, bars and shops in town, but Ron rejects all of them and instead we are driving down a less salubrious, nondescript street in industrial Ballard, with lots of drab construction work being undertaken around us and seemingly nothing of any interest to an afternoon tourist. Ron is very precise to Sarin about where to stop: 'Just up here, don't overshoot.'

Sarin is as confused as we are as to what site Ron could be leading us to, but Ron knows his city. In 2006, a construction project in Ballard planned to build a new shopping centre, which meant that a number of insignificant houses would need to be demolished by a corporate behemoth to make way for the new building. Despite all of her neighbours selling up and moving away, octogenarian Edith Macefield was a real estate hold-out and turned down a number of offers from the construction company to leave, eventually refusing a final offer of $1,000,000 to let them buy her chipboard house. The looming five-storey retail development had to literally be built around Macefield's 100-year-old tiny wooden farmhouse, as if the final jigsaw piece had been deliberately removed from the perimeter frame, leaving an awkward, unnatural, house-shaped gap.

Edith's story became the inspiration for the charming Pixar animated movie *Up*. And here we are standing outside the celebrity cartoon cubbyhole, now empty following Edith's death and looking very much like a condemned building. It is the quirkiest site I have ever visited and unsurprisingly there are no tourists here to spoil my tourist photograph. I ask Ron if he could also arrange for me to meet my favourite cartoon, Jessica Rabbit, but sadly she is not from around these parts. Instead I make do with the Tenth Doctor, who poses for a photo in front of the *Up* house.

Next, Ron takes us to see a troll under a bridge. It lives below a freeway underpass beneath Aurora Bridge and it is clutching a Volkswagen Beetle. It is twenty feet tall. I wait until some wayward children stop climbing on its head before taking my photo. I feel rather pleased. It is not every day one gets to see a troll under a bridge.

Ron is good. I have never had so much fun exploring a new place since a friend, whose house I was staying at in southwest France, gave me a tour of his property upon arrival and we found a naked French woman from the village sneaking a skinny dip in his pool. Ron is ticking a lot of boxes: he, too, is a Tom Hanks fan. We agree over tacos that if ever there was a year when Tom should stand for President as a third-party candidate, it is this year. Choosing between Donald Trump and Hillary Clinton is like choosing a favourite out of Josef Goebbels and Vladimir Putin. The Americans always like to outdo the Brits, so I fear that they could trump our moronic decision to leave the EU by deciding to elect the moronic Trump. Tom should be standing to give the American electorate an escape route. When Ron Howard was casting *Apollo 13*, he was struggling with the lead role, so he asked himself the question: which actor would everyone want to see return home safely from space? The answer then became obvious: Tom Hanks. Selfishly, Tom is not standing – but his house from *Sleepless in Seattle* still is. That is our next stop, after Ron leads us through a neighbourhood where he assures me, 'There's some great live music here.' There is no evidence of this, but from Gas Works Park, with my zoom lens, I do get to take a photograph of the houseboat from where Tom Hanks's pretend son called the radio station and Tom melted Meg Ryan's heart. It is no longer the remote floating home of the film, though: immediately behind it has grown a vibrant city of skyscrapers. Seattle is no longer sleeping.

Music and birdlife were my brief, vicariously through Steve to Ron. Music has been overlooked apart from dubious passing references, and birdlife in a city was always a tall order, but, as we leave the rust-orange gasworks which once supplied gas to the whole city but now have been preserved as testament to the city's past life and as a fabulous piece of installation art, a flash of electric blue catches my eye. It is a brilliant blue Steller's jay, a common bird with its unmistakable black head crest.

'Look, a bird,' says Ron knowledgeably.

Both boxes now ticked in his mind, we move on to the Pike Place Market for more melody- and ornithology-free activity.

I don't like coffee or tea. I don't see the point of tea. It is a bland and insipid drink, made interesting only by turning it into sugared milk. Even with my sweet tooth I wouldn't drink sugared milk. I do see the point of coffee – it at least has a taste – but I don't care for it. Nor does it have the rejuvenating impact on me which everyone claims is part of its appeal. I am of course in the minority. With a Starbucks now on almost every corner of every American city, it is hard to believe that any nation could drink more coffee than America, but in fact America, on a per capita coffee consumption basis, is not even in the top ten. According to the International Coffee Organization, the world's largest coffee consumers are the Finns, closely followed by the Norwegians. The Dutch are third, but I suspect they misunderstood what the survey meant by 'coffee shop' and treated it as a euphemism.

Coffee scares me. Even if I wanted to walk into a coffee shop to order a coffee, I wouldn't know how to. I am intimidated by the myriad types of coffee on offer and have no idea how to distinguish between any of the following: Americano; Cubano; Crema; Zorro; Doppio; Romano; Romario; Rivaldo; Espresso; Au Lait; Guillermo; Ristretto; Macchiato; Noisette; Lungo; Latte; Cortado; Cafu; Cappuccino; Frappuccino; Affogato; Kaká; Con Hielo; Mocha; Breve; Bombón; Flat White; Black Eye; Red Eye; Dead Eye; Lazy Eye. I have introduced a few legendary Brazilian footballers into that list but I suspect most people would not have noticed and would quite happily have ordered one and indeed received something from the barista, my point being that they all probably taste the same anyway.

The other reason I don't walk into coffee shops is the queues. I am not a patient man. These imaginary coffee flavours take so long to concoct that anyone who doesn't drink coffee, and who simply wants a blueberry muffin and a bottle of water, has to wait twenty minutes and politely observe the whole ridiculous, noisy, steamy ceremony. If someone ever opens a chain of coffee shops that doesn't sell coffee, then I will be the first in line, because there will be no queue. I blame Starbucks for all this. And that is our next stop.

Starbucks is a year younger than me. It was founded in 1971; I was founded in 1970. Starbucks first became profitable in the early 1980s; it took me considerably longer. I was focusing on Marillion, Depeche Mode, Thompson Twins and Ultravox when Starbucks was focusing on popularising darkly roasted coffee across the world. Named after the chief mate (Starbuck) in Herman Melville's *Moby Dick*, Starbucks originated in Seattle. Claimed by Ron to be the first ever Starbucks store (my research suggests it is the second, but now the oldest since the first store closed), I am standing outside 1912 Pike Place. Predictably, there is a queue. But even by coffee shop standards this is a long queue, snaking outside the store and around the block. I politely ease myself through the Japanese tourists, assuring them that I don't even drink coffee and just want to have a look inside. The only discernible difference to me is that this 'original' store has a more risqué logo. The twin-tailed mermaid is proudly exposing her breasts, whereas the more discreet logo of today has her hair hanging down to protect her modesty. Otherwise it pretty much sells the same impenetrable coffee varieties as any other Starbucks. I am tempted to order a Pele Macchiato, but it is too far to the end of the queue.

Cheese shops don't sell coffee, so there is no queue next door. I buy some cheese and say farewell to Ron and Sarin, who contrary to my expectations have both been terrific guides. They do, however, look bemused by their tip of a slab of cheddar each.

I obviously can't visit Seattle without checking out the music scene. My morning Red Bull hasn't worked. Neither has my run. The jet lag is kicking in. In fact, it is kicking my head in. We go to a grungy music venue called The Crocodile, to see a band called Hurray for the Riff Raff. Ron didn't organise this, obviously. I have never before fallen asleep standing up. At the bar. Ordering a craft beer. Jackie suggests we should go home as I am too tired, but I am also too stubborn. I have paid for the tickets; even though I have no idea who the band are and just like their name, I want to see them. We go to the outside smoking area for some fresh air, where I fall asleep again. I manage to hold out until the band eventually come on stage. They have a female lead singer of small stature but massive stage presence. She is wearing cowgirl boots, playing acoustic guitar and singing folk-rock with energy and enthusiasm. Her music is right up my street, but before she reaches the chorus of her second song, we are on a different street heading to bed. I can see plenty more of that type of thing in Nashville. But for now, I need to be Asleep in Seattle.

# CHAPTER FOURTEEN

*Car parks and golf courses – Port Angeles Senior & Community Center – Thank You Stephenie – metamorphosis – the glory of God – the two Geoffreys*

SOUNDTRACK: CHRISTINA PERRI – 'A THOUSAND YEARS'

The Mount Olympus I know is the highest mountain in Greece, from where Zeus used to unleash wrath and thunderbolts. It turns out there is another Mount Olympus in Washington state, surrounded by its own National Park, which today is going to be our first.

My run this morning consists of jogging down to the Seattle ferry terminal to work out how to drive there on the one-way system: it is not a long run but a satisfyingly practical piece of exercise with, for once, a purpose.

A car-ferry-hop across Puget Sound west of Seattle, and a pleasurable, twisting two-hour drive, deposits us in the flat grid town of Port Angeles, which serves as a gateway to Olympic National Park. I feel ill-informed that I have never heard of a National Park which encompasses nearly a million acres and is a designated World Heritage Site. But there are fifty-nine National Parks and in fact plenty of which I have never heard, such as Acadia, Big Bend, Congaree, Cuyahoga Valley and Dry

Tortugas, and that is only A to D. My knowledge of National Parks is in fact disappointingly mainstream, and tends towards the other end of the alphabet: Yellowstone, Yosemite and Zion.

We are staying at a place called Olympic Lodge. It is a sort of high-end motel, surrounded on one side by a car park and on the other by a golf course. Fortunately, our room overlooks the golf course. I am not a huge fan of golf, but I am less of a fan of parked cars. We unpack and drive in a straight line to the city of Port Angeles. It has the feel of a town rather than a city, and it is home to only 19,000 permanent residents.

Port Angeles is a confused place, struggling for identity. This is reflected in its very name, which is half-English, half-Spanish. It is a booming port, with giant tankers providing an impressive backdrop; it is an important portal to the Olympic Peninsula and even links the US and Canada with a ferry to Victoria, British Columbia. Yet it is also an obscure, slumbering lumber town which few people outside of Washington state have heard of despite its important historical ties with the Native Americans (whose sole purpose now, sadly, is to own the land upon which the casinos are built) and Abraham Lincoln (in the early months of the Civil War, Lincoln reputedly designated the obscure western village of Port Angeles as the Second Capital of the United States in case anything should happen to Washington DC). Finally, it is a quaint, intelligent, well-bred little town of closet hipsters, with a rebellious, artistic, bohemian streak. It smells of wood and I rather like it. I also rather like the range of craft beers readily available in each of its welcoming bars.

Taking a leaf out of Seattle Ron's tour book, I decide to do something quirky and outside of the guide books tonight. I have bought a book that has been recommended to me on three separate occasions in Seattle (including by Ron) called *The Boys in the Boat* by Daniel James Brown. Daniel James has sensibly distinguished himself from Dan Brown (and from the godfather of soul, James Brown) by using his full name, or I would not have bought it. It is an American *Chariots of Fire* but with oars instead of running spikes; a true account of how nine gritty working-class heroes from the University of Washington rowing club (so not that working class) beat Hitler's Aryan rowing team to win the gold medal at the 1936 Berlin Olympics.

The bookshop from which I bought it, Port Book and News on East First Street, Port Angeles, has a claim to fame which will impress the hell out of Meggie and Mimi: it is the store where Bella Swan had her first date with reformed bloodaholic Edward Cullen in Stephenie Meyer's book *Twilight*, which for some inexplicable reason made a star out of Robert Pattinson, a pasty-faced Englishman with the acting ability of a corpse. Book in hand, we stop off for a root beer float (nowhere sells Red Bull and I am running low on sugar) in a little white wooden café lit by late afternoon amber sunshine. The owner and two ladies eating cake agree between the three of them that they love my English accent. They have a collective age of around 250 years, and I lament that I had not come here in my twenties, or in their case in the 1920s. If only my voice had provoked such a magnetic response from the girls at Nottingham University.

I pick up the local newspaper, the *Peninsula Daily News*, and notice an article announcing that tonight, as part of the build-up for the Rio de Janeiro Olympic Games in a few weeks' time, the Olympic Peninsula Rowing Association will host an advance screening of a PBS documentary entitled *The Boys of*

'36, giving the story behind the book. It is a free event and will be held at the Port Angeles Senior & Community Center. The Olympic Peninsula Rowing Association is apparently excited to be presenting this programme, and a full house is anticipated. It is exactly the type of small-town experience, with small townsfolk, of which Ron and Woody Allen would approve. I am looking for nice, normal Americans and I should be able to find some here. Jackie can barely contain her excitement: the one thing she enjoys more than history books is documentaries about history books. I do some more speaking in English to keep the coffee shop ladies happy, and then head back to our lodge to get ready for my night at the community centre with the senior citizens of Port Angeles.

It is the middle of the night in England so I can't ask Charmaine to get me directions to the community centre. I have no internet signal in my room, so I resort to the medieval navigational technique of driving downtown and asking people. I am starting to think that Port Angeles is not a very community-spirited place after all, as no one knows where the community centre is. After a few sketchy directions, we find ourselves in a run-down neighbourhood of single-storey and in some cases single-room wooden houses, with front yards only big enough to house a 'TRUMP: MAKE AMERICA GREAT AGAIN' placard. I am baffled that benefits-class people from one of most remote western towns in America can connect with and support a bigoted billionaire from the opposite side of the country, who has as much in common with them as I do with bingo halls.

But it is to the bingo hall I resort to ask for directions to the Port Angeles Senior & Community Center. It is packed:

the senior members of the community seem to have more enthusiasm for bingo than for the community centre. The two cake-eaters are there, delighted to see me again, and in return for speaking more English to them and their friends, they give me precise directions to the community centre, one block away. I thank them in quintessential English, leave the car with the Trump supporters (it is only a hire car) and walk. There is no sign of any community at the community centre. There is also no sign of *The Boys of '36*. All of the doors are locked. I check the photograph of the newspaper article which I had taken on my phone; only now do I notice that the date of the newspaper is four days ago. I can't blame Charmaine or Jackie, so I blame the Anglophile lady in the coffee shop for not refreshing her newspapers on a daily basis. It is this attention to detail and ability to pass the blame that have made me such a successful lawyer.

I decide that I'm done with *The Boys in the Boat*, but the Stephenie Meyer local connection has piqued my interest. The next day, after my run around the golf course (Day 3 and I am still running like Forrest Gump), the receptionist at our lodge informs us that the nearby town of Forks is in fact where the *Twilight* trilogy was set. Although our tour of the National Parks is at risk of turning into a tour of celebrity houses, we decide to visit the eerie, grey town of the vampire movies to get some photographs of famous film locations for the kids.

It is a promising summer's day and the sky is clear and blue, but I can play around with the lighting on iPhotos and make it seem sepia and atmospheric. I begin to become suspicious at the entrance to Forks, where we are greeted by a cheery slatted sign amongst plush green foliage reading 'The City of Forks

Welcomes You'. I do not want welcoming, I want foreboding; I do not want a cheerful city, I want a small, spooky town; I do not want breezy locals, I want anaemic, gothic teenagers who grimace at me. Jackie remembers that Bella worked in Forks General Store, so we head there first. It has a parking lot for 300 (a lot of parking) and is the size of a large out-of-town Tesco. I am pretty sure this is not the store where the film was shot. We get back in the car and drive on to the visitors' centre to be put back on the right track (preferably a sinister dead-end track with tumbleweed). There are two battered red pick-ups outside it; one has the registration plate BELLA. I am pretty sure that these are not the actual pick-ups from the film either.

The lady in the visitors' centre is nice, for a deceitful old fraud. She tells us about Stephenie Meyer, and how grateful the city is that she selected Forks for the setting of her books, and how each year the city has a Stephenie Meyer Day, and how, if we want, for twenty dollars we can buy what looks like a home-made white multi-pack cotton T-shirt that now says in simple block capitals 'THANK YOU STEPHENIE' (an utterly mean-ingless piece of merchandise unless you happen to be there on the one day of the year that is Stephenie Meyer Day, or have a friend called Stephenie (unlikely given the idiotic spelling) who has done something kind and would appreciate your grat-itude being expressed by what you are wearing). She hands us an information sheet that looks like it was printed before Bill Gates, which lists all of the sites in the book, but none of the photographs looks familiar. At this point my keen legal mind and eye for detail finally come into play.

'You have been talking about the scenes in the *book*, but was any of the *film* actually shot here?'

She looks around furtively and leans in to me, lowering her voice to a whisper.

'Stephenie never actually visited Forks before she wrote the book, honey, but she wanted to set it in a remote western town. The book was set here, but when the film producers came, they didn't think it was eerie enough.'

From what I have seen of this bright, well-meaning place, I am inclined to agree with the producers.

'So where were the films actually shot?'

'Oregon.'

Upon realising we are in the wrong state, we leave forking Forks.

Not only am I done with *The Boys in the Boat*, I am also now done with *Twilight*. I never liked the stupid films anyway. But before we leave, I WhatsApp Meggie and Mimi a photograph of the Tenth Doctor standing on the red pick-up with the sun gleaming on its bonnet: they will never know. Meggie replies: 'Isn't it meant to be greyer?' I ignore her question as I think she might have rumbled me.

The false dawn to our day improves as we drive on through pine forests to First Beach at La Push. It is located in the Quileute Indian Reservation, which is as satisfyingly spine-chilling as Forks should have been. Genuinely battered pick-ups stand in the front yards of genuinely battered single-storey wooden houses. There is no grid system here; the houses look like they have been blown in, *Wizard of Oz*-style. It is the type of town where it would be difficult to distinguish between the before and after photographs, were it ever to be hit by a tsunami (for which it genuinely has road signs that read 'TSUNAMI EVAC-UATION ROUTE' – let's hope the road signs survive the tidal wave). We pull up on a gravel track with a forbidding sign saying 'No Parking Without a Permit'. The permit in question could well be a hunting permit, for a man hunt. Ours is the only car here. The air temperature is ten degrees colder. I feel vulnerable so I let Jackie get out of the car first. A rolling grey sea mist has all but concealed the smattering of small islands we have come to see. A spindly tree rises out of the rocks and driftwood at the end of the track, and the beginning of the sea, it is all that we can see before the ocean fades into mist. A bald eagle lands on one of its branches, looks me unnervingly in the eye and flies off over the rocks before I can retrieve my camera from the boot. It feels like an omen. This place has an unearthly quality and the producers of *Twilight* should have tried here before Oregon.

From where the eagle flew towards, a human head, enveloped by vapour, emerges out of the rocks. Whether or not he is a full Quileute Indian I don't know, but he is certainly of Native American origin. He looks like Chief Bromden from *One Flew Over the Cuckoo's Nest* and has the lined, weathered face a portrait artist would prize. He fixes me with a wise, knowledgeable but kind gaze as he strides past and towards the harbour. Immediately, as if he has commanded it, the mist begins to evaporate and boat-less masts are reunited with their vessels.

The previously concealed view before me is now breathtaking: a clutter of craggy islands rising from the water like volcanic tips which would be equally at home with a Transylvanian castle atop them. A long, thin beach covered with natural driftwood sculptures connects the small islands. This lonely coastline has a supernatural air to it.

Although it says in my Moon guide to the Olympic Peninsula that the Quileute tribe have embraced tourism, La Push shows

no signs of this. It is utterly unspoiled. There are no tourist trap-
pings, no 'Thank You Stephenie' T-shirts, and we are the only
people here in August, their peak season. La Push is better off
for it. It is owned by the tribe and has a stagnant, timeless pace.
No longer canoe builders or whalers, these days the tribe quietly
go about their 21st-century business of operating an oceanfront
resort, a fish hatchery and a harbour. Meanwhile, anyone is free
to come and marvel at the eerie view of their First Beach. They
also seem to be run by a mystical chief with dual superpowers
of metamorphosis and meteorology.

There is an otherworldly beauty to Olympic National
Park. As we drive back along Highway 101 (an appropriately
Orwellian road number for this place), we stop off at the Hoh
Rainforest. It feels like a separate world to La Push. In place
of craggy coastline are deep-green, moss-draped, gargantuan
fir trees. We have moved from the starkness of *Twilight* to the
lushness of *Avatar*. The dark, mysterious rainforest retains
the spiritual quality with which the Native American Hoh
tribe must have connected for hundreds of years. There is a
modest visitors' centre, where I buy a *Birds of Washington Field
Guide* but only see one bird: an Eastern Kingbird; it fixes me
with the same wise, knowledgeable gaze as the Quileute chief
and the eagle. I wonder...

At the end of the day, I log on to WhatsApp and send Charmaine some photographs of the differing ecosystems of Olympic National Park: of the mist rising over the tree-topped James
Island at First Beach; of green maple trees in the Hoh Rainforest
against a perfect azure sky; and of the fast-flowing cyan and
white Hoh River, framed by spruce and pebbles. Consequent-
ly, she changes her WhatsApp profile photograph to my Hoh

River shot (a copyright infringement which I will overlook) and her status now reads: 'The heavens declare the glory of God. Thank you Lord for nature, which reflects your glory.' Whilst I don't necessarily agree with Charmaine's conclusion about the providence of the Olympic Peninsula, it is undoubtedly a very spiritual place and they were glorious photographs.

The next day, I want an early start, so I selflessly forgo my run. This is the only day I will miss. After an exhilarating drive alongside the Pacific Ocean on Route 101, with a stop-off at the magnificently named Ruby Beach (a rather dull grey beach), we arrive at Lake Quinault Lodge (neither dull or grey). In 1937, President Franklin Delano Roosevelt dined here and was so impressed by the view of Lake Quinault that he promptly declared the whole area a National Park. Declaring places as National Parks was in his blood: as I had taught the kids at the American Museum of Natural History in New York (a fact which they already knew from Robin Williams's performance in the educational documentary *Night at the Museum*), it was his distant cousin, and all-round better President, Theodore Roosevelt, who had founded the National Parks movement exactly 100 years prior to my trip, a centenary of which I was utterly ignorant until arriving. But for the purposes of this book, let's pretend I had planned it all along and that can be another reason why I am visiting the National Parks this year. Happy centenary.

Being a lawyer, I have to give a lot of conference and seminar talks and I always try to come up with a one-liner that will capture the audience's attention from the outset. My openings have nothing on Theodore Roosevelt's, though. When campaigning for the presidency in Milwaukee in October 1912, Teddy Roosevelt was shot in the chest moments before he was due to give an address. Instead of going to hospital, he insisted on giving his speech. His opening line was nothing special – 'Friends, I shall ask you to be as quiet as possible' – but his second line did the trick: 'I don't know whether you fully understand that I have just been shot.' He then unbuttoned his waistcoat to reveal his bloodstained shirt, stating, 'It takes more than that to kill a bull moose.' The audience were his after that, but Roosevelt had a much easier gig than me as he didn't have to talk about a topic as dull as the advantages of arbitration over litigation.

Both Teddy and FDR shared the privilege of having an un-usual name, something to which I can relate. Admittedly mine is not a spectacular name, but you would be surprised how unique it is. There are mercifully few Geoffreys in the world. I am my parents' first child. It baffles me that the two of them fixed upon Geoffrey as their first-choice name, but their second choice was Campion so I should probably be grateful for small mercies. The name Geoffrey does, however, have its advantages: I don't know any other Geoffreys, and I have certainly never met another Geoffrey Steward. I was the only Geoffrey in my school, I am the only Geoffrey at my firm, and I have made sure that I am the only Geoffrey in my family.

When you google 'Geoffrey Steward' (as I have done on oc-casion), I am the first hit (together with a rather earnest partner profile photograph at work), which my children think makes me famous. The disadvantages to the name Geoffrey are that it attracted a lot of Zippy from *Rainbow* impersonations in the 1970s West Park Primary School playground; Americans can't understand whether it is a first name or a surname; and no one can ever spell it properly, so much so that I always have to intro-duce myself as 'Geoffrey with a G; and Steward with a D' (not to everyone I meet, you understand, but only when required by officialdom). However, my introductory nomenclature explanation is not a patch on how one of my partners introduces himself: 'Morgan: that's big M; small organ.'

When we check in at Lake Quinault Lodge, I am disappointed to learn that Steve has screwed up. This is a hotel where we have decided to treat ourselves before a week of very basic accommodation on a boat. But Jackie, cougar-like, pounces upon the fact that we are only given a standard room, despite having paid for a 'lakeside fireplace room' (the fireplace being an essential extra in August).

'No, sir, I have the booking here. Your agent has booked you a standard room for two nights.'

Dolores is a large, authoritative lady with the sense of humour of a Border Protector and with whom I am reluctant to pick a disagreement, so I politely explain that we are in fact only here for one night and that we are meant to have a lakeside fireplace room. She checks her system and calmly explains that whilst all of the fireplace rooms are taken, there is a chillier and disabled room available with a lakeside view which she can upgrade us to because of the mix-up (which skilfully she has made me feel responsible for). I accept her offer.

The lower climate, special needs room does indeed have a beautiful lakeside view and I suggest to Jackie that perhaps we don't need a fireplace after all. She challenges my masculinity for not fighting harder for our 'real room'; I would rather that than taking on Dolores. But no sooner have we unpacked than the concierge knocks on the door and says that there has been another mix-up and Dolores would like to see me again at reception. It feels like I have been called to see the headmaster.

I approach her with trepidation, worried that we might have bumped someone in a wheelchair, but it is good news.

'I got your name wrong,' explains Dolores.

'Don't worry,' I say, smiling, 'I get that a lot, like Roosevelt.'

She doesn't smile back.

'There is another man staying here with your name and I assumed you were his booking. It's my bad.'

I abhor that phrase, largely due to its grammatical bastardisation, but on this occasion I let it pass as it carries with it some unexpected news which throws me and leaves me emotionally confused. Whilst I am pleased that we will finally get the fireplace we so warmly deserve, I find myself becoming very possessive of my name.

'Are you positive he has the same name as me? I am Geoffrey with a G and Steward with a D.'

'He's near enough. He's Jeffrey with a J and Stewart with a T.'

This development makes me feel a whole lot better. It's nothing like my name. His introductory name explanation doesn't even rhyme. I win on both counts: I have a better name and room than Jeffrey fucking Stewart, and a fireplace. As a result, I can now enjoy the rest of my night at Lake Quinault Lodge, content in the knowledge that I am unique to this hotel after all.

# A REGRESSIVE INTERLUDE

*Friends – team players – tossers*
SOUNDTRACK: OASIS – 'LIVE FOREVER'

Over the years, I have learned that the three most effective means to jettison superfluous friends picked up along the way are:

Get married

Have children

Get un-married

Only if they survive all three of those milestones are they worthy friends, worth retaining.

Four such friends of mine, who share over a hundred years of my friendship between them, are Glen, Chris, Gav and Gay Matt. If you ask an American to describe one of his best friends, you will receive a list of superlatives: he is an incredible guy, phenomenally successful, a creative thinker, a terrific team player, a wonderful father, an outstanding human being, the embodiment of perfection. Frankly, it will put you off his friend from the outset. Whereas if you ask an Englishman to describe one of his best friends, he will respond that he is 'a bit of a tosser'. This is as warm an endorsement for an Englishman as the list of superlatives is for an American. To me, Glen, Chris, Gav and Gay Matt are all tossers.

We were all in our early twenties during 'new laddism'. Political correctness had gone a bit too far during our university years and as we left there was a generational backlash against it, which coincided with a purple patch of British music, art and fashion. Young, working men wanted to assert themselves and say that it was acceptable for guys in their twenties to overtly enjoy football, drinking and the female form. We all read *Loaded* magazine and Nick Hornby, we all watched *TFI Friday* and *Fantasy Football*, we all laughed at *Men Behaving Badly* and *Shooting Stars*, we all listened to Oasis and the *Trainspotting* soundtrack (apart from Glen, who knew nothing about music), we all idolised Gazza and Cantona (apart from Glen, who knew nothing about football). But after a few years, as with political correctness, new laddism had itself run its course and become crass and tiresome. Oasis released a disappointing third studio album, Chris Evans became a cock, Vic and Bob weren't as funny any more, Gazza signed for Rangers and Cantona shrugged his shoulders and walked away from football altogether; the internet replaced *Loaded* and online porn was occupying all of our spare time; and we all ran out of steam, settled down and got married, bought houses or did both. Equilibrium had been restored after a happy hedonistic hurrah.

It was at around this time that Gay Matt became a homosexual. When we were at university, he didn't have a prefix. He went out of his way to be as heterosexual as possible. He used to play and watch rugby, often downing pints whilst doing both; before going out for post-match drinks he would listen to the aggressively masculine 'Bat Out of Hell'; and whilst out drinking he would be aggressively masculine, starting fights with anyone in Nottingham who bumped into his friends on the dance floor or who bumped into his pint. After graduating, he went to work in Hong Kong and came back wanting to be known as Matthew and as a homosexual. His friends all thought this development was splendid; not only did we now have a gay friend (which was fashionably original back then), but he was also the most unexpected of all of our friends to be gay (Chris was far more likely), which made it tremendously funny as well. We embraced his gayness with open arms, but we could never embrace the name Matthew.

Gay Matt is getting married today, the day I fly from Seattle to Alaska, to his Caribbean partner of twenty years. This is my only regret of my whole trip: missing my first big fat gay wedding and a reunion with my oldest and dearest university friends. Just before taking off, I send him a text from Seattle airport offering him some advice as a seasoned and bruised ex-married straight man.

'Dear Gay Matt, a successful marriage is all about give and take. I am sure you will therefore have a very successful marriage as you have been giving and taking for twenty years.'

I land in Alaska to a text from Chris. It is a photo of Gav at the wedding, sticking up his middle finger at me. The tosser.

# CHAPTER FIFTEEN

*Lanyards – the correct spelling – a paranoid psychologist –*
*skiing in Texas – microlight crash – poisonous berries*
SOUNDTRACK: THE SILVER SEAS – 'ALASKA'

I am being branded. In a windowless town hall in Juneau, they
are handing out name tag lanyards at the start of our south-
east Alaskan 'UnCruise' cruise. It was a very early start to drive
back to Seattle airport, so I had no choice but to forgo my run
again. I promise myself that it really won't happen again, until I
remember that I am going to be on a boat for a week. I will revive
my daily runs when back on land. I don't want to overdo it.

'Geoff?'

'Yup,' I say, rising from my seat, but I am beaten to the lanyard by someone else claiming my name.

'That's the English spelling,' I say confidently, 'so it must be
mine.'

But, uncannily, twice in two days I have found an American
who has stolen my name (and lanyard), and this time he has
even spelled it correctly.

'It looks like we have two Geoffs,' concludes Matt, our expedition organiser, who has the biceps of a baboon and the
charisma of a clam.

'In which case I shall be known as Geoff One,' I joke.

'We were rootin' for ya, Geoff,' says my neighbour as I return to my seat lanyard-less; he is a craggy, muscular, reptilian San Diego passenger called Larry (I know this because he already has his lanyard), whom I like immediately from his impish smile and the fact he used the word 'rootin''. His glamorous Japanese/ Hawaiian wife (her father must have stayed over after bombing Pearl Harbor), Susu, giggles beside him, I like her as well.

Steve the sabbatical planner has taken advantage of me again. I have never done a cruise for two reasons: I don't like boats, and I don't like people who like boats. A number of my partners enjoy sailing and tying pastel jumpers around their necks at our annual partners' conference. To me, cruise ships represent organised geriatrics and Las Vegas artifice. Steve had assured me that UnCruise would be different, aimed at nimbler, funkier, more adventurous people who want to participate in the Alaskan wildlife rather than observe it from a bingo hall. Their smaller ships are more manoeuvrable and offer the opportunity to get up close and personal with the glaciers, whales and bears: ours is to be an unglamorous 160-foot vessel called the *Wilderness Adventurer*. I had signed up during a hurried meeting with Steve back in January, and it currently feels as adventurous as lawn bowling.

Looking around the orientation room, I am feeling a misrepresentation claim coming on against Steve. Larry may be muscular but his muscles are twenty years older than mine and he is one of the younger-looking retirees. There are only two other couples younger than Jackie and me. Also seated at our table are an unlikely older couple from North Carolina, who don't seem to like each other very much: a placid, pliable, roly-poly squeezable stress-ball called Bob who is a dead-ringer for Radar from the 1970s/1980s television show *M\*A\*S\*H*, and a difficult, high-maintenance lady called Pam, a dead-ringer for a paranoid psychologist in need of some self-diagnosis.

I am quickly learning that when participating in a cruise, you need to exercise great caution and judgement when choosing your seat at the orientation meeting, because the people you first meet and speak to will immediately shape-shift into barnacles and will thereafter be impossible to shake off. Bob and Pam are hardened cruisers (and, I suspect, swingers): Bob is looking for some naïve first-timers to offload Pam onto for the week; Pam is looking for a daughter or a pet to adopt. Jackie appears to tick both boxes.

There is not much to do in Juneau, other than to board your ship. It has a population of only thirty thousand, or the equivalent of Middlesbrough FC's packed Riverside Stadium when they are playing a decent team. (At this point, I enjoy a certain smugness in bringing up Middlesbrough in the Alaska chapter. James Cook navigated and mapped part of Alaska in 1778, and came from Middlesbrough (nearly). Coming from a tropical climate such as Middlesbrough, he found the Alaskan winter a bit too chilly so he then headed to the Hawaiian islands to remind himself of home, but like home the natives were none too friendly and ate him.) There are as many bald eagles in Alaska as there are people in Juneau. Nonetheless, it is the state capital, demonstrating just how vast and empty this state is. In the summer season, there are three or four cruise liners in port every day, with up to three thousand passengers per ship. Mercifully, our *Wilderness Adventurer* has a total of only sixty passengers, but mercilessly two of them are Pam and Bob.

The cruise operators are canny. They ingest and ejaculate all of their passengers at Juneau. But their arrival and departure times in no way coincide with the flights in and out of Juneau. It must be their way of giving back to the local community, to provide a steady flow of tourists with nothing else to do for a few hours than walk up and down the one long strip of shops, eating king crab and buying tat. Juneau is an odd place: like the surrounding bear-life, it hibernates off-season. The strip is divided into the temporary shops at one end, which resemble picturesque old Wild West saloons and are inhabited by seasonal sellers who quite literally pack up shop in the winter, and local victuallers at the other, less attractive, end, who are there... for ever. Less attractive is how I would describe the residents of Juneau generally. I would not imagine that the telephone directory here contains many different surnames.

Jackie and I have to kill two hours and avoid being killed by a local. The shops at the seasonal end seem to sell only diamonds, for those ocean liner passengers who are so bored and so wealthy that with only a few hours to spend in Juneau, they spend it by loading their pockets with gems.

The shops at the local end are equally useless to me, as I have no desire for items patched together from bits of bear and otter. I do, however, find one important local store with a Red Bull fridge. This is my only chance to refuel before a week without wings. I am followed in by a local in a lumberjack shirt, who seems genuinely surprised at how a door works. People from Alaska (the 49th state) refer to the rest of America as the 'Lower 48', which I suspect is also the average IQ level of the people from Juneau. My lumberjack-shirted imbecile then stands at the till with no purpose and no intention to purchase, and instead settles in to watch me open the fridge door, the operation of which again seems to startle him. He laughs and says, 'Red Bull'. I daren't roll my eyes at the face-pierced shopkeeper in case she is his mother or his wife or both.

It is only 11 a.m. but we decide to abandon the shops and their delinquents and spend our remaining time in Juneau in a bar, with genuine swinging saloon doors (which must really confuse the locals, on both sides) called the World Famous Red Dog Saloon. I have never heard of it, but it is the best way to waste time in Juneau. There is a live (just about) musician, dressed in ill-fitting cowboy clothes and singing bad country and western songs in a bad Stetson, sitting alongside an unsubtle giant plastic jar (the size of body-builder supplements) labelled, rather optimistically and shoutily, 'TIPS!' There is sawdust on the floor, presumably to catch his spittle as he sings. I listen to his set, watch his arches of spit and pray to Charmaine's God that Nashville will be better than this. As we leave, I put twenty dollars in his jar and make a wish, but he keeps on playing.

We eventually board the ship to perfect blue skies and a placid ocean, uncharacteristic weather for rainy Juneau. We are shown to our modest but comfortable cabin, with our own toilet, the aroma of which reminds me of Glastonbury. Moments later, Pam and Bob are shown to the cabin next door but one. Of course they are. Bob is carrying a guitar. Wistfully, I look across at the other two floating cities currently in port and think how much easier it would be to escape from Pam on ships that size: more places to hide. I wonder if I could swim for it, using Bob's guitar as a float, but decide the water is probably too polar and it is too nice a guitar (it's a Martin).

After watching from deck as we set sail and leave Juneau to a sunset, we are called to dinner by Matt's monotone through the intercom system in our cabin. Larry and Susu join our table. I breathe a sigh of relief and my handshake is probably too exuberant in greeting them, given we have only exchanged one sentence to date. Perilously, there are two remaining seats. A Quentin Tarantino lookalike, with an enviable camera lens and an even more enviable wife, walks straight past us and joins a table with the only other young couple on the cruise. Pam and Bob join our table. Of course they do.

After the crew have been introduced to us by Chewbacca, we get to know each other better. Larry was the FD of a ski apparel company in Texas. He is a bright and successful guy; whilst starting a ski company in Texas might not sound like the brightest and most successful business decision, it turned out to be an entrepreneurial master stroke because Texas has a lot of wealthy people who travel north to ski but they want to buy their gear before they go. There are not many ski shops in Texas, just as there are not many waterski shops in Sheffield. It is hard to pinpoint Larry's age as he has militarily cropped hair and a frame that has been sculpted from granite. I try the indirect approach.

'How long have Susu and you been married?'

'Seven happy years,' he replies in his bass-baritone voice, softened with a wolfish smile and twinkling eyes.

Second marriage, I assume, but Susu laughs and quickly corrects him.

'We have been married thirty-three years this month, but Larry claims to have only been happy for seven of them.'

Larry and Susu are going to be good fun. Bob, on the other hand, is going to be un-fun and Pam is going to be unbearable.

Bob begins his long personal history by telling me that he was a Broadway performer. The highlight of his apparently unsuccessful stage career was being in the chorus looking at the back of Meryl Streep's head for two weeks, before she was famous. He is also a singer-songwriter and guitarist, in which field he has enjoyed a similar level of anonymity. I will find out why later on the cruise when we have a talent(less) night. He specialises in stories about himself, and tells me another one – something to do with a microlight crash in the Zambezi last year which nearly killed him, and I think he might have said that his foot fell off, but I am half-listening to a much more amusing story from Larry about grapefruit.

Freshly caught Dungeness crab is some of the best crabmeat in the world, alongside the other local speciality, Alaska king crab. Dungeness crab is on the menu to spoil us for the first night. It is rich and succulent, delicious. Pam doesn't like it and sends it back. She asks for berries instead. Tempted as he must be, Tavay, our Thai waiter, does not serve her poisonous ones. Had he done so, I would have doubled his tip.

With Pam on board, with no plank for her to walk, this could be a long week.

# CHAPTER SIXTEEN

*Bushwhacking – vodka martini – eagle hunter – Hooligan*
*Hollow – Tom lookalike – David Tennant lookalike*
SOUNDTRACK: DOWN LIKE SILVER – 'WOLVES'

'I wan'cha bench. Can I come into your cabin to read my
book every day?'

I wake up to Pam sitting on the bench in our room.

It is 7 a.m. and she has decided to pay us a wake-up call to
check out our cabin before breakfast. I didn't think to lock the
door on the ocean. We apparently have a smaller bed than her,
but she doesn't have a bench. Over dinner last night, I made
the mistake of telling her our itinerary after Alaska; she has
consulted with Bob overnight and they think it would be nice
if they came to see us in Nashville. They live in Durham, North
Carolina, which apparently is not far. I might have to call work
to start injunctive proceedings.

Aside from its natural beauty, the true appeal of Alaska, and
of the next week of our trip, is that there is no mobile signal and
no Wi-Fi. Even if I want to call the office to take out an injunction against Pam, I won't be able to. More attractively, even if
the office or clients want to call or email me, they won't be able
to. They will have to quietly seethe without me.

Meggie, Mimi and Shauna all believe that the purpose of visiting a place of great natural beauty is to Snapchat or Instagram photographs of it to their friends. They could not survive in the final frontier of Alaska without their devices and over-connectivity. The Tenth Doctor is my companion; social media is theirs. They are not alone. I recently read in *National Geographic* magazine that according to a survey by Destination Analysis, 71 per cent of millennials said they would be 'very uncomfortable' on a one-week vacation without connectivity. Fortunately, I don't have that problem: I don't have any of my millennials with me and am personally delighted at the lack of connectivity. It will help with my email diet and should therefore enable me to lose a weight off my mind.

As the will-o'-the-wisp mist clears over Ushk Bay off Chichagof Island, we set out on our first bushwhack. I have succeeded in persuading Pam that it will be too strenuous for her, but the quid pro quo is that I have allowed her to read her book on my bench instead. Bushwhacking does not in fact involve whacking any bushes. It is in essence a walk in the woods, with bears secretly watching and laughing at us. We have no machetes. We don't even have a penknife. Our guide has some deodorant to spray at a bear, should it threaten us with its odour. (I had originally thought she said hairspray, but it turns out it is bear spray, which sounds equally ineffective.) It hangs off her belt like a football referee's free-kick foam.

What a bushwhack involves is being dropped off on land by an open metal skiff and finding the natural game trails on islands unspoiled by human foot – until, that is, our wellington boots join the wolf, moose, deer and bear tracks. Our scat does not, however, join theirs. The greatest hazard is a path-blocking, Jurassic-looking plant called Devil's Club. It is easy to spot with its enormous leaves and treacherous spines, and grows up to ten feet. It is pricklier than Pam when another passenger speaks to Jackie, and like Pam is poisonous. It grows at the perfect height to grab onto when you stumble on a log and will rip your flesh clean off.

Our guide is a young (she reverses her baseball cap) girl called Taylor who was raised by wolves and prefers animal droppings to humans. She has a hawk-eye for a wolf track, but can't look anyone in the eye when she speaks. We are a necessary evil to enable her to explore the Alaskan forests at her leisure. She knows where we are but not where we are going. She is legally required to carry a GPS device, but she regards this as state interference and prefers to get lost using maps and a compass. Taylor is a scat specialist (her parents must be very proud) and she is able to verify that bears do indeed shit in the woods, and that if you poke a stick in it, it has a smell which matches its owner's size.

The oldest and oddest member of our trekking group is a delightful 72-year-old Chicago lady called Geri, who can barely walk on deck without falling over, not due to her age but due to her unnaturally awkward orangutan gait and the vodka martini coursing through her veins. Watching her walking on deck atop an ocean as smooth as glass makes me feel seasick. It is ambitious of her to think she can bushwhack, so she uses Jackie as a walking stick throughout. Taylor takes a Darwinian approach to guiding, marching off at pace with the word 'yonder' (and the bear spray) and expecting only the fittest to follow (the bear spray) and survive. Every now and again she shouts, 'Hey Yogi, it's Boo-Boo', to scare off the bears. That method is probably as effective as the hairspray.

I notice the feather of a bald eagle on the ground, so stoop to
pick it up. Taylor the she-wolf pounces.

'It's a criminal offence in Alaska to pick up an eagle feather. It
is one of the zero-tolerance measures which has resulted in the
recovery of the bald eagle population from the hunters.'

I feel admonished as a sadistic bald eagle huntsman.

'Will I be cautioned for looking at it?'

Taylor doesn't do humour. When she turns her back on me
and yonders off, I sneak the feather into my pocket so that I can
plant it in Pam's suitcase later. If I can find a few more, I will
make her a headdress.

Unexpectedly, out of the mass of prickly Sitka spruce and
feathery Western hemlock, we emerge into a clearing where
there is a disused log cabin, a storage shed and even an outside
toilet. Above the cabin is a crudely carved sign saying 'HOO-
LIGAN HOLLOW'. Inside, it has a kitchen where tins of Spam
are neatly arranged – it seems that bears might draw the line at
Spam. Bushwhacking Taylor speculates that it must have been
a squatter's retreat: 'Someone who wanted to get away from
humans', she sighs enviously. In my mind I start to hatch a plot
as to how Larry and I might lure Pam here. We could slice her
up, put her into rectangular-shaped cans, and drop the S. Alter-
natively, if we lured her here but let her live, I wouldn't feel any
guilt because if the bears don't like Spam, they would certainly
draw the line at eating Pam. Her fussy eating requirements and
inability to select a meal which appears on the menu would also
be cured by nothing but Spam to choose from. If she doesn't
make it out alive, Jon Krakauer can write a book about her
called *Into the Vile*. I would buy it but flick straight to the back
to make sure it had a tragic ending.

I spend the rest of the bushwhack not seeing bears and not seeing wolves. But Taylor is disproportionately excited about some tracks they have left in the wet mud. I suspect that she might have come out here early this morning with her plastic animal feet.

We conclude the bushwhack with a moment of quiet reflection. Taylor drags us out of the undergrowth and Western skunk cabbage into an opening, a muskeg (a grassy, peaty bog which takes thousands of years to form), and asks us all to space out, put away all electronic devices, stop talking and to allow our senses to take over. I suspect that this is the highlight for Taylor: she has been looking forward to asking us all to shut up for the past three hours. Jackie is at one with nature and she goes for a wee – she is in a bog, after all. I spend five minutes listening to bird song, inhaling the musky swampy smells (or possibly it's my polypropylene T-shirt, which has been straining to wick all of the moisture from my back and armpits), and vowing to do this more regularly when I return home. I am so inspired by the ability to stop and observe the tranquillity that I am moved to compose the following poem:

What is this life if, full of care,
We have no time to stand and stare.
No time to stand beneath the boughs
And stare as long as sheep or cows.
No time to see, when woods we pass,
Where squirrels hide their nuts in grass.
No time to see, in broad daylight,
Streams full of stars, like skies at night.
No time to turn at Beauty's glance,

And watch her feet, how they can dance.
No time to wait till her mouth can
Enrich that smile her eyes began.
A poor life this if, full of care,
We have no time to stand and stare.

As someone who has dabbled in intellectual property law, I should probably admit now, before I receive a pre-action letter of claim, that the Welsh poet W. H. Davies may have experienced identical sentiments before me. He is, however, out of copyright, having died over seventy years ago.

Back on the ship before dinner, a friendly couple from Indianapolis introduce themselves to me as Ted and Carrie. Pam is jealously watching from the other end of the bar. Ted is stocky and bearded, with a red face which could be weather-worn or alcohol-torn or both. He and Geri must share the same blood group. He always wears shorts, in Alaska, regardless of the temperature. He is interested that I am English. He has been to England once. He was in the army in the early 1970s. He didn't believe in the draft, so he made himself some money on the side by becoming a drug dealer in Amsterdam, paid someone to do his army duties (apparently you could that in the 1970s), and hit the road Jack Kerouac-style, driving across Europe in a Datsun 240z which he spray-painted bronze to make it look like a Corvette Stingray. His recollection of his road trip is hazy because he had been under the influence of his own merchandise for much of the time. He thinks he has been to Belgium; he has definitely been to Paris. He can't remember where in England he has been, but it was somewhere up north. He would like to go to Ireland but he is scared of driving on the other side of the road, which amuses me as he is a robust hunting type and a fully signed-up member of the NRA. It is no surprise that he is an ardent Trump supporter and another person who volunteers to me that Hillary Clinton is a murderer. I tell him that a New York taxi driver told me this as well. Out of interest, I ask who she has murdered.

'Hell, enwan who crasses her. Prably twen'y or thirdy rivals now she's had killed.'

I decide that one pre-dinner drink with Ted is enough, and go to join Larry and Susu's table. Bob's echolocation alerts him to my movements and he joins us without me noticing. Pam closely follows, demanding to know who I have been talking to, why and what about. I tell her I was talking to a confederate about ammunition.

'You need to be careful what you say around Republicans,' she warns me.

Bob is like the BBC. The repeats immediately follow the original broadcast. Larry is now getting the Zambezi microlight story with both barrels, because he had the good sense to be talking to Jackie about grapefruit when it was originally aired the previous evening. I check Bob's feet under the table and they are both still there: I must have misheard him last night. At the end of the story, when dessert is being served, Larry notes that if it had been Susu who had been involved in a near-fatal microlight accident, he would have drawn the African doctor's attention to the DNR instruction which he has inscribed into her passport, and that he would have been sitting by her bedside in hospital, whispering, 'Go to the light, Susu, go to the light.'

Pam gives a disapproving glare to Larry. Theirs is evolving into an interesting relationship. For a psychologist, she is not very skilled at reading people. She leans into me and tells me that she finds him misogynistic, but she couldn't be more wrong. He and Susu are as tight as a well-rehearsed band: Larry is the front man, constantly performing and riffing; Susu is the rhythm section, skilfully setting Larry's tempo. She never takes offence at his mealtime jokes at her expense, partly because it is obvious that behind the machismo is a man very much in love with his wife, and partly because she is too busy taking photographs of every course to post on Facebook and misses half of his gags.

Later on, in the main lounge's bar, which has the feel of a neighbourhood pub and is run by a welcoming English bar-maid called Leigh, I get chatting to a softly (to the point of seductively) spoken, gentlemanly, self-confessed IT nerd (which impresses me as he is not far off my mother's age and she can't send an email) from San Francisco called Tom, who is still wearing full waterproofs in case we sink. He is there with his doppelgänger called Bryan (also in waterproofs), who I assume is his brother or his reflection but turns out to be the second husband of his oldest friend from university, Diane, who must have had designs on Tom at some stage but has set-tled for his lookalike. I ask Tom's wife, Nina (but pronounced Niner, rhyming with 'ocean liner', because she is American), whether she finds herself attracted to Bryan as well, but appar-ently not. It seems everyone is drawn to Tom, including Jackie, who describes him slightly giddily as very charming, her eyes kaleidoscope spinning like Mowgli when hypnotised by Kaa the snake in Disney's *The Jungle Book*. Nina and Diane both have arthritis (wait until I have words with Steve), which has its advantages for Tom and Bryan, as they get to do all of the daytime hiking and kayaking activities without their wives. I bet Bob wishes he had arthritis; after his microlight crash, he might get lucky.

'Whatcha all talkin' about?' interrupts Pam, before asking me if Jackie and I can help her get into a wetsuit tomorrow as she has signed up for the snorkelling. Even by Pam's standards, this is an odd request. Shoehorning Pam's skin into a gossamer-strength Arctic wetsuit would be like trying to force toothpaste back into its tube. Small pieces will go in, but most of it will go all over my hands. I try to ignore the fact that she has now linked arms with me and turn back to Tom and Nina.

Tom tells me that now he has spoken to me, I am not as weird as he had first thought. This comes from left field for such a generous, old-school guy, but he explains that he had earlier seen me taking iPhone photographs of an orange doll in front of the Dawes Glacier whilst everyone else was marvelling at the calving thunder of its crumbling blue ice. I tersely explain that it is not a doll; it is the Tenth Doctor, David Tennant. Nina gets excited and tells me that I had reminded her of someone and she has now realised that it is David Tennant. I go to bed happy (I normally get Jack Dee), but for the rest of the cruise notice that Nina might have a crush on me; I am worried that she herself looks a bit like Kathy Bates.

# CHAPTER SEVENTEEN

*Ranger Dan – Gloomy Knob – Buzz Lightyear – turning gears*
*– gasping moss abduction – driftwood – the Captain's Dinner*
*– abandon ship – talcum powder*
SOUNDTRACK: THE LEMONHEADS – 'THE OUTDOOR TYPE'

There is a frisson of excitement in the air. A real-life park ranger is coming on board for two days: a bona fide outdoor superhero, in a four-pinched peaked hat. Jackie has washed her hair especially. Pam's pheromones are directed more towards me and she has taken to leaving her cabin curtains open so that she can see me as I sneak past and then pounce on me like a female wolf spider; she gets me in her clutches and asks me if I will go out in the kayak with her, as Bob is not strong enough to paddle. I decline on the basis that I too am quite aroused by the prospect of Ranger Dan and don't want to miss his boarding. I picture him launching from the sea like Godzilla and landing on the deck, glistening.

In 1915, at the National Park Conference, Colonel L. M. Brett, acting superintendent of Yellowstone, declared the following criteria for the selection of park rangers:

An applicant for the position of ranger must be between

147

twenty-one and forty years of age, of good character and correct habits, of sound physique and capable of enduring hardships; tactful in handling people; possess a common-school education; able to ride and care for horses; know how to cook simple food; have had experience in outdoor life; be a good shot with rifle and pistol; and have some knowledge of trail construction and fighting forest fires.

A week after the conference, parks general superintendent Mark Daniels told the *Denver Post* that the men who get involved in the National Park Service should also 'know about animals and birds and trees. They must be capable of caring for a lost baby or giving first aid to the wounded tourist. They must be sober men, absolutely healthy. They must be courteous and good tempered.' In short, park rangers are the master race. Unlike those Americans who lose their babies in the woods.

Ranger Dan certainly looks the part. He is young, handsome and erect. He knows he has the first two qualities but has probably never experienced the third. His uniform is pressed and his badge is shiny. He wears sunglasses below deck. But that is where his superhuman qualities end. We are sailing through an area known as 'Gloomy Knob', a description which could equally apply to Ranger Dan. It quickly becomes apparent that he has spent too much time outdoors, with only himself and the sea otters for company. Not only has he run out of things to say to himself, but he has also bored himself rigid. My ice-breaker, as tradition requires, is unsuccessful. I ask him if he can go fetch his hat so that I can wear it for a selfie. He earnestly replies that not only has he not brought the Montana Peak on board, but had he done so it would be a regulatory violation, sir, to allow me to wear it. I end the conversation there, with a lie, telling him that I am looking forward to his seminar on 'The Life of Glacier Bay' in the forward lounge. The notice board says 'Join Ranger Daniel!' It is astutely written because he is clearly not folksy enough to be a Dan, and the exclamation mark carries with it a didactic plea of desperation, as in 'Don't leave me here on my own with Ranger Daniel!!!' As Ranger Dan takes the mic, Jackie sensibly decides that now would be a good time to pack. I opt to stay for some masochistic monotony.

His seminar does not disappoint me. 'The Life of Glacier Bay' is not the life of the party. I learn only two things: I learn that sea otters are the hairiest mammal on earth (apart from our expedition leader, Matt); and I learn what gears turning on a cruise ship sound like. I was trying really hard to listen to his seminar but all I could hear was blah blah blah and the steady turning of the gears, a sound which, for the first time on the cruise, has pushed itself to my frontal lobe.

At dinner that evening, I catch Ranger Dan in the queue, tell him how much I enjoyed his seminar, and point out Pam to him, informing him that she is a National Parks enthusiast and that he should sit with her and tell her all about the history of his waterproof uniform and peaked hat. I feel I have done the whole cruise a favour when he takes one of the many empty seats on Pam and Bob's table.

As I walk past to get dessert, I hear Ranger Dan talking to Pam in his best Buzz Lightyear voice.

Before the National Park Service existed, cavalry units of the US Army patrolled the parks, and after the service was established it made sense to model the uniform on familiar military gear, with green trousers and coat and a grey shirt. I am proud to wear the uniform, ma'am, as it is a signal that I can give information and be trusted.

He talks about nothing but himself. Hopefully Pam will learn from this. Bob is still talking about Meryl Streep's backside and seems unfazed that no one is listening. But all that is about to change for Bob.

After dinner, the guides try something venturesome: an open mic talent night. This is brave for two reasons: there are only about thirty people in the bar, and most of them are pensioners or children (they must be stowaways as I haven't seen them all week and they all belong to one family, presumably from Juneau). We start with a girl whose parents own six Burger King franchises and think, as only parents can, that she can sing. Their taste in musical ability is as sophisticated as their palettes. Larry listens with the face of someone having root canal surgery. I then get to witness a genuine Susan Boyle moment: the surprise act of the evening is a university student who performs animal noises: they are awful but she knows it and I enjoy her carefree crazy courage; her grand finale is a whale which is actually quite good. Next up is Burger King's whopper sister on the violin: she is either tuning up or taking her first lesson in public. Larry is now having colonic irrigation. This is un-music at its very best.

I never thought I would say this, but Bob saves the day. He might have failed in everything he has turned his hand to – script-writing, acting, producing – but his failure as a songwriter is the highlight of the evening and possibly of my life so far. At my request, he plays a song I heard him play earlier on the cruise when no one else was listening. I had assumed he

wouldn't fall for it, but he is clearly too flattered by this unprecedented request for some of his own material. He picks up his Martin (while Geri picks up her martini) and performs a song he wrote himself called 'Get outta my back door'. Containing sexism fresh from the nineteenth century, it is like an offensive Gilbert & Sullivan, and tells the tale of a man who goes fishing and orders his wife to be gone by the time he returns. It is a triumph, for me. The room is awkwardly silent throughout, in disbelief rather than admiration, and the icing on the cake is that Pam, seemingly blissfully ignorant of being the inspiration for the song, is singing harmony, in the wrong key, like the caterwauling backing singer in the laughing version of Elvis Presley's 'Are You Lonesome Tonight?' But here, only Larry and I are laughing. This may well prove to be the pinnacle of my sabbatical. I am already regretting not videoing it, as it would go viral.

The next day starts with no one having signed up for Ranger Dan's 'Junior Ranger' talk. It seems that the uninspired, unmusical children on board have better judgement than all of the adults. It transpires that mistakenly Jackie and I have signed up for his rainforest walk. We had assumed that Taylor the mountain goat would be our guide, but she has been usurped by Ranger Dan, presumably as the only way he can now secure attendance at one of his events is to get people to sign up before his participation is advertised.

His rainforest walk starts with some drama. He tears a piece of moss from the ground.

'When I first saw a ranger do this, I gasped,' he says, in the excitable tone of a dentist identifying the teeth in your mouth, 'but then I learned that moss has no roots and you can return it like this.' With a flourish, he tosses the moss to the ground from which it was so cruelly plucked.

With the excitement building to feverishness amongst our passengers after the phoney moss abduction, Ranger Dan points to a log on the ground.

'Who can tell me where this log comes from?' he asks, forgetting that we are not his junior rangers.

I am tempted to say the captain, but I suspect that park rangers don't watch *Star Trek*. No one else is interested enough to proffer an answer.

'I will give you a clue,' he says desperately, 'it's not driftwood.'

Uncharacteristically, his knowledge of pathing level objects has failed him.

'No, wait, I have given the answer away,' he corrects himself. 'It is in fact driftwood.'

I doubt that I will ever forgive him his error. My disappointment is second only to learning that Santa Claus does not exist. I trusted Ranger Dan, with his butch badge, but now he has betrayed me. I begin to doubt that the spray attached to his belt will ever be able to ward off the poisonous mushrooms that he shows us from a safe distance. I am too angry with Ranger Dan to partake in his next guessing game, which again has a log identifying theme, but this time it is not driftwood; it is a fallen branch. Were it not so rotten and covered in soft yellow lichen, I would club him over the head with it.

At the end of the amble, he apologises that he always sets such a cracking pace. I point to the moss which has grown on my shoes during his walk.

We can only have one skiff on the water at any given time in Glacier Bay National Park, so we have to return to the ship in relay. When I get back on board, I move Pam's magnet from 'ashore' to 'aboard' in the hope that they'll leave her at Bartlett Cove for the remainder of eternity. My plan is foiled and she arrives for dinner, buzzing around Jackie like a wasp at a picnic, but Jackie sells her a brilliant dummy with the salad course and swerves to the safety of Larry and Susu's pre-arranged table for four.

Tonight is the final meal on the ship, known as the Captain's Dinner. Captain Don Johnson has let himself go since his *Miami Vice* career but he has kept us steady as she goes for the week and avoided the icebergs. I suggest to him that he should sit with Pam, who has always wanted to know how to drive a boat. He duly takes her off our hands but, before the meal, has to do the closing address. It is a controversial start, as he reminds us what the expected tip is for the staff, under the pretence that everyone keeps asking him for this information (I haven't seen him all week so I for one didn't ask him – perhaps others, however, were overcome with the urge to rush onto the bridge to ask to give him more money). He is short on material so then proceeds to introduce the crew, half of whom we know intimately as we have been following their backsides up cliffs and through bush for a week. But he is at pains to emphasise that it is a team effort and that there are many people behind the scenes who have made for a successful voyage. He saves for last the guy who washes the dishes. He gives him a big build-up. He is the unsung hero of the voyage. Without him, we would definitely have hit icebergs. His name is, unfortunately, not known by Captain Don, but he is a pivotal washer-upper and a great guy. We clap him, whoever he is. Dave, someone whispers to Captain Don, it's Dave; too late, his moment has passed.

I have more final drinks than I had anticipated. I gave Leigh the English barmaid a good tip (never allow anyone called Pam on your cruises again) so have been getting free alcohol in return. I find Monkey Matt's microphone. I joke with Jeremy (the more handsome version of Quentin Tarantino) and Margarita (his wife, a Prussian princess) that I could do a mock announcement from Matt. Jeremy continues the joke by saying 'Iceberg Abandon Ship, Iceberg Abandon Ship.' I flick the switch to on, just in time for his repetition. Jessica the tour co-ordinator comes rushing in – it is the first time I have seen her as well but I don't feel the urge to tip her – and confiscates the microphone from me. She claims that it was getting piped into every cabin, but that can't be right as Larry and Susu have not rushed upstairs from steerage.

Alaska has been magnificent. I have enjoyed Larry's dinner-time storytelling; we agree that there is no need to meet again, however, as he has used up all of his best material and we can keep in touch by liking Susu's Facebook meals. I have seen calving crumbling glaciers, ice-topped mountains, feeding humpbacked whales, clumsy tufted puffins, belching sea lions, pink rivers rich with salmon, the fresh faeces (but not faces) of wolves and bears, and a life-size park ranger doll. But the enduring image from the trip, for ever etched into my mind's eye, is going to be walking past Pam's cabin earlier tonight, with her light on and curtains still open, and seeing her applying talcum powder to her back-lit sea otter. The breathtaking beauty of Alaska has been erased for me in an instant.

# CHAPTER EIGHTEEN

*Katharine Ross – Katharine Ross – Katharine Ross*
*– Katharine Ross – Katharine Ross – Katharine Ross*
SOUNDTRACK: BURT BACHARACH
*– 'RAINDROPS KEEP FALLIN' ON MY HEAD'*

In 1998, to commemorate the first 100 years of American movies, the American Film Institute published a definitive (in their view) selection of the 100 greatest American movies of all time. More than 1,500 leaders from the American film community, in their collective wisdom, decided that *Butch Cassidy and the Sundance Kid* was only the 50th greatest. I deduce that the American Film Institute cannot be very wise. They ranked *Snow White and the Seven Dwarfs* at no. 49. At no. 3 was *The Godfather* (but *The Godfather II*, which everyone knows is a much better movie, did not feature); at no. 2 was *Casablanca* (because of two lines, one of which was never actually said in the movie); and at no. 1, predictably, was *Citizen Kane* (on the basis that movie critics everywhere have to rank it at no. 1 for fear of being ostracised by all of their fellow critics who have now had to endure the turgid film for the past seventy-five years and therefore want everyone else to share in their misery, in much the same way as priests encourage others to become priests).

In truth, the greatest three American movies of all time are *The Great Escape*, *Star Wars: Episode IV – A New Hope* and, still at no. 1 after all these years, *Butch Cassidy and the Sundance Kid*. It made an indelible impression on me at the age of eleven or twelve when I was first allowed to stay up to watch it all the way through. It had all I could possibly ask for in a movie: the insuperable buddy chemistry between two of the three greatest Hollywood actors of their generation, Robert Redford and Paul Newman (the other being of course Steve McQueen, who was more of a loner and less into buddy films); the perfect Burt Bacharach soundtrack; a playful script with some wonderful one-liners ('I swear, if Sweetface told me that I rode out of town ten minutes ago, I'd believe him'); and the magnificent scenery of my next stop, Utah. And then of course there was the light of my life, fire of my loins, Katharine Ross.

Everyone remembers the iconic scene where Paul Newman (Butch Cassidy) wakes up Robert Redford (the Sundance Kid)'s lover, played to perfection by flawless Katharine, by making ghost sounds and whistling outside the bedroom which she is sharing with Sundance (in the eyes of the American Film Institute, his whistling can't have been as good as that of the seven dwarfs). He then rides her around on the handlebars of the futuristic invention, a bicycle, to the soundtrack of 'Raindrops Keep Fallin' on My Head'. When Butch returns her to Sundance's log cabin, having crashed the bicycle, Sundance asks what he's been doing. 'Stealin' your woman', replies Newman confrontationally. 'Take her', says Redford. 'Well, you're a romantic bastard, I'll give you that', concludes Newman.

Everyone also remembers the closing scene, where the crack posse, who have been chasing the outlaws throughout the film for a string of playful train robberies ('Who are those guys?'), finally track them down and surround them in Bolivia. After the mandatory shoot-out, when both are badly injured, Butch turns to Sundance, with no hope of escape, and asks whether their nemesis, bounty hunter Lefors, is in the surrounding posse; Sundance replies that he isn't, and Butch ends the film with the greatest closing line of all time: 'Oh, good. For a moment there, I thought we were in trouble.' A line which puts to shame the comparatively lame optimism of 'Louie, I think this is the beginning of a beautiful friendship.'

The action then halts with the brilliant sepia freeze-frame of Newman and Redford charging out of the building, their guns blazing; Newman looking ever the upright gentleman outlaw, firing the gun stiffly in his right hand; Redford, more dangerous, is crouched and moustachioed, firing both pistols at the same time; to the reverberating sound of the posse and the Bolivian Army riddling them both with bullets. Importantly to me, both as an eleven- or twelve-year-old and as a 46-year-old, you never see Butch or Sundance die. They must have survived because, even in the rain, Butch kept singing.

But neither of those scenes was the one that became ingrained on my eleven- or twelve-year-old brain. The one that I will always remember is the earlier 'keep goin', teacher lady' scene for two reasons: first, for the embarrassment of having to watch it with my parents two or three times immediately before and during puberty; and second, because it caused me to fall in love with Katharine Ross.

It is dusk and misty; eerie like Oregon but not like Forks.

Katharine ascends the three steps to her log cabin, wearing a long black skirt and white blouse. Inside, she lights a gas lamp which casts a dim light. She begins to undress, in shadow, taking off her frill-necked, shoulder-puffed blouse. The scratchiness of old film spool silence raises the level of foreboding. She turns and screams. Materialising from the darkness is Sundance, sitting on a chair in her cabin, smartly dressed in jacket, waistcoat and tie, fingers interlinked across his chest. He calmly nods at her.

'Keep goin', teacher lady.'

She stands before him, frozen. Sundance reaches for his pistol.

'It's OK, don't mind me.'

Resigned to her fate, she undoes what has now become a long white (black/white continuity issue there) pioneer dress beneath her blouse and lets it fall to the floor, revealing a short, buttoned-up, lace slip.

Sundance soaks in the view.

There is then another continuity issue and Katharine is now holding the discarded dress against herself to protect her modesty.

'Let down your hair,' instructs Sundance.

To do so, Katharine has to drop the dress, again. Perhaps that is why she had picked it up while the cameraman wasn't looking.

'Shake your head.'

She complies, creating the tussled siren look so popular in Hollywood at the time, whilst simultaneously causing an im-pressionable eleven- or twelve-year-old in Hartlepool to try to conceal from his parents an erection in his pyjama trousers. But Sundance has not yet finished with her. It was not all about her hairstyle. He sighs with displeasure, pulls back the trigger and motions for her to continue undressing.

Close-up of Katharine's face; fear in her eye; moisture on her lip (Nigella Lawson-like), tussled hair (Nigella Lawson-like).

She unbuttons her final layer and stands before him, close-up on her barely lit cleavage.

Sundance undoes his gun belt. The build-up has been tense and things are turning sinister. He stands up, walks over to her, holds her by her waist, and opens her top further.

Then comes the twist.

'You know what I wish?' says the perilously trapped school teacher to the heartthrob gunman.

'What?'

'That once you'd get here on time.'

And she throws her arms around his neck and kisses him gratefully.

The pair have been playing with us; it was all just a little harmless pre-arranged rape roleplay. It turns out that Katharine Ross has been dating Robert Redford all along. Nonetheless, it was always a tense moment watching it with my parents, when I was eleven or twelve. Times have changed and yes, the scene is sexist and yes, rape scenarios should not be tried at home, but it has a brooding eroticism and would still remain an awkward moment if ever I watched it with my kids (which is unlikely as they refuse to watch 'old' films and only make exceptions for Tom Hanks in *Big* and *Splash*). But that is why it is such a well-judged and well-performed scene. The tension still works fifty years later (despite the continuity flaws), and Katharine Ross is still the most beautiful actress of all time.

In the hope that I can turn Jackie into Katharine Ross, our next destination is Sundance Mountain Resort in Utah, near the pass-through-and-keep-going-or-the-Mormons-will-get-you town of Provo. Robert Redford fell in love with the mountainous and canyonous (neologism, copyright Geoff Steward) area during filming and, with the money he earned from the movie, in 1968 purchased 5,000 acres beneath the breathtaking Mount Timpanogos and named it after his Utah-born character.

In the early twentieth century, a family of Scottish immigrants called Stewart (almost a great name) set up a homestead here, and a second generation of Stewarts then developed the mountain into a ski resort named Timp Haven. Redford used it as his own homestead until, in 1981, he devised the Sundance Institute, dedicated to the development of independent artists. The institute's Sundance Film Festival, held at the resort, has evolved into the well-known showcase for independent film-makers (who know a lot more about movies than the American Film Institute). Secretly, I am hoping that Katharine Ross still lives here and that she will be in my log cabin waiting for me in her frontier schoolmistress outfit.

It is gone midnight by the time we arrive at our wooden cabin. I might have waited most of my life to be on location with the Sundance Kid, but I am too tired to take in our surroundings after a full day of travel from Alaska (the highlight of which was the uncharacteristically humorous Air Alaska air hostess who, when giving the safety drill before the flight back to Seattle, recommended that in the event of landing on water we should all try to put on our life jackets a little quicker than her demonstrator colleague, otherwise we would drown). I inspect all of the rooms in our new log home, but Katharine definitely isn't there.

I check WhatsApp before going to sleep. Jeremy, with the enviable lens, has sent me photographs of a mother black bear and her three cubs crossing the road in Juneau. I bushwhacked for a week and saw nothing; he goes for a stroll around the city shortly after we were deposited on land and, judging by the proximity of his photos, gets invited into a bear cave for some milk and honey. I decide it's best not to tell Jackie, and drift into sleep with a deep sense of injustice and irritation.

The sun streaming through the wooden slats wakes me early the next morning. After dreaming of Katharine Ross, I am feeling amorous. So I sneak out of the cabin and, Paul Newman-style, circle it, shouting whooo-aaah like a pantomime ghost and whistling 'Raindrops Keep Fallin' on My Head'. When I come back inside, Jackie tells me to feck off for waking her up. I know from experience that she can only safely be woken if it is snowing outside or if a celebrity has died. I suggest we should hire a mountain bike for the day, and that we only need one as she can ride on the handlebars. She tells me to feck off again. Paul Newman and Robert Redford didn't have to put up with such back-chat from their women, but, like I say, times have changed.

As we walk down the mountain trail to breakfast, with the sun beating down ten degrees hotter than in Alaska, and the fresh scent of Febreze pine filling my nostrils, I send Jeremy a photograph of a pretty orange moth (to trump his bear family from last night) and Charmaine a photograph of a sunflower, set against the imposing, rugged red canyon, that I swear wasn't there last night. The time difference is favourable and she replies almost immediately: 'The Earth is truly the Lord.' I don't reply as this is a Mormon state and it would be unwise to challenge the authority of Jesus Christ here; after Edward Snowden, I don't know who might be reading my texts and I don't want the Church of Jesus Christ of Latter-Day Saints hounding me out of Utah and taking Jackie as another one of their wives.

Utah is the hottest state in the US today, maxing out at thirty-eight degrees centigrade. We decide to take it easy and take the 38-minute chairlift ride to the top of Bishop's Bowl, offering views of Provo Canyon, Utah Lake, Mount Timpanogos and the rolling Wasatch hills.

Redford's environmental consciousness is evident through-out the mountain resort. All of the wooden buildings are subtle and natural and merge harmoniously with the surrounding evergreens and the gentle North Fork stream running through. Sundance was created with preservation as a priority and the canyon looks much like it did when it was inhabited by the Ute tribe (with the exception of the chairlift and the zip-wire ride, both of which I feel the Ute tribe would have enjoyed). It is a tranquil place, where nature and man can be in harmony, as long as man can be in control. According to the bumf in our cabin, 'The Redford Family Nature and Wildlife Preserve pro-tects 860 acres of scenic vistas and canyons to provide a safe environment for the mule deer, grouse, wild turkeys, songbirds and raptors, and a sanctuary for future generations.' Redford is also quoted as saying: 'Our commitment to Sundance has always been to develop little and preserve a great deal.'

Which is why I am irritated by a Mexican family with around sixty-seven round children standing behind me in the queue for the chairlift. The youngest, pudgiest brat is entertaining his vile siblings by letting the pretty orange moths rest on his chunky arm and then squashing rather than preserving them. When he kills the first one, I look disapprovingly at his parents and give them my Paddington Bear hard stare. No reaction. When he kills his second, I say to Jackie, at a volume designed to be heard by his parents, 'Did you see that? That boy is killing the moths.' Jackie looks away; she senses and wants to avoid confrontation – her eyes tell me to shush. When Twinkie Fingers gets his hat-trick, I intervene: 'Stop killing the moths, you little turd.'

One of his Snickers-sponsored older brothers corrects me: 'They're butterflies, not moths.' But my poetic description of his brother goes unchallenged. His father stays quiet; he is also wearing his Mr Potato Head shush-eyes.

This is a ski resort in the winter and one of the hottest states in the US in the summer. Robert Redford was wiser than the American Film Institute by purchasing it. I am currently 6,200 feet above sea level, the very sea that until recently I was float-ing on in Alaska. I have gone from being at eye level with the sea to being lung-crushingly high above its level. The newly dis-covered puniness of my lungs and shortness of my breath hands me the perfect excuse to avoid reinstituting my daily run (now that I am off the boat) and to replenish with Red Bull the lost energy caused by the thin air. It is also a good excuse to abandon any lingering plans I had to climb Everest or Kilimanjaro in my lifetime, or to do a 2.5-mile hike from the top of the chairlift to Stewart Falls. I opt instead to sample a tangerine-flavoured craft beer at Bearclaw Cabin, which sits atop Bishop's Bowl at the top of the chairlift. It is much better for my contracted lungs.

There are no other canyon viewers up here. We have the scenery to ourselves. I feel like one of the original pioneers looking out across the vast territory, just without a horse. I take some great shots of the Tenth Doctor standing on the wooden veranda, mountains in the background, looking like the new sheriff in town. The only other person up here is a giant basketball-playing barman. I have to look up to see his name badge, which disappointingly informs me that he is yet another Jeff Stewart. I can accept that the Stewart family owned the original homestead here and he is no doubt a descendant and entitled to continue the family name, but did he really have to be called Jeff? I begin to suspect a conspiracy and can't enjoy my beer. The Mexican moth-murdering mob eventually catch up, having tested the weight limit of the chairlift to its extremes. I hope that they are here to try out the zip wire, as there is no way that will hold them. I descend in a sulk about the seemingly ubiquitous nature of my name in America, trying to cheer myself by picturing the moth-murderer plunging to his death from the zip wire as the butterflies and moths float on by, flicking V signs with their proboscises.

At the bottom, there is an exciting development. Jackie has a good phone signal for the first time in a week.

She has a voicemail message from Sam, our dog-lady, who is half-human, half-canine and who, with her twin sister (half-canine, half-human), runs the Hounds Hotel in the South Downs. We have two miniature dachshunds: Layla (named after Eric Clapton), whose dual purpose in life is to chase after her ball and to look for her confiscated ball; and Karma (named after John Lennon or Radiohead but definitely not Culture Club), whose sole purpose is to outwit humans. They are sisters, but the genes were distributed unevenly. Layla, like Mary, has the looks; Karma, like Joe, has the brains. Dachshunds are ridiculous dogs. They are impossibly cute with their pretty faces, floppy ears, elongated sea lion bodies and Tyrannosaurus Rex arms, but such in-breeding comes at a cost: they are an unfeasibly stupid breed who can't follow the simplest training instruction (such as 'shit outside the house'). Karma is the exception. She is unnervingly studious: she watches and learns, second-guessing my next move like a *Jurassic Park* Velociraptor. If I am going to put her outside for a wee, she will sense it and immediately piss on the carpet; if I am leaving the house and about to lock her in the kitchen, she will hide my keys. She is calculating and likes to rationalise her next move.

The voicemail message from Sam bears bad news. When Layla ran after a ball inadvertently thrown into a hornets' nest, she retrieved her ball and ran away very quickly, whilst Karma, unfamiliar with hornets, wanted to learn about them so stopped to study their behaviour, and received fifteen stings to her head. Jackie immediately googles 'dachshunds with bee stings' and I would urge you to do the same; Jackie is concerned to find out the impact on our dog's health, whereas I am drawn to the images. The best ones are the dachshunds stung on either the nose or the mouth. Their faces swell to give them the appearance of Marlon Brando with cotton wool stuffed in his cheeks in *The Godfather*. I doubt I could laugh so hard at any other photographs, except perhaps the swelling head of my Mexican child-nemesis.

Once I have spoken to the emergency vet and been relieved of £500, Jackie wants to stay where the signal is strong to call my spare-kids. I tell her I will meet her back at our cabin. When she returns, it is dusk with a mountain mist; I have turned the lights off and am sitting silhouetted in an armchair with my feet up on the wooden bench at the bottom of our bed. I have even put on my one and only smart jacket and white linen shirt. I form a pistol with my hand.

'Keep goin', teacher lady.'

'Would ya feck off.'

# CHAPTER NINETEEN

*Yoghurt attack – babies' startled arms – Solitude – guess the gas – GPS error – the karate kid – alternate teeth – Jedidiah – inn-sitters – an accident involving Thomas Edison*

SOUNDTRACK: GEOFF LOVE ORCHESTRA
– THEME MUSIC FROM THE BIG COUNTRY

American Yoplaits come upside down, ejaculate yoghurt all over the chest of your clean T-shirt when you open them, and have an overhanging lip that then causes your spoon to catapult more yoghurt into your face. This is how my day begins.

It is 6 a.m. (too early for my daily run, which I decide to defer until tomorrow) and we are leaving Sundance for a flight from Salt Lake City to San Francisco and then a Californian road trip to Yosemite. When I check out, the day takes a more promising turn. I have nothing to pay on our cabin, despite eating and drinking at the restaurant and buying a cap bearing the legend 'Sundance' which I will never again wear; instead, the Sundance Mountain Resort owes me twenty-nine dollars. Something to do with overcharging me on the original booking. In the same way I don't in other hotels when I notice a meal or a minibar Red Bull missing from the final bill, I am not going to quibble. Let the seller beware.

The original drive to Sundance was at night. I could feel a looming presence as the road wound upwards, but it was a starless night and the mountains were hiding their faces from me, modestly cloaked in shadow and obscurity. The drive back to Salt Lake City is at dawn. As we get on Interstate 15, the full moon is dropping behind a newly revealed, staggering, jagged landscape. The canyons are blushing pink, like they have been caught doing something they shouldn't be doing to their ravines. Somewhere out there, coyotes are howling and cowboys are cooking breakfast beans. I recognise the scenery: it is like every Western movie I have ever watched. It is also like the Big Thunder Mountain ride in Disneyland, but the rocks aren't made of plastic, and they are more obviously shaped like penises. It is all rather wonderful. You can come again, Utah.

Jackie is a nervous passenger. The freeway has five lanes, and is transporting huge double-trailer trucks which like to make a sandwich filling of me by overtaking on both sides. She tells me off for watching the moon and the trucks instead of the road. When each of my children were babies, I used to enjoy watching them in their baby-carrier as their little eyes got heavier and heavier until they quietly drifted off to sleep; I would then clap my hands or slam a door, making their startled little arms instinctively shoot up over their little heads. Every now and again, when we have trucks on either side, I jab the foot brake sharply to recreate the same effect with Jackie's little arms.

We pass a road sign giving a choice of BRIGHTON or SOLITUDE. I give myself a wry smile. Brighton, England, is where I spent my purgatory period of solitude between *decree nisi* and *decree absolute*. I wonder to myself what possessed the original settler to name the town 'Solitude'. I reflect on this and decide that it can't just have been one loner who named an entire town. One person cannot constitute a town; and if he really did want to be left alone in solitude, why would he put it on the map by naming it? There must have been a group of settlers who all came up with the name 'Solitude', which means that the town was a misnomer from the outset. I ask myself what type of person would think that the best possible name for a new settlement in the New World was Solitude, but then I remember that my parents fixed upon the name Geoffrey. Whoever it was must have had the same dreary outlook as my elusive New York diarist, Kalman Kaplan, who is beginning to irritate me with his rudeness in not replying to my email. I amuse myself as I drive past Solitude devising equally unwelcoming town names such as Ineptitude, Ingratitude or, my personal favourite, Turpitude.

American gas stations play a fun guessing game with you. When I take my kids and spare-kids out for dinner, at the end of the meal we always play 'Guess the Bill'. Whoever is closest doesn't have to use their pocket money to pay for their own meal. US gas stations have developed and improved this game. You have to guess how much gasoline it will take to fill the tank of your hire car; pay in advance; and then insert the fuel to see how close you can get. I guess $40 but only run up $20. For the second time today, the establishment ends up owing me money. This is still the land of opportunity. It is not even 7 a.m. and I am up by almost $50.

The money I have made on the journey quickly evaporates at Salt Lake City airport when I leave our personal and brand-new $300 GPS unit in the hire car. Jackie decides that as I am the driver, this is definitely my fault. She may have a point, although throughout the trip it has been her responsibility to carry the fucking thing in her fucking hand luggage. We don't speak on the flight but this enables me to read more of *The Boys in the Boat*. Like Depeche Mode, I enjoy the silence.

The next stage is the road trip, driving from San Francisco to Yosemite (with a hired and inferior GPS device), and Jackie starts to hyperventilate like a birthing mother. The cause of this extreme breathing is the seven-mile San Mateo–Hayward Bridge across San Francisco Bay. I threaten to sedate her if she continues to leap out of her skin every time a truck passes by. She is making me nervous as I drive. I try to take her mind off the traffic by explaining that this is the earthquake capital of America, but then realise that revealing this whilst driving on a man-made floating road is not helping. I stop talking and turn on the car radio to a public service advertisement about a man who as a child always wanted to be a karate champion but when he grew up realised that the only person worth emulating was Jesus Christ. I had often wondered what had happened to Ralph Macchio.

The first two hours of our drive are very dull; not what I had expected of a Californian road trip. Interstate 580 is the Bob of highways, boring and endless, and each identical roadside town indistinctly merges into the other, with only McDonald's and Taco Bell to mark the theoretical boundaries. There is nothing for me to look at other than the road, which is probably just as well to avoid Jackie having another panic attack. After a couple of road-concentrating hours, we approach Modesto and I recall to Jackie that I have heard of Modesto and that it has some kind of connection with John Steinbeck but I can't remember what; I query whether it was a town which the migrating Joad family passed through in *The Grapes of Wrath*, but Jackie can't help as she only reads *Where's Wally?* books. She informs me that she thought Steinbeck was Scandinavian, not American.

'Didn't he write *East of Sweden?*'

It's time to stop.

The choice of freeway dining is not fine, so we pull in for our first (and hopefully only) McDonald's of the trip. The only good thing about McDonald's is its free Wi-Fi. The Steinbeck connection is bugging me, so I google it: Modesto was his birthplace and family home. I am excited. I suggest to Jackie that we could visit his house, which is now a restaurant. Jackie looks at me as if she would rather eat her own vomit, which would be more nutritious than her all-day breakfast McMuffin.

A young couple in the corner look like they are still part of the dust bowl migration. He has a dirty baseball cap on the wrong way round, a ginger beard, and is wearing long baggy shorts and oversized shoes that resemble what a vagrant circus clown might wear. She looks like the religious antagonist with bad teeth out of *Orange Is the New Black*. I ask Jackie if she remembers the opening scene of *Pulp Fiction*. She doesn't; good. I am sure I hear him call her 'honey bunny'. I suggest we leave, quickly.

Steinbeck's house must have been east-facing. The road west of Modesto, which we have just completed, is straight and three-laned, the scenery flat and uninspiring, and everywhere looks the same; east of Modesto (not as good a title as 'East of Eden') is the dust bowl territory that inspired Steinbeck. It is the magnificent drive that I expected of California. The landscape is transformed to parched yellow and tinder-dry. It is as if the set to Steinbeck's novel begins on his very doorstep. The single-lane road waves gently, presumably following the original trail of the 1930s migrant covered-wagons, as I drive past miles and miles of wrathful vineyards running parallel to the Union Pacific Railroad. As we start to twist upwards with the mountains now visible in the distance, the sky darkens ominously.

I am vaguely aware that there have been some summer fires in California, but I have not been following the news as closely as I should have been (I am on sabbatical); GPS tells me the nearest petrol stations but not the nearest bush fire. I bet my swanky new TomTom would have been more helpful, were it not sitting in a sodding hire car in Salt Lake City. It is really getting very dark now; the sun has been snuffed out by a sluggish smoke drifting across it. Now both the ground and the air have a greyish tint.

I am beginning to wonder why there are no more vehicles on the road. I once had a similar experience in the Lot Valley, in south-west France, when I went cycling on a beautiful sunny day, with the roads as empty as an alien invasion, oblivious to the fact that somewhere nearby, a smug French weatherman, speaking only in smug French, had issued a severe weather warning. In blissful ignorance, revelling in the sunshine and the roads free of French motorists, I cycled straight into an asteroid storm. As hailstones the size and constancy of cricket balls bounced off the road, I took shelter beneath the porch of a sympathetic local, who was kind enough to give me a glass of Ricard but not kind enough to invite me inside. I have always felt that this incident perfectly summarises the approach of the French to hospitality. Just enough for you to be grateful, even though what they are really saying is drink your drink and 'va te faire foutre'.

I don't mention the possible bush fire to Jackie, as the

earthquakes didn't go down so well. But fortunately it is not a fire; obligingly, the dark smoke is in fact a dust storm. It is as if Steinbeck himself is scripting this for me. It is probably not quite as bad as the great dust storms of 1936 – the grapes and crops we pass will survive – but it is enough for me to feel I don't now need to visit his house or reread any of his books.

I pull off the arid road and am punched in the face by heat and dust as I get out of the car. I have stopped to take a photograph of a single-storey white wooden shack, which is half-veranda, half-living space, on the top of a hill, surrounded by scorched yellow grass and dark, forbidding sky. Despite the desperation of the location, the Stars and Stripes flutter optimistically at the bottom of a loose, meandering track leading up to the homestead, together with a sign advertising freshly dusted strawberries for sale. One other car emerges from the dust, coming from the opposite direction. It is a red pick-up which is more genuinely battered than anything Forks could offer. It also pulls up at the bottom of the driveway, fluffing up a cloud of powdered earth. I quickly put the Tenth Doctor back into my pocket: Californians might think it odd to see a 46-year-old man trying to get a five-inch poseable time traveller to pose for a selfie in a dust storm.

'Purty or ugly?' asks the old crone who is driving, through her alternate teeth.

In the hope that she is not a special-interest prostitute, I assume she is talking about the landscape rather than herself.

'It's beautiful,' I say, holding up my camera in a gesture of approving tourism.

'Too yella! Come back in the spring.'

And with that, she drives off up the winding road to what

I assume must be her home and strawberry farm. Unlike the passengers from our Alaskan cruise, who all offered for us to come and stay with them if ever we are in town, I think the crone's offer might be genuine. In fact, it is more of an order than an offer.

The landscape slowly moistens and grows from flat and yellow, to undulating, then mountainous, green, brown and even pink. There are no bears crossing the road yet, but it can only be a matter of time, because we are nearing Yosemite.

A five-minute drive from the entrance to the National Park, we are going to be staying at a bed and breakfast called Tin Lizzie, at the village of Fish Camp (which comprises a fishing pond and a general store which sells all the essentials: bread, M&Ms and fishing tackle). The B&B is so named because the owner is a dealer in antiquities who also collects Ford Model As and Model Ts. Tin Lizzie was a derogatory term for the Model T, a car initially ridiculed for being made of cheap materials and for not being very masculine, until it beat all other contenders at a butch Colorado car rally due to its excellent build-quality and surprising ability to off-road, and went on to sell over 15 million units between 1908 and 1927. With the Model T, Henry Ford not only achieved his aim of becoming a billionaire but also managed to:

> build a car for the great multitude. It will be large enough for the family, but small enough for the individual to run and care for. It will be constructed of the best materials, by the best men to be hired, after the simplest designs that modern engineering can devise. But it will be so low in price that no man making a good salary will be unable to own one – and

enjoy with his family the blessing of hours of pleasure in God's great open spaces.

Where better of God's great open spaces (Charmaine and the Mormons will be proud of me) to be able to drive an original Model T, a hundred years later, than in Yosemite National Park? That is what Tin Lizzie offers, as well as a lovely replica 1890s Victorian white wooden, red-roofed property. It looks like an Edward Hopper watercolour. When we arrive, the double garage on the bottom floor of the house, beside an external staircase and handrail leading to the entrance veranda on the first floor, is open to reveal the Model T as a beacon to guide us home. A hundred years ago, we might have struggled to find the right property, as a Model T sat in most garages.

We are met by the welcoming couple who run the B&B as 'time-away inn-sitters'. This is not a job (or indeed a combi-nation of words) I have ever heard of. What it means is that they travel around the world enjoying free accommodation by looking after and running other people's B&Bs on a sea-son-by-season basis. They spent the last year doing the same thing in Costa Rica. They are 'in the mountains' (i.e. Yosemite) from April until October. They introduce themselves as Jeb and Carmen. I mishear and am excited to achieve one of my objec-tives of the trip: to meet my first Jedidiah.

'Not Jedidiah' is in his fifties, tall and well built with a com-pletely bald, symmetrical head, a gentle grey goatee beard and warm, welcoming blue eyes. He is a softly spoken man of lan-guid movement and action. He could quite easily have risen from the same ground as the unhurried Yosemite pines but he is in fact from Seattle (he presumably left when Bill Gates and his friends were getting all energetic and entrepreneurial).

Carmen is in her late forties (with solid breasts considerably younger), glamorous and has more urgency and organisational instinct about her, which is due to her Germanic roots, having grown up in Frankfurt. As a pair (the couple, not her breasts), they make the perfect inn-sitters. I suspect that Jeb does most of the sitting: he is witty and casual; she is business-like and orderly.

We are shown to our cottage at the rear of the property. Jeb opts for the suitcase on wheels whilst I struggle with the heavy and awkward hold-all; he usefully points out a dish of chocolates once we are inside, whereas Carmen establishes what time we would like breakfast and what kind of bagels we prefer.

Our cottage is tastefully appointed, as estate agents would say. As is my entitlement as a paying guest, as soon as Jeb and Carmen have left, I nose around all of the interesting objects in the bedroom and sitting room. There are framed original Ford Model T advertisements to middle-class America, including one which is ahead of its time in terms of political correctness. It is encouraging 'the woman in business' to purchase a 'Ford closed car' for her personal use. For only $525 for a coupé, the car will enable her to 'to conserve minutes, to expedite her affairs, to widen the scope of her activities'. The implicit encouragement of women to use their new automobiles to commit infidelities is also ahead of its time in terms of sexual liberties.

I find a comedy record called 'The Little Ford Rambled Right Along' with words and music by C. R. Foster and Byron Gay. Henry Ford had of course been ahead of his time with factory assembly lines, but I hadn't realised that he had also product-placed his automobiles in songs. I had thought that Sigue Sigue Sputnik were the first to do this. They were a ridiculous and failed 1980s new wave, glam-punk band with extravagant haircuts and a BDSM fetish. They wore torn fishnet stockings over their faces and leather jock-straps over their trousers like superheroes, and were reputedly signed up by EMI for £1 million as a marketing gimmick to promote their first single, 'Love Missile F1-11'. As a gullible thirteen-year-old, I had fallen for the hype and purchased their debut album; the best part of which was the product placement advertisements between each track (I still recall 'Studio Line from L'Oréal, fixing gel, strong hold' and wonder why my brain retains this shit but can't recall my children's years of birth). But it seems that Henry Ford had got there first with product placement in records. 'The Little Ford Rambled Right Along' professes itself to be 'the greatest comedy song sensation'. Certainly Sigue Sigue Sputnik could not challenge that claim.

I root around for a record player in the cottage but can't find one, so instead I go on YouTube in the downstairs living room and find a 1915 recording of the song. It involves a Ford crashing into everything (fences, telegraph poles, ditches, mules and preachers), but the perky little Ford keeps rambling right along and sounding its irritating horn repeatedly throughout the song. It was no doubt a very funny song a hundred years ago, but Jackie doesn't appreciate it today and shouts at me from the bedroom upstairs to turn down that shit as she is trying to sleep.

I poke around in a wooden cabinet housing a few books: *Henry Ford and Benjamin B. Lovett: The Dancing Billionaire and the Dancing Master*; *The Truth about Henry Ford*; and *The Holy Bible*. I am beginning to wonder if I might have inadvertently wandered into a religious cult, as I did once in Tintagel, Cornwall, when I accidentally stayed in a hotel run by Scientologists who think they are King Arthur and His Knights of the Round Table. Although Jeb is handsome and charismatic enough to be a cult leader, nothing would ever get done.

I am getting bored of the Ford memorabilia, so cast around more widely and stumble across by far my most exciting find in the room. It is a small, innocuous wooden box which I had missed on my first scout, but when I look inside, it is an original Edison 'Gem Phonograph'. In addition to pioneering the AC alternating current, the lightbulb and the motion picture camera, US inventor Thomas Edison also invented the phonograph, enabling not only the mechanical recording of sound (which had been done before) but also the reproduction of sound (which hadn't). Like Henry Ford, he also mastered mass production. Seattle's Bill Gates and Paul G. Allen may be feeling smug for developing the Windows software that I am currently using to write this book, but Edison contributed the electricity that my laptop is using, the artificial light that I am working by and the recorded music which I am listening to (on my headphones now, to avoid further interrupting Jackie's dozing). Most importantly, without him, there would also be no Tom Hanks.

To a music fan such as myself, the Gem Phonograph is ground zero. I have never seen one before. As is again my right as a paying guest, I start to fiddle with it. I find what I had initially thought was a vase next to it but I now realise is the flaring horn. I successfully attach it, so that the box now resembles a smaller version of the HMV logo. This attachment is quite an achievement for me. Encouraged by my success, I dive back into the cabinet housing the books and find the winder. I also successfully attach this. All ready to go, I wind the winder and watch the stylus fly off and disintegrate on the floor. It is only afterwards, with the help of Google (which also would not have existed without Edison) that I learn that an Edison cylinder phonograph should never be played without first attaching the cylinder containing the recorded material.

I look up Edison Gem Phonographs on eBay and find one for sale for $995. No GPS and now no Gem Phonograph. I am down $1,300 on a day that had such a promising start. I am beginning to understand how Kalman Kaplan must have felt: 'Changed mind about a million-dollar week – looks like complete disaster. A million-dollar week? Was completely fooled.' But the more he doesn't reply to my email, the more I am losing sympathy for him.

# CHAPTER TWENTY

*Sacagawea – Post-it navigational tool – missing Clark's point*
*– Jack Frost – Gangnam bears – a village made of curry*
*˙ – Model T – bear back-up*

SOUNDTRACK: LED ZEPPELIN – 'MISTY MOUNTAIN HOP'

**M**eriwether Lewis and William Clark had Sacagawea as their tracker and guide when making history and pushing west to the Pacific Ocean with their Thomas Jefferson-commissioned expedition across Yosemite (something which my children already knew about without the American Museum of Natural History, thanks again to the unexpectedly educational *Night at the Museum*). Jackie and I, on the other hand, have nothing more than a yellow Post-it note from Jeb, listing where we should visit in Yosemite Valley. We don't have a map, our phones have no signal, and our water bottles are now empty. We are looking for Clark Point, the one place in Yosemite for which there are no signposts.

Jeb lied to me. Twice. First, he told me that it is only a moderate hike from Yosemite Valley up the Mist Trail to the top of Vernal Fall. Three hundred granite steps might be a moderate hike for the indigenous, ubiquitous California ground squirrel, but it is not moderate for a 46-year-old lawyer with more sweat in his body than the waterfall he is visiting. I stop every twenty steps or so to take on water and, when my water is finished, to pretend to take yet another photograph of the waterfall or look through my binoculars. If only I had taken a Red Bull at the bottom of the waterfall, I would not be receiving such condescending looks from overtaking squirrels.

Having eventually reached the top, heaving and blowing, my calf muscles shot, and realising that a waterfall in fact looks much better from the bottom than the top, I decide that I do not want to take the perilous steps back down or to compete with the torrent of homogenous hikers and smug squirrels coming up. I opt to keep going upwards to Clark Point. There are people swimming in the fast-flowing river leading to Vernal Fall, right beside the DANGER: DO NOT SWIM signs. Given their reordering of people's names, it is possible that the visiting Americans might have read this sign as DO SWIM: DANGER NOT. I hang around to eat my trail bar and to watch, but none of the swimmers gets into any real difficulty so I move on. Jeb had recommended Clark Point. It is no. 2 on his Post-it note guide. This is Jeb's second lie. There is no Clark Point, just like there is no Keyser Söze. There are intermittent information boards for hardened hikers, sketchy maps and signposts, but nowhere is there any mention of Clark Point. Even Sacagawea could not have found Clark Point. I doubt William Clark himself knew his Point.

We take a wrong turn, walk for another mile or so and end up at Nevada Fall. Jackie concludes this is my fault. I counter that if she hadn't lost the GPS then I might be able to find Clark Point. The ensuing silence is a bonus as it enables me to listen to the rather pleasant birdsong.

Retracing our steps from Nevada Fall (which was very beautiful, but not when you are only looking for one waterfall), I spot a fit young American Indian couple up ahead who look like they know what they are doing. Sadly, they are not Native Americans, but Californians with family in real India – had they been Native Americans, they would have been able to inform me that the National Park should in fact be called Ahwahnee (meaning 'the place of the gaping mouth') rather than Yosemite (referring to the displaced tribe and meaning 'they are killers', which is a less tourist-friendly name). He has both a map and a charged phone with Google maps. She is in running gear. I abandon Jackie to any hungry bears and catch them up to ask if they have heard of Clark Point. They haven't, and neither has their Google maps, but they have heard of Brexit. I have no time or oxygen for any more discussion about the baffling stupidity of some of my friends, neighbours and partners, but explain that Clark Point is meant to be an alternative route to the Mist Trail back down to Trailhead. He says that he knows where I mean and that they are heading in the same direction. He asks if we should wait for Jackie; after careful consideration I agree that we probably should.

Following another twenty minutes of ascension, we reach two roads that diverge in a yellow wood.

'It's like Jack Frost,' says the Indian girl breezily. 'We'll take the one less travelled by.'

'Thanks,' I say breathlessly.

They point us in the right direction, which mercifully is pointing downhill, and we part ways. Because they have been so helpful, I manage to resist correcting her poetry reference to Robert Frost. To do so was almost as difficult as the Mist

Trail itself. Now that we are walking downhill and can breathe again, I can at least enjoy the majestic Neolithic valley, and soak in the view across its meadows and meandering river. I hadn't noticed them so much on the way up, as I was concentrating so hard on breathing. Yosemite is breathtaking, literally and metaphorically.

If you want to learn about the geology of the artfully sculpted Sierra Nevada mountains, can I come to your lesson, please? Jeb's Post-it note doesn't really help me, but it is probably something to do with vaguely recollected words from distant school days, words such as upper mantle, magma, sedimentary rocks, oceanic crust, continental crust, subduction, tectonic forces, batholith, glaciation and lots of millions of years. Regrettably, all that I can remember about geology was my geography field trip to High Force, a waterfall on the River Tees near my school, where I risked my life for the sake of geology. By English standards, it is a spectacular waterfall, with the whole of the River Tees plunging over a precipice. Mr Rushforth, my geography teacher, felt that the best way to demonstrate both the height and the force of High Force was to let teenage boys dangle head-first over the same precipice, sitting on the backs of their legs to anchor them. He was a man of considerable frame, and also fame within my school for his bold teaching methods. His fame amongst Yarm School boys was eventually usurped by my German teacher and coach of the rowing team, who earned national tabloid coverage for repeatedly exposing himself to women on trains. You just don't get daring teachers like those two any more.

Reunited with the car after three hours of hiking, we spend the next hour doing some drive-by shooting. Not in the

American college sense (it is the school holidays so not yet the season for college shootings), but in the photography sense. I have had enough of arduous treks, so opt for getting the rest of my Ansel Adams-style photographs from the comfort of the dodgy Dodge we have hired, which claims to have only 19,000 miles on its clock yet has no USB port or jack-to-jack input, still has a CD player, and was probably around during the tectonic formative years of Yosemite. I will tell friends and relatives that we trekked right across Yosemite Valley. They will never know differently from my photographs and I doubt they will ever read this book to find out the truth.

El Capitan is the largest granite monolith in the world, towering over my five feet eight inches at more than 3,000 feet against the blue Californian sky. It is intimidating to drive the valley road in the shadow of its looming mouth. The background granite rocks are like the decayed teeth of an Irish bar singer; the pine trees in the foreground forming the rotting, unflossed gums. I am going off on one here, devising silly similes and now aimlessly attempting alliteration. Who am I kidding? You don't need me to try to describe the beauty of Yosemite to you. Get off your backside and go and see it for yourself; you won't regret it. If you don't make it there, then you need only read one book: John Muir's *My First Summer in the Sierra*. His poetically spiritual descriptions of Yosemite remain unmatched a hundred years later: 'Marvellous cliffs, marvellous in sheer dizzy depth and sculpture, types of endurance. Thousands of years have they stood in the sky exposed to rain, snow, frost, earthquake and avalanche, yet they still wear the bloom of youth.'

My apologies for that little interruption of trying to write a descriptive piece. From now on I promise to stick to my irreverent, irrelevant, unrehearsed, unresearched stream of consciousness. That is what we have both become accustomed to and we seem to be getting along just fine as we are.

The car in front slams on its brakes.

'Bears,' I say to Jackie, and do the same. Her little arms fling into the air with now satisfying familiarity.

Sadly, it isn't bears. It's humans. Two of them. Scaling El Capitan, the most vertical rock face in the world. It was admittedly quite a long shot to think bears could operate karabiners and belays. Now I feel miserable and inadequate and console my insecurities by petulantly suggesting to Jackie that the Mist Trail must be just as hard. I have my binoculars with me but hadn't thought I would be using them to watch humans dangling on a string. Other cars stop to see what we are looking at and to borrow our binoculars and soon there is a small crowd of us craning our necks upwards to watch the tiny human yo-yos. For all I know, behind us a family of black bears are dancing Gangnam-style.

After the exertion of watching the thrill-seeking rock-climbers, we have built up an appetite so go for lunch at Curry Village. This is not as promising as it sounds. It proves to be as disappointing as the FREE CASH signs at unaffiliated cash withdrawal machines, and it is in fact not named after Indian food, but after some joker called David Curry who established a camp here in 1899 which now comprises 400 tent cabins and has been deceiving hungry hikers ever since. Camp David would have been a less misleading name than Curry Village. I overcome my curry setback and make do with pizza and a side order of squirrel.

In the afternoon, we leave the valley to visit the noble Glacier

Point. I am very proud of my driving ability for not falling off the edge of the Glacier Point road, a dizzying, spiralling road with such spectacular views that it draws me like a lemming off a cliff. Jackie doesn't get to see the view from the road as she has to act as my eyes whilst my own are feasting on the scenery. That is the type of teamwork that makes ours such a successful partnership: she watches the road, I steer. I feel safer when the handbrake is on in the car park and conclude that this must be one of the best views in America, overlooking Half Dome, Yosemite Falls, Royal Arches and North Dome.

Jackie needs the toilet but the retching Japanese tourist exiting the chemical loo in the car park tightens her bladder for a while longer. As we are short of time, we enjoy the scenery, take some photos (including one of the Tenth Doctor dangling, Mr Rushforth-style, off the top of a precipice) and get back in our car to finish our Post-it-note self-tour of Yosemite by driving to a closed road which Jeb has recommended to park on as a shortcut, which shaves off an hour of hiking to Sentinel Dome. Jeb's laziness is beginning to work to my advantage. This is a great tip; we park up and only have to walk five minutes to reach the peak of this iconic granite formation. I overtake the overheating hikers struggling up the face of the Dome with the smugness and agility of a California ground squirrel.

Having used the lemming analogy earlier, I feel obliged to research whether they do in fact commit mass suicide by jumping off cliffs. Unsurprisingly, I learn that it is just an urban myth, but the origin of the myth does take me by surprise. In 1958, squeaky-clean, cuddly animal-loving Walt Disney made a film about Alaska called *White Wilderness*. It featured a segment about lemmings, an adorable short-tailed vole, which was dragging a bit; so the dream-makers at Disney decided to sex it up by buying some tame lemmings from local Inuit children and flinging them off a cliff into the ocean, closing the sequence with a final shot showing the ocean awash with freshly murdered Chip 'n' Dales. Imagine how much fun the film-makers must have had making that, reprehensible as it was (obviously).

So I was wrong with my lemming analogy; I was also wrong about Glacier Point offering the best view of Yosemite Valley. Sentinel Dome is higher than Glacier Point and offers even more wide-reaching views from its summit. There is no crowd up here and we are able to take some time to stand and stare, in silence, as the wolfish Taylor had urged us to do. Someone has left a rucksack. Unlike back in London, I am fairly confident it won't be holding improvised explosive devices, but rather the camera, water, trail bars and possibly car keys of some hapless husband who will shortly be getting it in the neck from his wife and sent back up to retrieve it, with no sex for him tonight. It could have been worse; he could have left it at the top of the Mist Trail and be expected to have sex afterwards.

To make up for his bogus Clark Point directions, Jeb takes us out in the Model T when we return to Tin Lizzie, with the promise that we can drive it. Unlike my fifteen-year-old Land Rover Discovery, it starts first time. Like a good dogger, Jeb wants to take us where we can't be seen from a main road. He sits up front, in the middle of both seats, with Jackie and me sitting on the back-seat leather sofa without seat belts; his massive shoulders arched, his sunscreen-polished head gleaming in the late red Californian sunshine, he is at one with the vehicle. It is only twenty brake-horsepower, a pace which suits Jeb. He tells us how the brakes failed when he was letting a twelve-year-old customer drive. Twelve-year-olds don't panic. Nor is the word panic in Jeb's vocabulary. Panic requires a sense of urgency; he has replaced the word panic with the word poise.

He pulls in on a quiet dirt track and lets me drive. It is uneventful. Then it's Jackie's turn.

Jackie has never driven in America. She has never driven on the right-hand side of the road. She has never driven a car with gears. She is the equivalent of the twelve-year-old customer, but with a much, much keener sense of panic, panic, PANIC.

Jeb talks her carefully though the controls and how to make the car move. Push the silver button on the floor to start the engine; press down the left pedal all the way to the floor; slowly pull down the lever on the steering wheel.

She tries. The car stalls. I smile.

'You didn't press down the left pedal to the floor.'

'You didn't tell me to press the feckin' pedal; you just said to pull down the lever.'

I am enjoying this. Watching is more fun than receiving.

Jeb is enjoying this too, because nothing flusters him. He laughs that Jackie sounds exactly like Carmen. He comments that if anything goes wrong, I don't have to worry about my insurance because everything will be his fault.

Jackie eventually listens properly to the instructions and gets the car moving, but too fast for her liking. Although she is sitting in front of me, I know the fear-filled eyes that she will be wearing right now. She wears the same eyes on the nursery ski slopes. She gives out to Jeb because he hasn't told her how to brake. He tells her she doesn't need to brake as we are barely moving. Jackie is having none of it; she presses every pedal until the car halts and stalls, again. It might not have been for very long, but the first car she has ever driven in the States was the first ever mass-produced car in the States. That is a quite a cool thing.

Yosemite, like Alaska, has let us down on the bear front. The remaining cities of Beverly Hills, Nashville and Savannah are unlikely to remedy our bear deficiency, although when planning this trip and telling Jackie that I wanted to go to Savannah, she googled 'savanna' and was misled into believing that we were going to be going on a safari (the perils of a search engine and an Irish education). Alas, even African savannas don't have bears, so she would have been disappointed either way. Larry and Jeremy both saw bears crossing the road in Juneau without us, and when we return to Tin Lizzie this evening we learn that a smug young French couple also staying there have had three separate bear sightings today, crossing the road in Yosemite in the same areas that we visited. The most I have seen is a wild turkey crossing the road in Sundance, so I resign myself to having to settle for the birdlife in Costa Rica (where I will be looking for the most spectacularly named bird of all time, the resplendent quetzal).

When I return to our cottage, my bear disappointment turns to bare relief. Jackie has joined a Facebook page for the *Wilderness Adventurer* so that she can keep in touch with Susu's meals, and someone has posted a news article on there about a bear attack on one of UnCruise's bushwhack guides two days ago. Fortunately, it wasn't Taylor but it was one of her colleagues on the sister ship, the *Wilderness Explorer*. They had been trekking in the same place where we had been whacking the week before, Sitka Bay, with two guides (rather than our one). The 41-year-old female lead guide had taken a similar 'yonder' approach to

Taylor, with four or five of the faster walkers up front with her, and they had become separated from the rest of the group (the likes of Geri and the other root-stumblers), with the other guide at the rear. The lead guide had rounded a semi-blind corner and inadvertently entered the path of a sow and her cub, some fifteen feet away; she shouted 'Bear, back up', an instruction the passengers, unsurprisingly, followed immediately, leaving her isolated.

The report is hazy about what followed, but what appears to have happened is unprecedented: the bear reared up and attacked immediately, without warning, such that the lead guide was unable to un-holster her bear spray from her belt before the bear started mauling her. She did the right thing (she was well trained in how to be mauled) and lay on her front with her arms protecting her head whilst the bear focused its attack upon her backpack and, unfortunately, her legs. Unlike Ranger Dan, the 22-year-old guide at the back was a genuine superhero (and literal 'bear back-up') and, having heard the bear's groan, sprinted to the front with his bear spray to take on the bear, successfully (it turns out the spray does actually repel bears); he then applied first aid and radioed the ship, who scrambled further first aid from the crew and a rescue helicopter from Juneau. The lead guide survived the attack but has bad lacerations to her legs. None of the guests on the hike was injured.

Aside from obvious concern for the guide and the impact the attack must have had on the passengers (even Pam might have stopped complaining that she prefers her lasagne portion to be the crusty, corner bit), two further thoughts strike me. First, Jackie and I had been hiking there only a week before, actively seeking bears. What were we thinking? We were the intruders in bear habitat, in what is genuinely the final frontier on earth. It is surprising such attacks have not happened more frequently. Second, the boy at the rear, the bear back-up who had saved his colleague's life with a canister, is not much older than Meggie, Mimi, Jamie and Shauna. Yet they can't get the lid off a can of ravioli between them.

I am now grateful that the most I saw in Alaska was berry feast bear scat. I resolve not to search for bears any more. That should be easy as our next stop is Los Angeles.

At this juncture, I hope it is not too insensitive and inappropriate to refer to a sign at Fort Steele Campground in Canada that Google spews out at me. The sign reads as follows:

### WARNING

Due to the frequency of human-bear encounters, the BC Fish and Wildlife Branch is advising hikers, hunters, fishermen and any persons that use the out-of-doors in a recreational or work-related function to take extra precautions while in the field.

We advise the outdoorsman to wear little noisy bells on clothing so as to give advance warning to any bears that might be close by so you don't take them by surprise.

We also advise anyone using the out-of-doors to carry 'Pepper Spray' with him in case of an encounter with a bear.

Outdoorsmen should also be on the watch for fresh bear activity, and be able to tell the difference between black bear faeces and grizzly bear faeces. Black bear faeces is smaller and contains lots of berries and squirrel fur. Grizzly bear shit has bells in it and smells like pepper.

# CHAPTER TWENTY-ONE

*Benzodiazepine – high end – elevator shades – white roses*
*– Odd Job and Jar Jar – corruption, celebrity*
*and film noir – becoming a VIP*
SOUNDTRACK: SHERYL CROW – 'ALL I WANNA DO'

If New York is a movie set, then LA provides the soundtrack.
We drive past signs for Santa Monica Boulevard (Sheryl Crow – 'All I wanna do is have some fun, until the sun comes up over Santa Monica Boulevard') and Mulholland Drive (the Gaslight Anthem – 'I used to drive you all around with the radio on, through the mist on Mulholland'). I slipped some benzodiazepine into Jackie's tea this morning as we left Tin Lizzie so she behaves on the long drive from Yosemite to Beverly Hills and even relaxes enough to play a game of Solitaire on her phone, rather than panicking that we are in a real-life game of Frogger as we enter LA.

Jackie always has to read the hotel bumf as soon as we get into the room, usually to find out the Wi-Fi password and what stuff is available for free. She remains calm enough when we check into the Mr C hotel in Beverly Hills to say nothing more than a casual 'Oooh look, they have an earthquake procedure.' That benzodiazepine is good stuff.

We are in the city of angels and beautiful people. I need to beautify myself. I put on my navy (to make me look slim), short-sleeved Hugo Boss linen shirt, and my brown Tommy Hilfiger (to make me look preppy) shorts, which I purchased in Greenwich Village, New York, under the approving gaze of Mimi and my mother, especially for an occasion such as this. Boss and Hilfiger no less. Could I be any more Beverly Hills?

'Can you give me a recommendation for somewhere to eat on Rodeo Drive?' I ask the concierge. I have done my research; I know that Rodeo Drive is just up the road from where we are staying. It is meant to be quite nice.

The concierge looks a bit awkward. He is also staring at Jackie's forehead which, after three mosquito bites on the Mist Trail, has now swollen to resemble a dolphin's.

'Rodeo Drive is very high end, sir.'

I feel like Julia Roberts in *Pretty Woman*, only much better dressed.

'Would you prefer an Italian? I can recommend a good Italian, parallel to Rodeo.'

He also offers us a car to the Rodeo Drive shopping area to do some sightseeing. I disapprove of his brazenly disapproving tone so give him some back.

'How many miles is it?'

'Miles? It's four blocks, sir.'

I decline the car, and tell him that I survived the Mist Trail's granite steps so can probably handle a walk of four blocks. I ask if I will need bear spray. He looks relieved to see the back of me and to have a real beautiful person with a beautiful bank balance check in behind me.

It turns out that he was right. We are a bit underdressed

for Rodeo Drive. Boss and Hilfiger just don't cut the mustard. Instead, we find a perfectly pleasant low-end restaurant called the Cheesecake Factory, where our camp waiter makes us feel much more welcome by flirting with both Jackie and me. After our meal, my plate but not Jackie's gets cleared by another waiter, and when our camp one returns he screams and says, 'Oh my God, have you eaten your plate?' Jackie almost chokes with laughter on her parmesan chicken and he says it's OK, he knows CPR.

I don't see any bears but I do see a raccoon crossing the road on the way back to the hotel. It's a poor substitute: Hilfiger instead of Versace.

I wake early the next morning and, overcome with LA fitness, decide to go for a run again. It has been a while since my daily run, but in my defence I have been a bit busy. The guy sharing the lift down with me is wearing a sharp suit and shades. I ask him if it's too bright for him in the lift. He looks up and down at my non-matching running gear (and my legs, which were once queried by a friend who was uncertain whether they were mine or whether I was riding a chicken). I probably shouldn't have mixed black Nike and navy Reebok. Behind the darkness of his sunglasses he must be giving me the withering look received across Hollywood by English D-listers such as Vinnie Jones.

I step out of the hotel into a perfect Beverly Hills morning. The erect palm trees lining the boulevard penetrate a flawless blue sky and outside even feels air-conditioned. I start my run by turning down South Rodeo Drive. Each driveway contains at least two European cars, because European cars are more exclusive on South Rodeo Drive: usually a Maserati, Mercedes or Porsche. White roses are this season's required flora, overhanging the pavement from every perfect garden. I stop to smell one and consider stealing it for Jackie, but am put off by the sign on the automatically sprinkled lawn advertising the armed (yes, armed – also automatic, no doubt) security response provided by ADT. It is then that I notice a single black and gold Nike basketball boot on the manicured verge, presumably marking the spot from where the last person who plucked a white rose was forcibly removed. Nothing in South Rodeo Drive is out of place, so the boot must have been left here as a deterrent. I am surprised it was not a whole leg. I start running again, only faster.

A guy with a leaf blower is clearing the street, which is just as well as I might have tripped on a stray leaf and scratched my Omega Globemaster.

Original Salvador Dali sculptures stand on the pavement opposite the *Pretty Woman* Beverly Wilshire hotel, outside the shopping area of Rodeo Drive occupied by Stefano Ricci, Fendi, Louis Vuitton, Cartier, Gucci, Prada, Tiffany & Co. and good old Tom (Ford) and Harry (Winston). 'High-end' stores, as our concierge would say. For me, though, it is just Vegas for shoppers.

The parallel Beverly Drive is no doubt where the concierge would recommend for my browsing, as there is a Roots, a North Face and a Sunglass Hut. I think to myself that Larry could have made a fortune selling ski gear at grossly inflated prices here.

I take a right down Santa Monica Boulevard because all I wanna do is have some fun. But it takes me fifteen minutes to cross the road, which I treat as my warm-down. I decide to walk the same route back to my hotel, as the external air-con is starting to fail and I don't want globules of my sweat to mess up South Rodeo Drive's sidewalk.

In the lift down to breakfast, Jackie asks me why I am wearing shades. I give her a withering look behind my blacked-out safety curtain.

Steve has booked us on an LA insiders tour. The driver arrives on time in a shiny new SUV. Steve has told me to expect a man called John. There is no way he is really called John; that must be his witness protection name. He looks like Odd Job. I try to shake his hand but can't get mine around his. He doesn't speak. He must have mangled his tongue when eating his last car.

Our guide rocks up twelve minutes late. His name is Eric and he is tall and LA lean. He is wearing scruffy grey jeans, a faded blue T-shirt, beads, a hoop earring and trainers. For the first time in Beverly Hills, I feel overdressed in Boss and Hilfiger. He is in his late forties or early fifties but has suspiciously black, tightly curled hair, held on by his raised sunglasses, and a thinly trimmed salt 'n' pepper beard. He walks with a long, lazy stride like Jar Jar Binks (from the best-forgotten *Star Wars* prequels). He is third generation Angelean and it shows in his tone of voice and skin.

'What texture do you want for your tour, man?' asks Eric, in a trippy Californian drawl.

I like this question. It sounds like one of Russell T. Davies's 'tone meetings', which he introduced for every episode of *Doctor Who* to ensure it had the right look and feel for the script.

'Some architecture, some music, some celebrity Hollywood stuff for Jackie and I would like to meet Tom Hanks, please,' I respond, in clipped English. I wish I had said 'man' instead of 'please'.

Eric is pleased with the music request and ignores the Tom

Hanks request. It turns out he is an ex-mod and a ska fan. He used to hang out with David Wakeling of The Beat, or The English Beat as they were patriotically known in North America, no doubt due to some overzealous IP litigator (such as me) preventing them from using the name The Beat in the US. We drive to the Walt Disney Concert Hall, a spectacular stainless steel Frank Gehry creation of curvaceous panels designed to provide the perfect acoustic experience. It looks like the bastard anarchic child of the Sydney Opera House. After a few teething problems when the glare of its panels caused planes and automobiles to crash, tweaks were made with sandpaper to make it less fatal to residents. Regardless of its violence, it is a beautiful building. It also makes me look slim in my reflection.

'Do you like book stores and music stores?' asks Eric. John remains menacingly silent and focused up front.

Eric is playing in my sweet spot. Before Jackie can respond about the priority being celebrity spotting, I confirm that we do indeed both love book and music stores.

Our next stop is the Last Bookstore. On the way, I learn that Eric was a PR executive who, in his words, 'clipped his tie for ever'. (I still fold mine each night after work, but am now enjoying the carefree feeling of an open neck.) He then became a travel writer and just happens to have with him a copy of his box of tour cards called *LA City Walks*, published by Chronicle Books. I feel like we are in safe hands. He literally wrote the book on LA tours. I don't tell him about this travelogue because I don't want him to feel threatened by the competition. Instead, I covertly note down on my iPhone anything cool or memorable that he says about his city, to steal for my own book.

I also learn that his girlfriend is a salsa dancer. I am not surprised that he has a girlfriend rather than (or perhaps as well as) a wife. Nor am I surprised that she is a salsa dancer. He has the look of a Latin dancer himself and if his name had been Rodolpho that wouldn't have surprised me either.

As we walk the neighbourhood of the Last Bookstore, I witness the different approaches of the many homeless to extract money from us. One greets us with 'Good morning, good afternoon and good evening, haha.' The next mutters to Jackie, 'A husband strangled his wife… to death.' Friendship and fear may well be what LA is all about.

I ask Eric what LA is all about. He answers me concisely by saying it is best captured in two movies, *LA Confidential* and *Chinatown*, because the city is about corruption, celebrity and film noir. That sounds about right. Thanks, Eric, I will steal that for my book.

We drive on to Amoeba Music and dismay is writ large across Jackie's face. Eric and I are in our element, though. He buys a The Who poster (note to other bands: starting your band name with the definite article makes it annoyingly difficult to describe a single piece of merchandise). I have come all the way to the west coast of North America, so I want a memento: I buy a The Cure T-shirt (see previous note). The Cure come from Crawley, ten minutes from where I live.

I also buy a Led Zeppelin 1977 US tour T-shirt which I change into for a photograph of me in front of the Hollywood sign. I text it to Meggie and ask if she feels guilty yet. She responds that she is currently standing in a field at V Festival watching Justin Bieber so will ask him to come round to see my guitars instead of Jimmy.

Hollywood Boulevard and Bel-Air are disappointing. The

Hollywood Walk of Fame is full of walkers (a typo would have been equally accurate here), and I can't find Tom Hanks's star, or Tom Hanks himself, anywhere. How can Donald Trump be here on the pavement (if only...) but not Tom? We drive past what I am told are the stars' (directors', producers' and A-list actors') houses in Bel-Air, but there is no evidence of that, as all I can see are forbidding gates and walls. I get the merest glimpse of the Playboy mansion, in much the same way that I used to steal mere glimpses of the magazine centrefolds in the newsagent's on Park Road in Hartlepool as a teenager. We have waited four hours, but finally Odd Job speaks as we drive past the house of Bernie Ecclestone, the Formula One supremo.

'His mother-in-law has just been kidnapped. I once drove her,' he growls.

I can't see his eyes behind his sunglasses but his satisfied tone of voice tells me that either he doesn't like Ecclestone (perhaps he didn't give a generous enough tip), or that the two events are linked and he currently has her locked in the boot of his other car.

Our time is up and I say goodbye to Eric and lose my hand in John's. I tip him generously, as I don't want him to kidnap Jackie.

A day in LA is enough for me. For entirely voyeuristic reasons, it has been interesting to watch LA at play. It seems appropriate that we have driven by and seen most of it from an air-conditioned, blacked-out SUV. Like a catwalk model, and like John our driver, LA is keen to strike a pose but doesn't want to get to know you. As required by Raymond Chandler and film noir, I end up in the cocktail bar of our hotel, chatting to the neon-lit barman about dames and sipping an Old Fashioned through a straw too thin. Next to me sits a Middle Eastern lady too thin. But it is all so artificial: the barman is from Montana, not LA; it is a poor excuse for an Old Fashioned; and the Middle Eastern lady was born in Bradford. That one state can contain both the carefully preserved natural beauty of Yosemite and the recklessly pickled Botox of Beverly Hills demonstrates the vastness and the contradiction of this wonderfully confused country.

LA is an over-privileged child, constantly demanding attention: 'Look at me, look at me, look at how filthy rich and beautiful I am', so I ignore the spoilt little bastard and move on; but before doing so we spend the next day marching past the riff-raff to the front of the line with our VIP passes at Universal Studios. It's a small victory over the superficial, unwelcoming and impersonal people of LA.

# CHAPTER TWENTY-TWO

*Camaro – Heavy Metal Drummer – Iraq*
*– my The Cure T-shirt – Jimmy Page dies*
SOUNDTRACK: WILCO – 'HEAVY METAL DRUMMER'

**G**ibson welcomes me. Martin Guitars welcomes me. Even Johnny Cash welcomes me. I am only at the airport luggage carousel and already Nashville is my favourite city.

Excited by the quality of my billboard greetings, I upgrade the car rental. I am bored of Steve's sensible SUVs. The rhythm guitarist of LAP and ex-rhythm guitarist of Castro to Deodar has arrived in Music City for four days. He needs appropriate wheels; a bluesmobile. I upgrade to a Chevrolet Camaro. I don't know what that is but I am assured by the man from Hertz that it will be good fun. The boot is too small for the luggage and the front windscreen is too small for the hired GPS, but it looks sensational. It is only a fifteen-minute drive from Nashville airport to the Hermitage Hotel, with a speed limit of 30mph, so the Camaro will have to prove itself to me another day.

It is an appropriate car for another literary reason. I will eventually be driving it to Savannah, Georgia, and a Camaro is the sports car that Danny Hansford, the young man murdered in *Midnight in the Garden of Good and Evil* (played by Jude

Law in the movie), used to drive. I get into character and feel like Jude Law (with a few extra chins). This is the second time that has happened to me: I once slept in the same bed as Jude Law. He rented the same property in Cornwall as we did. It was an isolated barn conversion. Jude and his celebrity girlfriend needed space and isolation to avoid the paparazzi. Jackie and I needed space and isolation to avoid our six children, who were then all under the age of twelve.

The receptionist at the Hermitage Hotel is very pretty and welcoming, dual characteristics that LA could never achieve. She doesn't mind me being underdressed in my The Cure T-shirt – in fact, she compliments me on it – and recommends a venue on Lower Broadway where we can get high-end American finger food and great music. She does it in a non-patronising way. I thank her; but in Tennessee 'Thank you' is never the end of the conversation; she follows up with a courteous 'Absolutely'. I rather like that, as an enthusiastic endorsement of her willingness to assist, so I think I will say thank you a lot while I am here.

The bar is called Rippy's. Like everywhere on Lower Broadway, or Honky Tonk Row, as it is better known, a band is playing. I have lost two hours flying from LA, and missed lunch, so I am hungry and arrive for the early shift band. Despite that, they are terrific musicians. They do not get paid by the venue and do not receive a share of the bar money. Instead, they depend entirely upon voluntary contributions from the audience of twenty dollars per song request.

No one in the bar is requesting songs. This irritates me. There is something not right with a society that will pay more than a thousand dollars an hour for legal advice but is content to see jobbing musicians with incredible talent struggle to make a living.

The band claim that if a song is requested, they have to play it. I decide to take them up on this challenge. I request something by my favourite band, Wilco (from Chicago), who are a sort of twisted Americana but certainly not country music. Neither the male nor the female singer have heard of Wilco, but the bass player has. He has spent most of the set so far in his own core rhythm zone (watching the dusk bats circling the schoolhouse outside) but agrees to do an impromptu solo set on acoustic guitar. He introduces the song by explaining that he served in Iraq at a time before iPods, and took four CDs with him. One of them was *Yankee Hotel Foxtrot* by Wilco, so the band mean a lot to him. He claims he has never sung or played it before but he then performs a flawless version of 'Heavy Metal Drummer'. He gets a raucous response, entirely from me. The rest of the bar is concentrating on its fried food.

The band return and play some more traditional country music, but still there are no requests. Bolstered by the success of my first request, and now three beers down, I get bolder. Bold enough to eat bread-crumbed catfish in a basket. Bold enough to request something by The Cure, whom nobody could ever accuse of writing country music. The band consults; I hear them jamming an introduction I recognise. But the bass player is not happy. He swaps his bass with the lead guitarist's Telecaster and takes over again. Not only does he play the rhythm and lead parts, he also sings 'Friday I'm in Love'. The bass player! My covers band play that song and it took me an entire day to learn just the rhythm part. I have well and truly arrived in Music City.

Continuing to single-handedly pay the band's wages for the

night, I then lose my credibility and the respect of the band. Having gained kudos with the bass player with my first two outstanding requests, I next request 'The Devil Went Down to Georgia'. It turns out that this is the most requested song on Lower Broadway and that bands are so bored of it that they charge $100 to play it. I agree to put up the first twenty dollars, but the miserable sods at the other tables don't want to chip in. They are presumably as bored of it as the band is. After a promising start, I leave the bar feeling chastened by the predictability and mediocrity of my final song request. I leave the band a further twenty dollars as an apology.

It is over 4,000 miles from Crawley to Nashville, but it becomes apparent that the home of country music loves my Crawley band T-shirt. As I leave Rippy's Bar & Grill, the doorman tells me I have a great The Cure T-shirt. The gay hairdresser in the salon next door to my hotel enjoys my The Cure T-shirt, and also enjoys massaging my head a bit too much. I close my eyes and pretend he is Katharine Ross. A guy I walk past in the street stops me to tell me that he likes my The Cure T-shirt, but he doesn't comment on my new haircut. Jackie and I end the evening at an outdoor Kurt Vile gig as part of the free 'Live on the Green' music festival, and even the merchandise T-shirt vendor likes my The Cure T-shirt. I feel I have proved my point. The Cure are a great band, much loved in America, but they really could do without the definite article. It is too cumbersome in narrative form.

Kurt is a professional musician whose latest album I have and like, but he is arrogant, his vocals are not great and the mix is poor. I know which free gig I prefer. The band in the bar put on a better show but probably didn't even break even tonight.

As we pass the pretty hotel receptionist, she says, 'Good night.'

'Thank you,' I say.

'Absolutely.'

The next day, two unexpected things happen.

First, I reverse the Camaro into a bollard at General Jackson's house (also, confusingly, called the Hermitage). It is not my fault as the car has no side or rear-view windows. Ray Charles would have parity with me in trying to reverse park this thing. It is a car designed to go forwards only. Andrew Jackson, the People's President, and great general of the 1812 War, who defeated the British at the Battle of New Orleans, would have enjoyed watching another Englishman retreating unsuccessfully.

Second, Jimmy Page dies. Not in the same terminal way as David Bowie and Prince; in truth, he is still breathing, but what I mean is that he becomes dead to me. I will explain in a moment.

One of Steve's odder decisions has been to arrange a private tour guide to take us around former President Jackson's plantation home, eleven miles outside of Nashville. I say 'take us'; we are in fact supposed to give her a lift to the Hermitage but there is no back seat in the Camaro and it is too hot to strap her to the roof, so she has to drive herself there. Her name is Becky and she is doing a Master's in history at the University of Nashville, but General Jackson is clearly not the subject of her thesis.

On the official tour of the Hermitage, we (including Becky) learn that at the age of fourteen, Jackson was an orphan, and his two brothers had died in the Revolutionary War. Faced with such adversity, he did the only sensible thing in the circumstances to redeem his prospects and gain respect: he became a lawyer. This was back in 1787, when lawyers, rightly, were respected in the upper echelons of polite society rather than chased and seethed at. He then cemented his place in that society by marrying the daughter of one of the founding fathers of Nashville, twice.

For a lawyer, he had an uncharacteristically hot-headed reputation for violence and a disregard for the law. When I get cross with one of my associates, I tend to give them some bad feedback. When 'Old Hickory', as a judge no less, got cross with people, he brawled with and caned them, and he was a veteran of at least thirteen duels, killing the best shot in the country and prominent duellist Charles Dickinson. Realising that a violent temper was not best suited for a career on the Tennessee Superior Court circuit, he decided he was better equipped for the military. He became major general of the Tennessee militia, and promptly whupped the British at the Battle of New Orleans. The fact that the British had already surrendered two weeks previously and handed in their weapons was a mere technicality, as was the fact that his wife Rachel had previously married someone else (hence having to marry her twice, before and after her divorce). America had a new hero, and in 1829 he became the 7th President. A violent bully and adulterer becoming President of the United States; it could never happen today.

He had a very nice house, though, which he ran as a cotton plantation, 'owning' over a hundred slaves, including one celebrity slave called Alfred who was born a slave at the Hermitage and remained there after emancipation, becoming the first tour guide when the property was opened to the public. Alfred lived at the Hermitage longer than anyone else, black or white, and died there, aged ninety-nine, in 1901. He would therefore have been a considerably better tour guide than Becky, who gives me the impression that Jackie and I are not alone in this being our inaugural visit. I buy her lunch in the museum café, show interest in her thesis (don't ask me what it is about), tip her (don't ask me why) and say goodbye. It has been like escorting one of my children around all morning, but with marginally less stupid questions than Joe's. Now that I have relinquished my parental responsibility, it is time to spend all afternoon doing what I came to Nashville to do: drinking in a honky-tonk bar.

It is here that I realise Jimmy Page is no longer the greatest guitarist in the world. I am sitting in Robert's, watching his successor. The Moon tourist guide book told me to go to Robert's. It described it as the city's best honky-tonk. It used to sell cowboy boots and shoes, and they are still on display, but I don't need either as I have just bought a genuine Nashville cowboy leather belt, with an extravagant buckle. I am wearing it with my Tommy Hilfiger shorts and my sandals, to ensure I fit in with the other cowboys.

Moon also tells me that there is something about the energy of Robert's that makes it feel different. Moon knows its stuff. The double bass player has the facial expressions and the zeal of Jim Carrey, has laid his instrument sideways on the stage and is standing on it whilst maniacally plucking its strings; the band leader and lead singer, Don Kelley, is wearing a cowboy equivalent of Slash's hat over his eyes and, unlike Kurt Vile, has owned the crowd from the opening song; the drummer is dressed like a vaudeville gun-slinger and considerably upstages my belt; and the lead guitarist pulls mock heavy metal poses, is a Jack Black lookalike and a Jimmy Page defeating guitar god. He also has the vocal range of Roy Orbison and Johnny Cash combined, and is the first person I have ever seen perform a male/female duet on his own. I have watched a lot of bands over the years: class acts such as Nik Kershaw, Transvision Vamp (I had tickets for The Smiths on the same night and unforgivably elected, as a student led by my hormones, to see Wendy James instead of Morrissey), the Macc Lads and Rolf Harris (Rolf, I trusted you; I even invested in your artwork, a collection which no longer requires insurance); but this band is tighter and putting on a better show than any I have ever seen.

Two ladies from Chicago ask to join our bar table; they are both in their sixties and love my English accent. One of them has been fraternising with a Tennessee local called Jack Daniel since breakfast. She is a vacuum-dried version of Jamie Lee Curtis with approximately eight teeth, and a few of them are only just hanging on. She repeatedly tells me that Jackie and I are 'good people', whilst touching my bare thigh inappropriately highly.

The Don Kelley Band have a crowd-pleasing set-list, including Johnny Cash, Credence Clearwater Revival, Rawhide and a song I haven't heard since my Radio 2 family childhood: 'The Auctioneer' by Leroy Van Dyke. The double bass player not only plays double bass like Jerry Lee Lewis on speed, but also performs tongue-twisting verbal gymnastics with the lyrics of the alacritous auction chant.

I put a generous tip into the bucket during the interval, partly because I have enjoyed the lead guitarist so much and partly because the double bass player told me that he liked my The Cure T-shirt. However, I don't make any requests; I have lost confidence in that regard.

When I get back to the room, I text Meggie to tell her that Jimmy is no longer welcome in my home. I get some question marks in response.

# CHAPTER TWENTY-THREE

*GCSEs – driving lessons – James Last and Johnny Cash*
*– gospel and mint – the Death Star – behind the curtain*
*– US marshal – tea lady – strobe seizure*
SOUNDTRACK: JOHNNY CASH – 'HURT'

I am a terrible parent. It is GCSE results day and I am not in the country to receive Mimi's results with her. Mimi is more competitive than all of my other children, spare-children, Roy Keane and Usain Bolt put together and has heaped the pressure upon herself during revision. I am worried that no matter what she gets she will be dissatisfied (a bit like Pam at meal times on the *Wilderness Adventurer*). When I speak to her at 3 a.m. Nashville time, I am relieved to learn that my concerns prove unfounded. She has gotten (as we say in America) all A*s, even in art, which is quite an achievement if I were to show you some of her erratic juvenile scribblings. I refrain from mentioning that exams have got much easier since my day and instead affectionately tell her that she is a freak, that no one should get ten A*s, but that she is my freak and that I am very proud of her (admittedly, I would be more proud if she played in a band). She has considerably outshone my own academic achievements. I suggest that Mimi should celebrate by getting drunk and going nuts at Reading Festival; she deserves it after all of the hard work she has put in. She agrees with me. I caution her not to do drugs or get pregnant. I am a terrific parent.

My dad died when he was only fifty-six years old. He had one of the early lung transplants, in 1991 at the Freeman Hospital in Newcastle. It gave him an extra seven years. He was a smoker. But he was also unlucky. He had alpha-1-antitrypsin deficiency. Although you have probably never heard of antitrypsin, it is in fact the rhythm guitarist of breathing. It is a protein produced by your liver that, as you read this, is being released into your blood to control your enzyme activity and prevent healthy lung tissue from being damaged. Its deficiency leads to lung disease, shortness of breath, a hacking cough, wheezing, and a medical gas cylinder by your armchair; nicotine throws emphysema into the mix of what is already a lethal cocktail.

We had the usual clashes between son and father in the teenage years, not helped by his illness. I regularly used to get ejected from his car and have to walk back from my driving lessons with him as a result of disagreements about the speed at which I should drive or the route we should take. At that time, we didn't seem to have an awful lot in common, except for one unifying male country vocalist.

My parents were in their twenties through the 1960s, the greatest period in British musical history. Unfortunately, they didn't start buying records until the easy-listening 1970s. The records I grew up with therefore comprised: the Carpenters, Bread, Abba, Simon & Garfunkel and a bizarre favourite of theirs, James Last. He was a big band leader from Germany who arranged questionable pop hits in a big band-style mash-up. 'Rivers of Babylon' would merge into 'Dancing in the City' into 'Night Fever', masking the link with canned party applause and a uniform tempo. This was truly awful stuff, bordering on child abuse. They had vinyl copies of *Make the Party Last, James Last Plays Abba, James Last: The Best of Non-Stop Dancing* and of course *James Last Christmas Dancing.* It would be piped out through a fake wooden sideboard which was a record player in disguise (very much in vogue at the time), with side drawers which pulled out to be small, ineffective speakers. It was the age of the cassette, so my sister and I had to endure his non-stop party hits as the soundtrack to our Blackpool holidays as well.

The saviour was Johnny Cash. Dad was a fan and had a copy of the *Johnny Cash at Folsom Prison* LP. This was a game-changer for me and began my love of country music.

After an inedible breakfast of grits (a corn-based staple food-stuff in the Deep South, which looks like thick, lumpy porridge but tastes like thick, lumpy sick), I thank the pretty hotel receptionist (who, like Jackie, seems to be getting prettier every day) for directions to the Johnny Cash Museum.

'Absolutely.'

The museum is relatively new and, fittingly, is located next to a cowboy boot store. The man who inspects our entrance ticket has taken the job in order to meet new people. It takes us ten minutes to get past him and into the museum, having answered questions on Jackie's Irish childhood, Brexit and The Beatles.

Even if you are not a Johnny Cash fan I would urge you to visit the museum, but only if you are already in Nashville (my injunction would fall short of suggesting that it is worth making the trip especially). It is a social history of America through the '50s, '60s, '70s, '80s, '90s and noughties, as lived through the surly man in black. I watch some reruns of *The Johnny Cash*

*Show* from the 1970s, and a Christmas special of Johnny sitting around a Christmas tree strumming his guitar transports me back to sweeter, simpler, less urgent, non-chargeable times.

Nobody's Christmases can match your own childhood Christmases, or rather my own childhood Christmases in Hartlepool. My sister and I would rush downstairs to the lounge on Christmas morning to find two blue pillowcases fastened with clothes pegs to a copper and bronze hostess trolley, presents spilling out onto the floor. On top of the trolley would be the remnants of fondant fancies (Hartlepool Santa preferred fondant fancies to mince pies) and a glass of whisky. My dad, blissfully unaware of the enzymes attacking his lungs, would be dressed in his buttoned-up blue stripy M&S pyjamas and my mum in a new dressing gown. As it was Christmas, there would probably be one of those opened chess piece wrappers on my dad's bedside table.

I had two grandmothers, called Gran Round the Corner, who lived round the corner, and London Gran, who lived in Surrey. Dad and I would go to pick up Gran Round the Corner before the present-opening ceremony began. Then, at eleven o'clock, Uncle George would come round to break my new toys, have Christmas lunch with us, and then relieve us of Gran Round the Corner by taking her home to Auntie Audrey for the rest of the day, so that we could concentrate on the Bond movie and the Quality Street. Seeing Johnny Cash at Christmas, the 1970s clothing, the carols with a country twang and the comfortably clichéd, saccharine nature of television in those days, embodies very happy childhood memories for me.

I manage not to blub at *The Johnny Cash Christmas Show*, but I have reached an age where I am very partial to my emotions overcoming me, usually in front of the television. I cry at sport-ing achievements (usually the Olympics or Middlesbrough winning something, so usually the Olympics); movies (any-thing from *Eddie the Eagle* to *The Notebook*); and anything on stage (the curtain call gets me every time, whether in the West End or at a school play sitting alongside my good friend Jimmy Page). I make the mistake of watching Johnny's music video to 'Hurt'. I have seen it countless times before but it is still the most moving music video ever made, charting the decline of Johnny's health from towering, charismatic American icon to decayed, Parkinson's-riddled husk. The talkative, friend-seeking usher hands me a tissue and detains me for another ten minutes of interrogation.

It is a consistently bright and brilliant day so, after my fill of Johnny and filled with nostalgia, I take a walk over the bridge to Eastern Nashville to take some photographs. Two boys in their twenties, one black and one white, are pulling a cart with a large wooden cross in it. One of them approaches me, offering a book and a sweet.

'Hello, sir, this is the gospel and this is a mint. Can you spare a few minutes to talk with us?'

'No thanks,' I reply with, in my view, considerable restraint, as they are interrupting my photography expedition.

'Where are you from, sir?'

'England,' I reply with, in my view, considerable restraint, as they are still interrupting my photography expedition.

'Ah, England, so I guess you don't believe in God?' I don't like his accusatory tone of voice.

'No, I'm sorry, I don't. And I'm busy.' I put the viewfinder to my eye to emphasise my atheism and my busyness.

'So who do you think made all of this that you are photographing?'

We are standing on the John Seigenthaler Bridge. It is a beautiful iron truss pedestrian bridge spanning the Cumberland River, which I still don't have a decent photograph of.

'Engineers,' I reply with, in my view, considerable accuracy and restraint.

'Sure, but who made you?'

I am not prepared to engage in a theological debate with them, as I know that is precisely what they want. They also want me to convert to God, which is not going to happen on a bridge in Nashville, and certainly not without Charmaine being present to witness it.

'Can I have that mint now?'

They turn their backs on me and walk away, like the priest and the Levite. It seems they didn't want to redeem me after all and they certainly didn't want to give me a mint.

When I get back to the hotel, I google the bridge and it turns out I was right. It was built by an engineer called Howard Jones (I also once saw him in concert, after Nik Kershaw), not by Our Lord.

In addition to being impossible to reverse park, I discover another design flaw with the Camaro. We are on our way to the Grand Ole Opry this evening when we witness our first biblical (but the bridge was still made by engineers) Tennessee rainfall, which is not the best time to learn that there are no rear windscreen wipers, probably because it has less of a rear windscreen than an armoured vehicle. Like Luke Skywalker attacking the Death Star in *Episode IV – A New Hope*, I have to trust the Force.

The Grand Ole Opry is a weekly country music live radio

show which has been taking place in Nashville for over ninety years. It wasn't grand or old when it started; it was first broadcast as the Opry in 1925 and it is now the longest-running live radio programme in the US. Yesterday I had visited the Ryman auditorium in central Nashville, which was the venue of the radio show from 1943 to 1974 (apologies for not telling you about that, but sometimes you just need to give me some space). The musical history seeps from its walls and church pew benches. Hank Williams 'joined' the Grand Ole Opry (it is also an elitist country music club for its regular performers and stars) in 1949 and played here; Elvis Presley performed here in 1954 but received only tepid applause (presumably the conservative country music elite did not approve of his gyrating pelvis); the great Johnny Cash was inducted in 1956 and then banned in 1965 for smashing all the stage lights during a performance. But in 1974, it was deemed too small a venue for the radio show it had helped popularise, so the show moved to a custom-built auditorium out of town called Opry House at Opryland USA, which is like Center Parcs for country and bluegrass fans.

I was all set to hate the current venue. I had loved the Ryman, which had character and heritage. Opry House sounded to me like the brainchild of sponsors and developers, rather than musicians like Jimmy and me. But as I approach Opry House, I have to admit I was wrong (something Jackie regularly but unsuccessfully tries to make me do). It is like *Star Trek: The Next Generation*: I know I shouldn't like it, but I do. It is a beautiful, imposing venue, far more suited to the popularity of the modern radio show.

I booked 'Behind the Curtain' passes a few months before the trip started. I am now feeling quite smug. This is going to be one of the highlights; Jackie and I are going to get to see the artists preparing to go onstage, and to actually stand onstage when the curtain rises, before being escorted to our premium front-row seats for the rest of the show.

My smugness is short-lived. It turns out we have no premium front-row seats to which to be escorted. I have indeed booked the thirty-minute 'Behind the Curtain' tour, but I should separately have booked tickets for the radio show, which I failed to do. At the moment, we are going backstage and then getting cowboy booted out of the back door. I knew I should have asked Charmaine to book this for me; this is my one contribution to the logistics of the trip and I have messed it up. Fortunately, there are still some seats available, tucked up high and right. I look down my nose at them, before then paying through the same nose.

We do the tour with a lady from Knoxville, Tennessee, who is a Sunday school teacher and will have a three-hour drive home tonight after the show. She has come here just to see her favourite artist, Brandy Clark, perform her two-song headline slot. After my experience on the bridge this morning with the mint-denying missionaries, I am not in the mood for Sunday school teachers, but she is such an enthusiastic fan of the Grand Ole Opry that it is difficult not to adopt her. She explains that Sunday school teaching is not her only job and that she is also (she lowers her voice at this stage) a US marshal. I often lower my voice apologetically when I reveal that I am a lawyer, but that is to avoid listeners-in hating me. I am more interested in her reason for lowering her voice and ask her if it is because she is on a stake-out. No, she assures me that she is just here to see Brandy and not to apprehend any fugitives. I tip her off about a drug dealer I know in Indianapolis called Ted, to whom she might want to pay a visit, but she informs me that Indianapolis is not her jurisdiction. I tell her that he won't be hard to spot as he drives the only bronze Datsun in the States, but she still can't be persuaded.

During the tour of the green room and the artists' dressing rooms, we get to witness the buzz of the build-up. It means a lot to all of the performers to be playing such a famous show and that is evident from the ripples of excitement behind the curtain: it's like Ranger Dan boarding the boat all over again. There are stage hands and session musicians rushing around everywhere. I get in the way of a polite old lady shuffling down the corridor to deliver tea to some of the musicians. Bless her, she is even dressed in denim-on-denim with a cowboy belt. I apologise and move out of the old dear's way; she says: 'Y'awl don't worry. I got plenty o' time. Y'awl have a good evenin' now.'

That's one of the things I love about Nashville. Everyone is so warm and welcoming; even the old tea lady, who could do without tourists blocking the corridor minutes before the show, is courteous (although I don't share her optimism as to how long she has left).

We are standing at the back of the stage when the curtain goes up. That voyeuristic Beverly Hills feeling returns, of spying on successful people from the wings, and I feel more comfortable when we are shown to our freshly purchased, lofty seats for the rest of the show.

When we sit down, I nudge Jackie. The old tea lady is halfway through a song.

It turns out that she is Connie Smith, country music royalty, one of Dolly Parton's biggest influences, Nashville legend, member of the Grand Ole Opry, and inductee in the Country Music Hall of Fame. I didn't recognise her. To be fair, I doubt she realised that she had just met the rhythm guitarist of East Kent's favourite indie covers band either. But like Jimmy said to me: at the end of the day, we are both just performers.

It is still very humid when we return to the hotel, which gives me an excuse to ask the pretty receptionist for a bottle of water.

'Thank you,' I say.

'Absolutely,' she says.

When I return to our room, there is a text from my ex-wife, the first one of my sabbatical. I must be in trouble. Her number is programmed into my phone under the name 'The Ex-Wife', accompanied by a photograph of a red Dalek: it is puerile but it always provides me with a light appetiser before I choke on the main course. She reports that Mimi had a seizure at the Reading Festival, which she puts down to alcohol and strobe lighting, and that she is refusing to come home. She informs me that I need to talk to Mimi when I get home. It seems that I am a terrible parent after all and that Mimi might have taken my celebration advice a bit too literally. As instructed, I diarise to talk to her to tell her to cease her seizures as they are very inconsiderate to her mother.

# CHAPTER TWENTY-FOUR

*Bluebird – seven hours – prisoner of war – mattresses*
SOUNDTRACK: NEIL YOUNG – '*GET BACK TO THE COUNTRY*'

It is with a heavy heart and increasingly heavy luggage (I felt compelled to buy books and T-shirts in Nashville) that I check out of the Hermitage Hotel. I have waited over twenty years to come to Nashville and it hasn't disappointed. The hotel has been elegant, the sunshine and the hospitality have been warm, and the music has been magnificent. I will miss the laid-back vibe of the city. Nashville is not a city that never sleeps, it is a city that only rises at dusk; the rest of the day it spends nursing a hangover or a bottle of Jack Daniel's. I will miss the fact that you can walk into any bar at any time and hear brilliant musicians. I will miss the soft drawl of the southern-fried accents. I will miss the street art and the prevalence of acoustic guitar imagery. I will miss the cowboy boot and hat superstores. I will miss Johnny Cash. But most of all I will miss the pretty receptionist.

'Thank you.'

'Absolutely.'

I drive to the iconic Bluebird Café. As it is a café, I have promised Jackie some breakfast there. As well as being a café, it is known as a 'listening room'. It is a no-pretence (LA would hate it) acoustic venue where the songwriters themselves (usually old and ugly) perform the songs which they have written for the stars (usually young or winners of *American Idol*, and in both cases lacking the talent to write their own songs). It features regularly in one of my new favourite programmes, the successful ABC drama *Nashville*. I started watching season 1 as research for this trip. I have been looking forward to visiting the Bluebird and bumping into Deacon Claybourne (upon whom I have a slight man crush; in fact, it's more than that: I want to be Deacon), Scarlett and Gunnar, Rayna James and that bitch Juliette Barnes. The café is in a nondescript row of shops on a freeway, which surprises me, but not as much as the fact that it is closed. It is 11 a.m.; how can a café be closed? Scarlett should be serving all-day breakfasts. But this is Nashville; breakfast doesn't start until 5 p.m. After some necessary cursing and blaming each other, we decide to drive to Savannah instead.

For the first time, Steve has messed up. Our itinerary says it is only a two- to three-hour drive from Nashville, Tennessee to Savannah, Georgia. Whilst it might take only a few hours to drive across counties in England, there are no states that can be crossed in that time, even in a V8 Chevrolet Camaro. The hired GPS informs me that it will in fact take seven hours, without stops. I begin the journey wondering if I can get a refund from Steve, or at least a free week in Nashville with the pretty receptionist.

Jackie spoils all my fun. The Camaro is a muscle car, designed for big, muscular people. Jackie is neither. She has lowered her passenger seat so that she can't see out of the front windscreen and therefore can't see the scary trucks whizzing past. The passenger door is like a prisoner-of-war fence to her.

She is not legal without a booster seat. No longer can I play the brake-stabbing, arm-throwing game.

So I am on my own, for eight hours with stops, with the radio and billboard advertisements enjoining me every ten minutes either to love Jesus or to enjoy softer mattresses. I find that an easy choice.

It is a long, unamusing day, but I do at least get to spend the night with a new woman, called Mary.

# CHAPTER TWENTY-FIVE

*Haunted hotel – the verb 'to of' – hip replacee – intergluteal cleft – Tom's bench – hospitable ATM machines – a generous offer*

SOUNDTRACK: BROKEN BELLS – 'LAZY WONDERLAND'

**M**ary Marshall is one of the many ghosts who live (you know what I mean) in Savannah, Georgia. However, the previous night, despite the fact I am sleeping in her bedroom, she did kindly let me have a good night's sleep at the Marshall House Hotel. Mary was the daughter of a prominent real estate dealer and the wife of a captain of the Savannah Volunteer Guards (which I assume was a sort of Dad's Army) during the American Revolution. She did well for herself out of her father's and husband's wills and became a shrewd businesswoman and property developer, as well as a socialite and a hostess (Savannah was very much a party town), and opened our building as a hotel in 1859. It was commandeered by the pyromaniac General Sherman as a Union hospital ward during the Civil War, but he managed to resist torching it, allowing Mary to continue as a hotelier until she died, and to haunt it to her heart's content thereafter.

It was named the eighth most haunted hotel in the world by *USA Today* in 2015. Pirates, sailors and Union Army soldiers have all haunted it. I am not convinced by the evidence on the hotel's website, which includes faucets dripping inexplicably (in my experience, that is as common as hotel bedroom lights inexplicably not turning off and hotel television remote controls inexplicably not doing what they are told) and children being heard running down the corridor late at night. If anyone has ever had the misfortune of staying in a hotel where my brood are residing, they will know that it is standard practice to dine late because they are on holiday and then, after a game of 'Guess the Bill', to have a race (handicapped by age) back to the hotel room.

Located in the historic district, it is one of Savannah's oldest hotels. It is recognised as a National Historic Building because it has retained many original features, most of which are injurious to me. I can only access the original wrought-iron balcony by clambering, ungraciously, out of the original sliding sash lead-weight wooden windows, catching my knee on the original window sill and tumbling shoulder first onto the original wooden floor of the balcony. Had I known how dangerous it was going to be to get onto the balcony for which I am paying extra, I would've stayed in a normal room and saved some cash.

There is no greater grammatical, linguistic (and, indeed, humanitarian) crime than using 'of' as a verb. As I have just demonstrated, 'I would have' is correctly abbreviated to 'I would've', not, as has slipped into the vernacular, 'I would of'. It is bad enough to say it, but to write it should be punished with crucifixion. David, my bearded, burly neighbour, insists on winding me up by ensuring that every text message he sends me contains the non-verb 'to of'. He also recently voted to leave the European Union purely to irritate me.

I abhor any mangling of the English language. However, the Americans can do whatever they like to their own version of our language. I have, for example, been enjoying 'Y'awl' in Nashville.

'Y'awl have a good stay.'

'Y'awl welcome.'

And, on the freeways, folksy electronic motorway signs reading:

'Y'awl fasten your seatbelts. It's the law.'

'Y'awl' must already be plural, as it means 'You all'. But the 'Y'awling' gets further mangled in Georgia, where I first hear it being pluralised.

'Y'awls have a good day,' wishes the smiling black concierge in Mary's hotel.

Today we are doing a five-hour walking tour of Savannah with a man who can barely walk. He has been waiting in reception for twenty minutes, as I was responsible for setting the alarm, which was one responsibility too far. His name is Mike and he is a cross between Colonel Sanders and Richard Attenborough's character, John Hammond, in *Jurassic Park*. He is walking with a stick and a matching limp. I ask him if he should be walking at all. He assures me that he is fine; he had a hip replacement three weeks ago, but yesterday he ditched the walking frame for a stick. He seems a nice man so I am pleased that we are able to help by providing him with his first post-op physiotherapy session. We wouldn't've (note the correct verb usage) got very far on a walking tour if he still needed the frame.

As it is, his pace is as blistering as Ranger Dan's, but that's fine as the Savannah semi-tropical humidity is punishing; it's like walking into the temperate house at Kew Gardens. I feel a drip of sweat make its way from the nape of my neck all the way down to my intergluteal cleft (or 'butt crack' in American), a strangely enjoyable experience. There is moisture in the air, condensation on my camera lens, and now my body wants to join in as Spanish moss starts to spore in my pants.

I first came to Savannah by accident in 1992. I had my Delta air pass and was meeting some fellow travellers in Atlanta. They were travelling more slowly by Greyhound bus and I had a few days to kill so I turned up at the airport at Atlanta asking to fly to Nashville. It was Thanksgiving (how was I to know?) and the Nashville flight was full, but nobody had family in Savannah (at least not that they cared about), so I hopped on that plane instead. It was a splendid decision as it became my favourite US city of my 1992 trip so I am delighted to be returning now.

I had been beguiled by the shaded squares and the colonial architecture all those years ago. I had stayed in the then newly opened youth hostel. It was a Victorian wooden-fronted building which in those more modest times felt to me like something out of *Gone with the Wind* and was grander than any other youth hostel I had ever stayed in. I recall wooden steps up to the entrance; a wooden veranda outside my room, accessible via sliding sash windows which I don't recall struggling with in my more agile days; trees full of Spanish moss; four-poster beds with mosquito nets; and high ceilings crowned with a fan which span me to sleep after a night of tequilas on the dock of the bay with the guy who ran the youth hostel and who was delighted to finally have some company.

Today, Mike is delighted that I enjoyed his city in 1992.

'Nobody came to Savannah in '92. It was a dying city back then.'

The fact that I had been the only paying guest in the youth hostel supported his point.

Three things have happened since then to revive Savannah. First, the Savannah College of Art and Design has invested a lot of money into property restoration in the historic district. Next to our hotel is the college itself and opposite is a beautiful movie theatre which it also owns, showing classic films such as tonight's *Seven Samurai*. It has the billboard and the façade of something out of the 1930s. It would be a very romantic first date were it not for its name, the perilous acronym SCAD.

Second is the international bestselling book by John Berendt, and the Clint Eastwood-directed movie, *Midnight in the Garden of Good and Evil*. The book was written a few years after I had visited. I had spent one night in Savannah, got drunk on tequilas, and largely forgotten about it. John Berendt had moved in, got to know the locals, and written an international bestseller about the city and its personalities. It is a wonderfully evocative, true-life account of the socialite scene of the last generation of great families to privately own the old ante-bellum (pre-Civil War) mansions, and covers the shooting of a local male prostitute by a respected antiques dealer and *nouveau riche* party host, Jim Williams (brilliantly played by Kevin Spacey in the movie), and the subsequent trial.

But the third, and most important, factor (in my eyes) behind the revival of Savannah since I was last there was good ole Tom Hanks. I started this trip by looking for his houseboat in Seattle, and the American leg of my sabbatical is now drawing to a close with me determined to find the bench he sat upon in the opening scene of *Forrest Gump*, when he gave his 'My mom always said life was like a box of chocolates' speech.

Mike is a respected local historian. He specialises in architectural and Civil War history. He looks crestfallen when he asks what we would most like to see and I reply, 'Tom Hanks's bus bench, please.'

Mike is a velvet-voiced, unrushed southerner. He is not going to transparently disapprove of my mainstream pop-culture taste. But he sucks through his teeth. I feel like I have let him down. In fact, he is about to let me down.

'The bench ain't there no more, y'awls. It was get'n vand'lised.'

I am naturally disappointed but I tell Mike that I will settle for the statue of the bird girl in the graveyard from *Midnight in the Garden of Good and Evil*.

'She ain't there no more neither. She was get'n vand'lised.'

Forrest's mom was right: you never know what you're gonna get. Savannah might be doing a great job, with the help of SCAD and the Historic Savannah Foundation, in renovating the historic sites, but who is taking care of the great movie sites? Social history needs protecting too, otherwise Tom's legacy will be forgotten. First FAO Schwarz and now this? Come on, Paul G. Allen over in Seattle, make some more investments in movie memorabilia.

We decide to get going on our tour before we get vandalised.

Savannah has a sultry, sticky climate, so the city is designed around providing tree-shade. As a result, it has its own palette: the extended, grasping reach of the live-oak shadows, the Spanish moss dangling like melting grapes, the palmetto trunks and the wreathed magnolia leaves all combine to create the unhealthy and sinister pallor of twilight grey and dappled green shadows in each of the twenty-two ornate, brick- and steel-clad squares. The moist, mossy squares are surrounded by architecturally unique townhouses (Georgian, Victorian, Greek revival and neo-classical) built of brick, stucco and Bath stone, with elegant external staircases, steel or wooden verandas and shuttered windows. For lighting, the squares are an artist's dream and a photographer's nightmare. I am wearing a light-green T-shirt, with dapples of darker green forming on my back, chest and underarms to match the palette of the squares. No antiperspirant can ever hope to contain my bodily moisture in this humidity. I dive into the shade of Chippewa Square for some respite.

James Oglethorpe, the English founder of the colony of Georgia, laid out the Savannah squares before the Civil War based on the design of Roman military encampments. He was an orderly man after my own heart. He liked squares, with fountains or statues in the middle, four administrative buildings laid out uniformly around the fountains or statues, and residential buildings slotting in behind. So he built twenty-four such squares to this plan (two of which have since been misplaced). He was the kind of man who, like me, would fold his ties. Not only was he a visionary town planner, but he was also an idealist and dreamt of Savannah being a utopia where everyone should be equal (a bit like Prince Charles's Poundbury in Dorset, built upon his princely principles of pre-war architecture and equality for all of his loyal subjects. Such new urbanism has not caught on, in the same way that Prince Charles won't if he ever becomes King). In order to achieve this ideal, Oglethorpe banned terrible vices such as the three Ls: large landholdings, liquor and even lawyers (OK, that's four Ls, but one of them is only an adjective).

For a while, things went to plan for Oglethorpe, with a ban on slavery passed in 1735, but then the white settlers of Savannah noticed that the neighbouring settlements of Charleston

and Atlanta were doing considerably better than they were because they could work their slaves as hard as they liked in the
cotton and tobacco fields and therefore increase production far
beyond their Savannahian neighbours, so within fifteen years
the utopian people of Savannah thought 'Bugger that' and decided that everyone could remain constitutionally equal as long
as they were not Native American or African. Although Britain
did not have slavery itself, it was quite happy to profit from the
slave trade, and the witty merchants and dockers of Liverpool
merrily supplied African slaves to Savannah. The local Yamac-
raw tribe were booted out west. To make it up to them, some of
the squares were named after them and their chief, Tomochichi,
was buried in one of them, underneath a vast monument to a
white railroad man named William Washington Gordon. The
city felt a little guilty that Tomochichi's tombstone was not his
own, so a boulder of granite now sits in the corner of Wright
Square, as a monument to the man beneath the railway man.

Why am I sharing all of my newfound, Mike-learned knowledge with you? Well, thank you for asking. It is because where
I am currently shaded, Chippewa Square, is the most important square for present purposes as it is also Gump Square. I
take a photo of the Tenth Doctor sitting on the wall behind the
spot where Forrest's bus bench should have been, in view of
the white wooden church spire over which the feather floats to
his feet in the opening scene. I am disappointed that the Tenth
Doctor's travels haven't yet gone viral, but his Forrest Gump
post gets six likes on Facebook, from half of my children and
half of my friends.

Of all the American cities I have ever visited, Savannah is the
only one where I would like to live. There are many American

cities I would not like to live in. St Louis, for example. I like St Louis and have a friend and former client who lives there, but if I lived there I would have to learn how to enjoy Budweiser, not least as they are my former client. Much as I love visiting New York, I couldn't live there either, as I would have to learn how to jog every day. Portland is a nice place, but Nike are there and I would have to learn how to be constantly upbeat and motivational. Sooner or later I would crack and have to insult someone.

The pace in Savannah is a little bit slower than elsewhere, which is just as well for a walking tour guide with a new hip. The humidity is not conducive to any sense of urgency. The six-minute chargeable unit would take around eleven minutes here, and would malfunction with dampness. There is an old 'New World' charm to the place and the people; it recalls gentler, simpler times. Even the ATMs are genteel and greet me with a chirpy 'Hello, Mr Steward' (quite an achievement given that most humans in the States can't work out which is my surname). If my sabbatical proves to be a career-ending decision, and the work, like my clothing, eventually dries up, or those of my partners with more finesse and political ambition than me have been using my period of absence to devise a Machiavellian exit strategy for me, perhaps I will return here for good; if I am still alive, I will live on Jones Street (the prettiest and shadiest street in the historic district), and if I don't make it here in this lifetime, then I will haunt Chippewa Square to demonstrate my disapproval of the removal of Forrest's bench.

Upon returning to Mary Marshall's room there are still no ghosts, but the spectre of David my neighbour is there to taunt and haunt me. He has texted to inform me that he has just returned from a two-week holiday in Cornwall and that I 'would of' enjoyed it.

I also have an email from Mimi's headmaster, congratulating me on her GCSE results and generously offering an academic scholarship for sixth form with one hand, but then ungenerously trying to take it away with the other by saying that it is traditional for parents to decline the fee reduction so that the money can be pumped back into the school. I have never been a traditionalist; the school's buildings do not need restoring like Savannah's; so I respond immediately, thanking him and confirming that I will be delighted to accept the fee reduction but that he should feel free to write to Mimi's mother to request a voluntary contribution to match it.

# CHAPTER TWENTY-SIX

*Fireworks and fantasies – a dust-up with a sheriff – a slow drive*
SOUNDTRACK: WAYLON JENNINGS – 'GOOD OL' BOYS'

South Carolinian truck drivers must crave Beach Boys excitation in their lives. The freeway north is long, straight, poorly surfaced and utterly tedious. But the entrepreneurial roadside vendors have carefully studied supply and demand in the area and deduced that there are two essential items required to provide the motivation and vitality needed for the truck drivers to complete their unswerving journeys: fireworks and sex toys. Every twenty miles or so, to break the tedium, the massive freeway billboards advertise 30 per cent off fireworks, and nearby adult fantasy superstores.

It is 10 a.m. and we have a seven-hour drive ahead of us. Steve's clock is a bit slow again. He has estimated the journey from Savannah to the Great Smoky Mountains as being three to four hours. GPS assertively disagrees with him by three hours. Knowing how bored Jackie gets on long journeys, I offer her the choice of a Roman candle, a rocket or a rabbit.

'Would ya feck off' is her inevitable reply.

I have found another problem with the Camaro. Four hundred and fifty brake-horsepower is quite a lot of horses. When I put my foot down to overtake a lane-hogging hog-truck driver, whose concentration has wandered due to sitting on his butt plug whilst writing his name in the air with a sparkler, I learn that my V8 car shoots forward in multiples of ten miles per hour. This may have something to do with the fact that, through boredom between sex superstores, I was fiddling with the paddle stick shift on the steering wheel without really knowing what I was doing. I might have inadvertently put it into sports mode.

I am not excusing what happens next; just saying that actually it is quite difficult, in an automatic car with the power of 450 automatic horses, to accelerate slowly. That's all.

Jackie and I both see him, but neither of us properly. Jackie thinks he is a broken-down police car (yes, you are thinking what I was thinking, but let's keep that to ourselves). I don't recall my own thoughts, other than the fact that I do register him in slow motion as he melodramatically wheel-spins out of the grass central reservation, kicking South Carolina dirt into the already murky air, his lights flashing importantly in a way that Border Protectors can only fantasise about.

I have little doubt that he had been having a quiet morning, watching obedient local motorists in their dull cars. It was probably too early for him to light the touch paper on a Catherine wheel. But my hired Camaro, accelerating in multiples of ten horses, provides him with the perfect opportunity to test his overreaction time.

'Do you think he's coming after me?' I ask Jackie, as he refuses to leave my rear-view mirror, blue light still flashing. I have never been pulled over for speeding before and America is probably not the best place to start. I am already picturing myself in an orange suit, with bad teeth.

'Of course he is, you were doing ninety-two.' I won't be calling her as a defence witness. She is far too disloyal.

'Sit up. It might be because you haven't got a booster seat.' If I go down, I am taking Jackie with me.

I eventually pull to a halt on the grass verge, as I haven't managed to shake him off.

'I'm going to video this,' says Jackie supportively, reaching for her iPhone.

'Don't be stupid,' I reply, 'don't reach for anything in your pocket.'

Ill-advisedly but politely, I open the driver door to cordially greet him. His car says 'Sheriff' on it and he looks mean. He is young and sturdy; like Ranger Dan but with real ammunition instead of hairspray.

'Get back in the ve-hic-ule, sir,' he urges me, and actually touches his gun holster. 'Get back in the ve-hi-cule.' At this stage, had I been black I would most probably have been shot in the head a few times to soften me up.

I actually don't need telling twice about getting back in my vehicle, and do as he says. He comes round to the passenger side and looks straight over Jackie's head at me.

'The reason I stopped you is you were doing eighty-five in a seventy zone.'

I half expect Jackie to correct him to ninety-two, but for once she remains loyal.

'I need to see your driver's licence and insurance, sir.'

I have my driver's licence and my car hire papers. I give him those, hoping that I won't need to use the trump card in my back pocket, the fact that I know a country music-loving US marshal in Knoxville, which must surely outrank his feeble sheriff's badge. She should be able to get me off if I need her.

He returns to his car and runs his checks on my driver's licence which confirm that I am neither Thelma nor Louise. It is my good fortune that his indolence now kicks in. He must realise the amount of paperwork required to charge and summons a Brit on holiday in a hired car. He comes back to the passenger side and still doesn't appear to have noticed the diminutive passenger hiding beneath him.

'Do you have any South Carolina identification, sir?' he asks, imploringly.

'I'm... er... terribly sorry,' I say in my quintessential Hugh Grant voice, 'but n-n-no, I don't, sheriff. I am f-from England, er, you see, on holiday.'

I am in luck.

'I'm just going to give you a caution this time. You don't need to come to the courthouse. Just watch your speed.'

'Thank you, sheriff.'

'Absolutely.'

His southern hospitality kicks in; in fact, despite wanting to imprison me, he is more likeable than the humourless Border Protectors and their fingerprint machines: 'Be careful re-entering the freeway and have a nice day, y'awl.' I am still unsure if he has seen Jackie but I now know that y'awl may in fact be singular.

He hands me a formal written 'Public Contact Warning' and it turns out I don't have a criminal record in Calhoun County, South Carolina, after all. He has been unable to read my driver's licence correctly and the person who has been cautioned is someone with the first name 'Steward' and the last name

'Geoffrey'. I enjoy, however, that his name is 'C. Duke'; hopefully he comes from Hazzard County. He has ticked the 'Speeding' box; Jackie is very lucky that he didn't see her or he could also have ticked the 'Booster seat violation' box.

For the rest of the journey, I tame my wild horses and drive at fifty miles per hour, which makes Steve's journey estimate even more fanciful.

# CHAPTER TWENTY-SEVEN

*Fold them jeans – Australian Alan – bumf deprivation – Kacey*
*Musgraves – milk and honey – flying bears – divine retribution*
SOUNDTRACK: KACEY MUSGRAVES – 'FOLLOW YOUR ARROW'

'**B**ear left,' says the GPS lady.
She is lying. There isn't one. What's more, the Great
Smoky Mountains National Park is our last chance to see a bear.
Despite the attack in Alaska, Jackie is becoming agitated at not
having seen one (from a distance), and I would rather travel
with an angry bear than an angry Irishwoman.

Jackie comes from a fairly fiery line of Irishwomen. This is
perhaps best illustrated by an exchange which took place between one of her cousins and his mother. The background to
what follows is that the nineteen-year-old son, still living with
his parents, had been out drinking, put his shirt in the wash
overnight and left his jeans on the chair. When his mother came
to wash the shirt the next morning, she was disgusted to discover lipstick on the collar. He managed to film her reaction on his
phone, so this is their verbatim transcript.

Mother: Don't talk to me.

Son: I wasn't with no one.

Mother: Archie, the evidence... if you were in court, the evidence is there.

Son: What? So I had a drink.

Mother: IT'S LIPSTICK!!!

Son: It's fucken drink; it's raspberry from the drink.

Mother: Is it now? It's lipstick and makeup.

Son: No, it's...

Mother: I don't give a FUCK what you say.

Son: I fell...

Mother: Go away.

Son: I fell, mam, onto vodka and razz.

Mother: Razz? Her name is fucken Razz. Stupid bastard.

Son: What?

Mother: FOLD THEM JEANS! Some slut, she has to be. I'm disgusted. Fucken lipstick and makeup.

Son: Yeh, no, but...

Mother: Ah shut up, ya wanker!

Jackie shares those genes, so that is why I want to keep her happy on the bear situation. I am optimistic, though. When I came to the Great Smoky Mountains twenty-five years ago, I saw and chased after a black bear. I was travelling with a rough-hewn Australian outbacker called Alan, for whom good sport was catching venomous snakes between his toes. As I was driving, he saw a line of cars parked by the roadside and correctly deduced that there must be a bear nearby, so before my natural cowardice could kick in I found myself running into the pine forest, but with the good sense of letting Alan go slightly ahead, chasing the bear back to its lair. My National Park passport informs me that the Great Smoky Mountains National Park has one of the largest populations of black bears of any similar-sized area in North

America. For Jackie's sake (and therefore my own), I hope that is right. I also hope that they still run away from people.

We are staying at a place overlooking the Great Smoky Mountains called Blackberry Farm. It is unlike any farms where I grew up and there is not a tractor in sight. This is Steve's money-shot: the most lavish hotel of the sabbatical. Indeed, the most lavish hotel I have ever stayed in. It is slightly cruel of Steve to pick a hotel name which will remind me of the work emails mounting in my hand-held device, but I can forgive him this oversight. It is a long way from the Dalmeny Hotel, Lytham St Annes, but I still recall that as being the happiest hotel on earth (largely due to the fact that it had a Space Invaders machine, a ballroom where we kids could dance with our parents, and the lovely waitress called Wendy). In place of tractors, Blackberry Farm has golf buggies and a fleet of Lexus SUVs to transport around the estate those guests whose legs are too valuable to use.

Jackie's bear-deprived mood is not improved by the fact that there is no bumf in the room for her to read. I say room; it is in fact a wooden home called Indigo Bunting (after a spectacularly blue local bird), with a bathroom bigger than both my and my sister's childhood bedrooms combined. I know from experience that the best way to improve Jackie's mood is to feed her or put her to sleep, so we summon a Lexus to take us to the Barn for dinner. It is the first place on our trip where a jacket is required for dinner, so I retrieve my crumpled Tommy Hilfiger from the bottom of my bag and try to remember how to use an iron. As there is no bumf, Jackie goes straight onto Google. She shows me the prices of the rooms. I lose my appetite, burn my jacket with the iron and resolve to have words with Steve, as he has probably hit his annual target from this commission alone.

As well as its astronomical prices, Blackberry Farm is well known for its artisan kitchen and what is known as foothill cuisine. The hotel is all-inclusive, rightly so at these prices, so uncharacteristically I allow Jackie to have a starter *and* a dessert. The food is so presentable and inventive that even Jackie is taking photographs of every course, which she sends to Susu, including one which is a mini-garden in a fish tank, sitting on top of which are the two mushrooms for our consumption. Jackie had erroneously thought that, within the fish tank garden, there were live snails for me to pick as my starter. I arrange the Tenth Doctor in the garden photo for Larry's benefit. The food isn't our only treat tonight: Steve has a musical surprise in store for us which causes me to forgive him for the room rate.

For the conservative country music genre, Kacey Musgraves is controversial. Her melodies are classic country but her lyrics are provocative. She sings about homosexuality, marijuana, sluts, hustlers, Bible belt towns, embarrassing family members and biscuits. She has been a favourite of my spare-daughter Shauna and my youngest daughter Mary since I introduced them to her music a few years ago. Mary merrily sings along in the car without realising she is announcing her coming out as a lesbian. Incredibly, just for Jackie and me, Steve has arranged for Kacey to stay at Blackberry Farm tonight and to play an intimate, free, unplugged gig, which makes up for our Bluebird Café disappointment. The venue is one of those classic American burnt-red stables. It is lit by hundreds of candles and is an idyllic scene of milk and honey. Some other guests have been admitted, which is a slight disappointment, but I will tolerate them.

I lied. I won't tolerate all of them. Sitting at the prime table nearest the stage is a whooping and hollering mountain of a guy in his early forties, dressed in tightly straining tweed, with the physique of someone overpaid and overfed. He appears to know the family who own Blackberry Farm and has an ugly air of entitlement about him, demonstrated by the way he slovenly and clumsily strode to his table just in time for the show and for everyone else to see him arrive. I wonder if he might know Kacey but, gratifyingly, when she walks onstage, she ignores his whoops and overlooks his hollers. She doesn't seem to recognise me either, which is surprising for a gig arranged exclusively for me by Steve, but I will let that pass. I like her even more for blanking the attention-seeking fat-ass at the front. He is most probably a lawyer. I have most probably had dealings with him by conference call (if I did, it would have taken over an hour). But as I have pledged to like all Americans again, I wish only a small ulcer upon his deserving body.

Kacey puts on a fabulous acoustic show. Her pitch is perfect; her persona is warm, self effacing and witty. But no matter what angle I try to view her from, the bulbous pumpkin at the front impinges my view, nodding his rotund head and patting his knee with an untraditional sense of timing. At the end of the show he marches straight to the stage door, unapologetically bumping into a table of middle-aged rich people, sloshing their drinks. He gives his name and expects to meet her, but is denied access and sheepishly looks behind to see if anyone has noticed. I have. So have the middle-aged rich people. The milk and honey tastes sweet enough to lure me to my bed.

The next day, we drive into the Great Smoky Mountains. Our sole purpose is to see bears. Just one will do.

At the entrance to the National Park, I stop at a tourist

information stand run by three retirees. I ask whether there have been any bear sightings today. There was one this morning by the dumpster down the road, but Jackie doesn't fancy spending the day in a bin. I ask where else we might see them and I am told to look up in the trees.

'You have flying bears?' I ask. I may be English but I am not gullible.

She assures me that the small black bears spend most of their time up in the trees.

On the Cades Cove Loop Road, we stop to walk a trail. There is a disused barn. Jackie goes round the back of it but I stay put on the lookout for flying bears. She re-emerges excited. She must have seen one.

'Come and look at all the butterflies.'

Butterflies don't excite me unless there are millions of them lifting a bear or letting a Mexican child plummet from a zip wire, so I decline. Two ladies behind us on the trail show a polite interest in Jackie's butterflies and they too go round the back of the barn while we continue up the trail.

We stop at an abandoned picture-postcard white wooden Missionary Baptist Church, which pre-dates the Civil War but ceased being used at the end of World War II. The interior is well cared for and has not been allowed to fall into ruin; it even has pews, an altar and a Bible. I get Jackie to take a photo of me holding the Bible and jabbing my finger like a television evangelist to an empty congregation, which I send to Charmaine. She replies immediately, admonishing me for mocking God and urging me to beg forgiveness as I don't want divine punishment. I know, however, that there is no need, as Charmaine will be praying for my soul tonight and, let's face it, He is more likely to listen to her.

As usual, Charmaine is right, and the Lord exacts his punishment upon me more swiftly than I had anticipated. As we return from the church, we pass the two butterfly ladies.

'Be careful as you walk back,' one of them warns. 'We just saw a bear cub, and its mother must still be nearby.'

Had I stopped to see the butterflies, we would have seen the bear cub as well. Jackie doesn't talk to me for the rest of the day, other than to tell me that the Great Smoky Mountains are 'feckin' shite' and to fold my jeans.

# CHAPTER TWENTY-EIGHT

*Bear dreams – dirty magazines – the Queen – hurricanes*
*and jazz brogues – Dragon Con – shin bath*
SOUNDTRACK: ARLO GUTHRIE – 'CITY OF NEW ORLEANS'

Jackie wakes up cross with me. But not for yesterday's costly butterfly/bear incident. This is something entirely new, which is impossible for me to defend. She was blissfully dreaming about a mother bear and three cubs running across the road to her childhood family home in Knockanore, Ireland, when my alarm woke her up and ruined it. I often get into trouble for what I do in Jackie's dreams, so it makes a change for an extraneous device to be blameworthy, but that's not how Jackie sees it: it was me who set the alarm the night before, so it was me who ruined her dream.

The drive from Blackberry Farm to Atlanta is across familiar territory. It is a sedate journey because we are crossing Calhoun County again and I don't want to tempt Sheriff Duke into changing his mind about that courthouse appearance. We drive past the city of Cleveland and my mind starts to time-travel back to the 1980s.

Cleveland, you see, is my defunct home county. I grew up there. But after I left, it ceased to exist. Hartlepool is like the perineum; it is now in a no-man's land, somewhere between Durham and North Yorkshire. Perhaps, like Brigadoon, Cleveland will come back every hundred years, and childhood friends and the playground 'kiss, cuddle or torture' girls will still be there waiting for me. I hope so. If you want to buy shoes, or something for less than a pound, or ideally shoes for less than a pound, then visit Hartlepool. If you want to walk through some of the most beautiful, uncelebrated countryside in England, in your new discount shoes, then visit the Cleveland Hills. As far as I am aware, although my county has died, its hills survive; perhaps they should have taken Prince's approach and renamed themselves 'The Hills Formerly Known as Cleveland'. Such thoughts take me into a state of conscious subconscious. I believe my eyes are still watching the freeway (Jackie may disagree), but I am thinking about Jack Maughan (my Cleveland county badminton and all-round life coach), Alison Waters (for those who have been paying attention), Roseberry Topping and Haverton Hill.

Roseberry Topping might be insignificant in scale compared with El Capitan and the canyons of Utah, but it is a picturesque hill with a distinctive overhanging peak (like a baby Matterhorn) and its significance to me is off the scale, as it signifies my teenage years. It is a less pleasant hill when you have to run up it in the snow, dressed only in a white vest and shorts, which is what I used to have to do once a year in the 1980s as punishment for doing too well in the Yarm School inter-house cross-country race. The top ten from each house got to scale Roseberry Topping, with Mr Woods and Mr Logan (our medium-portly games masters) standing at the top (having taken the easier route via the school minibus) in their sheepskins, shouting encouragement, as farmers shout encouragement to their herd at the abattoir. I never came first, but I laid that demon to rest in my university years when I took a girlfriend up there.

Haverton Hill didn't feature on my cross-country route, but I did manage to get my best friend at Yarm, Mike Turnbull, dumped by his girlfriend because of Haverton Hill.

Mike and I became best friends for no better reason than his surname began with T. For any American readers, my surname begins with S. So we had to sit next to each other in every lesson. We got off to a frosty start. Mike was one of those pupils who thought schooling was a collaborative effort. I was one of those pupils who barricaded his test paper with every available limb to prevent my cheating neighbour from copying the correct answer. But eventually we found some common ground: I would let Mike copy my work, and in return he wouldn't beat me up and would share his dirty magazines with me. It was those magazines which got him into trouble with his girlfriend.

Mike was the eldest in our year. He looked a decade older than the rest of us, which is why newsagents tended to serve him (magazines, cigarettes, alcohol). He was a good person to be best friends with. He was also the first to drive. He had a red and white Mark 2 Ford Escort with a black spoiler (on the back and, remarkably, the front as well), brake lights in the rear window, and rallying fog lights on the bumper; the interior was equally distasteful, with furry dice, furry grey seat covers, and furry cushions on the back seat. Despite driving such an idiotic car, he was also the first of my friends to have a girlfriend and, importantly, the first of my friends to have a girlfriend who would have sex.

This was in the days before texting and sexting, when love

letters were the most exciting form of communication in the playground. Yarm was an all-boys school and Mike would typically date sisters of boys at school, as it made it easier to deliver love letters through a go-between. Glen and I were staying at Mike's one weekend and we decided that we should adopt Mike's preferred collaborative approach and all write a love letter to his girlfriend. I provided the words; Glen provided the pencil illustrations (from one of Mike's stash of dirty magazines). At the time, I was experimenting with poetry and I didn't think there was anything offensive in comparing her breasts to Haverton Hill. Admittedly, it wasn't a great simile as there is only one Haverton Hill, which I later discovered isn't a hill at all but rather a former industrial estate and shipyard near Billingham. However, Glen's pencil illustrations had genuine artistic merit. She disagreed. Later that week, unflattered by the comparison of her figure with an ICI ammonia and nitrate plant, she dumped Mike by letter and he had to fight her brother by the walled garden (the mandated location for all break-time scraps). Mike always won his fights, which is another reason why he was a good friend to have.

Mike still lives in Yarm and is still taking the collaborative approach. He is a successful accountant and owns five accountancy practices, which can't be down to his own mathematical ability, as he could never count. Earlier this year, I took Joe and Mary to Yarm School and in the impressive newly built theatre auditorium there, Mike had a surprise for me: he had arranged for name plates on two of the seats – Steward and Turnbull, still sitting side by side thirty years later. I am thinking of all this as I drive past Cleveland, North Carolina.

Before I get too nostalgic and crash the car, I pull off the freeway for gas. I am getting the hang of the guess-your-future-bill game and plump for forty dollars. I am less than three dollars off, which is satisfying as this is the last time I will get to play it. I can't resist telling Kalpesh, the Indian petrol station attendant, that I have just achieved a new personal best.

In a heavy Indian accent reminiscent of Apu from *The Simpsons*, Kalpesh asks me where I am from. When I tell him England, he becomes excited and tells me that England is his favourite country.

'Have you been?' I ask.

'No, never.'

I like Kalpesh. And I can relate to how he feels about England. Nashville has always been one of my favourite cities in the States, albeit I had never been. Fortunately, it lived up to my expectations on this trip. Kalpesh sees some alien notes in my wallet and asks me if I have any English pound notes. I explain that we only have pound coins now, but I take out a five-pound note to show him. He asks if he can hold it, as he has never touched one before, assuring me that he will return it.

'The Queen. She is my favourite English person.'

I don't take offence.

As England ticks so many boxes for Kalpesh, I tell him he can keep the five-pound note. I also tell him that if he ever comes to England, to make sure he visits the Cleveland Hills. He tells me I have made his day. None of my clients ever tells me that, but in fact the day-making has been mutual with Kalpesh. I picture him showing my five-pound note to his wife and kids that evening and then framing it above his fireplace, and I feel good.

The best thing about Atlanta airport is a courtesy bus driver called Isaiah (still not quite Jedidiah, but I now have a Jeb and an Isaiah, which is near enough). If ever you find yourself at Atlanta airport, needing to stay overnight, then I would encourage you to seek him out. You can't miss him. He will be the most extravagantly dressed driver at the hotel courtesy bus depot after the monorail. Today he is wearing an oversize blue and white spotted bow tie, brown and white gangster jazz Gatsby brogues, sunglasses and three gold-capped teeth. Somehow he has made his standard-issue bus driver uniform look like something off a 1930s Broadway musical. If he wasn't driving, he would be tap dancing with jazz hands. During the six-minute ride in his bus to our hotel, I learn that he comes from New Orleans; that today it is eleven years and four days since the flooding caused by Hurricane Katrina; that he will never forget that day (evidently true) because it was the day that he lost everything; that the insurance company refused to pay out on his destroyed home as the city is below sea level; that the water table is so high in southern Louisiana that the deceased can't be buried underground so are buried on top of the ground; that when the historic district was flooded, a lot of bodies were torn from their caskets and crypts; that families had to go looking for their loved ones' bodies when they disappeared from their cemeteries; and that Louis Armstrong was in one of the graveyards that flooded. I know more about Isaiah's life story than I do about my recently deceased next-door neighbour of ten years. I have enjoyed his extravagant dress sense and storytelling, so tip him extravagantly.

I appreciate that I have been spoilt by Steve's choices, with the luxury of hotels such as Sundance (rustic log cabin, minus Katharine Ross), Marshall House (old colonial elegance, plus ghosts) and Blackberry Farm (modern opulence, multiplied by country music stars). But I am from Cleveland; like Pip in *Great Expectations*, I can revert to type. And tonight, for my last night in the States, Steve has allowed me to rest my wallet with the frugality of the Westin Atlanta Airport Hotel (functional, plus beds) for a quick stopover before a week of R&R in Costa Rica.

The lobby is violently rowdy. It reminds me of Crawley shopping centre on a Saturday afternoon. The noise is due to two conventions in town: an ice hockey convention, and one which sounds a lot more interesting, Dragon Con, which is a cosplay convention for fantasy fans and is celebrating its 30th year this weekend. I assume that the cacophony must be due to the hockey fans. Dungeons & Dragons fans tend to be more reclusive, with even fewer friends than me.

I check in with the now traditional confusion from the receptionist as to which is my first name. Statistically, someone is due to get it right, but she defies the statistics.

Mercifully, our room is on the eighth floor, away from the clamour, and alongside the gaming fantasists. There is no balcony or veranda to sit out on; there is no rocking chair; there is no mountain or forest view; there is nothing but an empty fridge masquerading as a minibar with no plug. I am too afraid to go back down to the lobby so I tell Jackie I am going to spend the evening in the bath.

I wedge myself into the shin-high tub, bend my knees up and slide down to try to submerge my back, enjoying an unexpected massage on the way down from the scabby surface. It knocks the heads off a few mosquito bites that I picked up at Blackberry Farm. I would have been safer (and cleaner) in a wetsuit. When Jackie sees the awkward angle at which I am bathing, and recovers from the shock of seeing that I am not fully submerged, she decides to take her bath standing up.

When we take our chances downstairs to get something to eat, it turns out I was wrong about the noise. It is in fact attributable to Dragon Con. At the bar, characters from *Avatar* are waiting to be served alongside Superman, Wolverine and a Ninja Turtle. The Tenth Doctor would love this but sadly he is packed in a suitcase somewhere. I assure Jackie that if we stick around long enough, she will eventually see a bear; someone is bound to be dressed as Chewbacca (technically a Wookiee, but Jackie will never know the difference) or as an Armoured Bear from Philip Pullman's *His Dark Materials* trilogy. From her response, I don't think Jackie is falling for it.

'Feckin' bears, I'll give you feckin' bears.'

When we get back to the safety of our room, Jackie checks our schedule and notes that we need to get up early for the flight to Liberia (which I am worried might be in Africa not Costa Rica). I offer to set my alarm, but she tells me that she will set her own as I am bloody useless with alarms, which is ironic given how the day began.

# CHAPTER TWENTY-NINE

*Potholes – poverty – plot lines – Poppa Sloth – plunge pool*
*Soundtrack: The Turtles – 'Happy Together'*

'**W**e're all going to Costa Rica,' announces the excitable Caribbean cabin crewman with excellent teeth. 'There will be no Wi-Fi on board so you had better all just relax into vacation mode.' I am already two months into my three-month sabbatical and his injunction inadvertently causes my disobedient mind to do the opposite and return me to the office.

I haven't had any difficulty in detoxing from work. I had thought this would have been a problem given how many emails I receive each day (usually around 300) and given what a control freak Jackie and Charmaine (and my mother and my sister) tell me I am. But I trust Charmaine; she has been dealing with my emails and liberally scattering them amongst grateful partners and associates to ensure that they are being mopped up in my absence. I have been checking in remotely twice a week to see how much better they are all doing in my absence than in my presence. It turns out that American clients can cope without me at weekends after all. Their world hasn't ended yet, but let's see what happens if the man with the cat on his head gets elected.

A couple of glimmering moments at the firm while I have been away demonstrate that there is life beyond law: one of my favourite associates has emailed to inform me that she has extracted herself from the profession to become a musician and a potter in Bristol; and one of the more eccentric paralegals in my team (who wears a bowler hat and a goatee beard and bows every time he comes into my office) has emailed to proudly let me know that he has featured in the MailOnline for an amusing Facebook exchange he had with an airline price comparison website after it informed him that he would have to wait forty-seven years for a flight from Bangkok to Dubai.

When we land at Liberia airport (which I can confirm, like Savannah, is not in Africa), our Caribbean dental advertisement can't remember the time difference but that doesn't matter as I am now back in vacation mode. I have another month of not caring about billing figures, utilisation rates and chargeable units, so I am going to bloody well enjoy it.

A Costa Rican taxi driver greets us at the airport, claiming the improbable name of Steve, but he is not a good driver and it is not a good taxi. It is a red Toyota of the variety that has never been new. It has been created in a workshop from old parts (excluding suspension and shock absorbers) and makes Mike Turnbull's Mark 2 Ford Escort look like a work of art. Steve is not only not good; he is a terrible driver. He overtakes on corners whilst speaking on his cell phone and aiming for potholes, but inexplicably Jackie seems a lot more relaxed with his driving skills than with my own. She is sitting calmly, reading *The Girl on the Train*; she is halfway through it when she realises that there are three different narrators in the story. I read the book before we came away so she asks me to explain who is who and which one is married to Tom; I feign sleep. She should stick to *Where's Wally?*

Through my one half-open eye, I am taking in the new landscape and country. I have never been to Central America. The houses are roadside shacks made of whatever materials were to hand: some brick, some wood, some corrugated iron, some steel, some chicken wire, some Toyota suspension parts and shock absorbers, all finished off with a splash of magenta or cyan or mustard or a combination of all three. We pass one such multicoloured patchwork shack with six dead fridges outside it. No doubt they will feature soon in the construction of some other properties and cars.

Each little village has little more than a church, a football pitch and a Coca-Cola sign. Skeletal horses are wandering the streets and we nearly run over the dog off the front cover of J. M. Coetzee's book *Disgrace*. It had the good sense to not be standing in a pothole, otherwise Seasick Steve would almost certainly have hit it.

The children here seem happy enough, though. Those who are over the age of ten are playing around on motorbikes and scooters. The younger ones are riding on the saddle-less frames of push-bikes twice their size. The wheels of one bike are bigger than the boy riding it. All the playful children are smiling, despite being deprived of internet connectivity or social media. They seem to be able to socialise without media, and they can even climb trees. Father Christmas gifted Joe and Mary a bike each, two years ago, and they have sat in the garage ever since. I asked Mary why she never rides her bike and she told me it was because she had lost the charger.

Some ex-friends of mine in London once bought a child like

these, from Mexico. It was legitimate, not kidnap. They couldn't have children due to faulty ovaries so went through a Jewish adoption agency specialising in Mexican children. They became better friends of mine during the adoption process; so much so that they asked me to be a referee. I had to be interviewed by a social worker to attest to them being good, non-child-murdering people. They bought their child from a young Mexican girl who was a drug addict. I never met the child because my friendship was no longer required once the adoption process was completed and the papers said that a partner in a law firm had validated their credentials. That is the type of superficiality with which I have slowly come to terms in London.

Despite the unsuspended cars, the deep potholes, the undernourished farm animals, the oversized bikes, the roadside fridges and the DIY accommodation, Costa Rica topped the Happy Planet Index rankings in 2016 (having previously come top in 2009 and 2012 as well). Even though its economy is based primarily on farms and hotels, its people have higher well-being scores than in the US and the UK, have a better ecological footprint, and live longer. It is smaller than Scotland but is home to the greatest density of species in the world (which is what brought me here, as Haywards Heath only has badgers and squirrels). But perhaps Costa Rica's master stroke in achieving happiness and contentment is that it abolished its army in 1949 and has since reallocated defence funds to be spent on education, health and pensions. It is a surprisingly simple idea, but unlikely to be tried in England despite the fact that the last time we were invaded was in 1066.

Meanwhile, the perky cut-n-shut Toyota is merrily rambling along from pothole to crater. Daughter number two, Mimi, got terrible motion sickness as a small child. Her stomach was regularly emptied over herself, the back of my driver's car seat and the back of my head. She has passed it on to me. From the age of forty I have struggled whenever I am on the passenger side. When I went to Universal Studios in LA, what I didn't admit to earlier is that I felt sick on the Simpsons Ride in Krustyland. It is four and half minutes of animation and motion simulation aimed at young children; four and a half minutes for which I had my eyes closed to avoid me barfing on the ten-year-old beside me. The final thirty minutes of off-roading with Seasick Steve are even worse than the Simpsons Ride. The tarmac has disappeared; so has my inner ear and equilibrium. It is the type of road that can reconfigure your internal organs and shake wheels off their axles. I close my eyes; not, this time, to avoid describing the plot of Jackie's book to her, but rather to avoid throwing up my newly dislodged spleen. Fortunately, I have not eaten today as I only had a Red Bull for breakfast at Atlanta airport; the breakfast of champions.

'Nicoya' in the Nahuatl (Aztec) language means 'with water on both sides'. 'Peninsula' in the English language means 'with water on both sides'. We are staying on a tautology: the Nicoya Peninsula. An impressive 26 per cent of Costa Rica enjoys some form of environmental protection: the government uses fossil fuel tax to pay for the protection of forests, and 99 per cent of its electricity is produced from renewable sources. Its laudable ecological footprint was first planted in the Nicoya Peninsula fifty years ago, with the preservation of the wetlands. Their latest success story is the reintroduction of the indigenous scarlet macaw. Where we are staying has a strong conservational emphasis. The Ara Project ('ara' means parrot in Spanish) is

located on the hotel's property and has been successful in rein-
troducing the scarlet macaws to their former ranges after they
had been wiped out by a combination of the wild bird pet trade,
habitat loss due to logging and agriculture, and illegal trapping
for food and feathers.

The macaw is the punk rocker of the bird world. It is a noisy,
brightly coloured attention seeker which leaves litter everywhere in the form of discarded almond carcasses. As I check in
to the hotel, my face wearing a pasty green hue, I am treated to
four of them streaking across the infinity pool and the brilliant
blue seascape. In flight they are unmistakable, as they announce
themselves with a harsh RAAAK RAAAK which is as tuneless
a song as my daughter Meggie can muster when singing along
with her headphones in.

The Hotel Punta Islita off-season has the feeling of *The Shining*
but in sunshine. A pan-pipe instrumental elevator-music version of 'Hotel California' obligingly supports my simile. There
are more staff here than guests, but cabin fever is yet to set in (I
hope). When I arrive, there is just one shouty American family,
half submerged in the pool bar: a father, two twenty-something
sons and one girlfriend whom they appear to share. The father
has the hair cover and the physique of a three-toed sloth. He is
suffering from the loud and stupid affliction which blights only
American tourists. His voice overpowers the screams of the
macaws; in the distance, a troop of howler monkeys, the loudest
land mammal on the planet, is feeling like a decibel-threatened
species; I am hoping that Poppa Sloth will drink too many coco
locos, topple off his submerged bar stool and drown himself
rather than the call of the macaws.

There is a welcome note from the manager in our chalet. I

am still feeling the effect of the Toyota shake-rattle-and-rally and get as far as 'Dear Steward Geoff' before rushing into our little back garden to throw up in a bush. Once I have done so, I realise how lush, green and vaporous the landscape is. A tiny hummingbird is darting between purple trumpet blooms, accompanied by black and red butterflies. A dull iguana is sun-bathing on the terracotta tiles of our roof, eyeballing me with the condescending authority of a High Court judge. It is rather nice out here, with views over the tree tops to the ocean, and there is a plunge pool. Overcome by the felicitation of my surroundings and the evacuation of my stomach lining, I enhance the nature on display by whipping off my shorts and T-shirt and plunging naked into the plunge pool.

Jackie is in no mood for dinner after that shock and now also feels nauseous, so we watch *Mission Impossible*, overdubbed in Spanish. I rather enjoy it. Tom Cruise is a lot more palatable and amusing with a lisping Spanish accent.

# CHAPTER THIRTY

*Bow-legged birding – Manakins and Motmots – American tourists*
*– an outstanding hermit crab joke – the great armadillo hoax*
SOUNDTRACK: MAVIS STAPLES – 'FAR CELESTIAL SHORE'

Biales is a former professional footballer and, refreshingly, I am now in a country where football is called football again, rather than soccer. It surprises me that he was a footballer, not because of his weight – that is forgivable as he had to retire due to an injury and is a Costa Rican, so happy and content in frame – but because he is so bow-legged. We are up in the mountains in the Nicoya Peninsula, so it is quite possible that he used to have to ride a horse to every game. He played in the same team as Joel Campbell of Arsenal, so he must have been a decent player. I am regretting agreeing to play in the local village football match later in the week.

'English, huh, which team do you support?'

'Middlesbrough.'

His expression is one to which I have become accustomed. I call it amused-confused. Not many people in the south-east of England support or admit to supporting Middlesbrough. Most of them don't even know where Middlesbrough is. Like Hartlepool, no county wants to claim ownership of it; it is bigger and uglier than Hartlepool, and all of the shoe shops have been boarded up because the local women tend to go barefoot to the maternity ward.

But today, Biales is not a footballer. It is 6 a.m. My stomach has settled and he is my birdwatching guide. He may have bandy legs, but at least he can walk unaided, which is an improvement on our Savannah tour guide.

As a child, I was an enthusiastic member of the YOC, the Young Ornithologists Club. I still pay my annual subscription to the RSPB. I know the difference between a treecreeper and a nuthatch, and I ensure that the goldfinches and bullfinches in my garden are better fed than my children. But I am in no sense a professional twitcher. I am as out of my league in Costa Rica as Middlesbrough are in the Premier League. It is one of the most biodiverse countries on the planet. It has over 900 known species of bird; that is estimated to be a staggering 10 per cent of the world's total avian population. To put that into perspective, Costa Rica has more bird species than the USA and Canada combined.

In a desperate attempt not to be bottom of the class, I mugged up last night, whilst watching Spanish Tom Cruise, in my *Birds of Costa Rica* (second edition) (I did tell you that I was a limb-barricading, test paper-covering swot), on the two classes of birds that made the strongest impression on me as a child in a distant country full of small dull brown birds: the colourful and sedentary trogons (dual characteristics which I am hoping will make them easy to spot this morning) and the holy grail of avian jewels, the hummingbirds, which I have always been enchanted by.

I needn't have worried about beating my classmates. There is only one other guest who has bothered to get up at 6 a.m. She is a heavy-footed, bird-scaring American. She doesn't have any binoculars and when Biales lends her his, she promptly starts to look at the other properties in the hills and asks, loudly, how much they cost. You see, the problem with Americans is that all of the nice ones tend to stay in their own country.

Biales quickly realises that I am a more willing recipient of his encyclopaedic bird identification knowledge than Sasquatch lady. He must have been a brilliant footballer, as he spots openings and shoots his telescope before the birds ever see us. He motions for me to look through his Swarovski spotting scope. Although he is favouring me, I sense that he is also testing me.

The image is perfect. Yellow belly, dark head, dark underbelly. I know this one.

'I'm not sure exactly which type,' I say modestly, 'but it's definitely a trogon.'

'Great kiskadee,' he replies, and I detect a slight tone of disappointment in his voice.

I have never even heard of kiskadee. I thought she sang 'Don't Go Breaking My Heart' with Elton John.

The American lady is facing the wrong direction, so she doesn't get a go on the Swarovski.

Before I have a chance to recompose myself, Biales has set up his tripod again and given me an open goal. I look through the lens. He increases the pressure on me.

'This is one of my favourites. A real superstar.'

It is a magnificent blue finch-like bird, with the bright morning sun illuminating its sapphire crown and nape. But I am stumped. I am about to wing it and hope that there is a 'blue finch' but then I remember the name of our chalet at Blackberry Farm. My lottery numbers have come up.

'Indigo bunting.'

'Close. Same family, but no, it's a blue grosbeak.'

I think Biales is beginning to understand why I support Middlesbrough. I have had the chances but haven't been able to put them away.

I have always enjoyed onomatopoeic words for their lack of imagination but also for their aural accuracy. Belch. Mumble. Dribble. Thwack. There are highly descriptive words which enhance the English language and, importantly, are tremendous fun to use in connection with elderly relatives. There are also some pretty unimaginative bird spotters who deserve equal praise for devising the likes of cuckoo, chiffchaff, hoopoe and kookaburra. But the person I would like to single out for praise, whoever he or she is, is the person who named our next bird.

It is a horrible crow-like bird with no redeeming qualities. It is not colourful. It has scruffy tail feathers. It steals food from other birds. It eats babies of other birds. It has a harsh, ugly call. It spends much of its time foraging around on the ground. For Harry Potter fans, it is the Dementor of the bird world. Unpopular with everyone, in footballing terms, it is Millwall. In legal terms, it is a tax lawyer. But there is one thing I like very much about this bird: its name. It is called the common grackle. 'Common' is nicely disrespectful, but it is the guttural ugliness and poetic indifference of the onomatopoeic 'grackle' that I most admire.

My favourite opening paragraph in any novel is Vladimir Nabokov's *Lolita*, where the narrator immediately demonstrates his obsession with the girl, through his love of the very sound of her name and the movement of his tongue in forming the word:

'Lo-lee-ta: the tip of the tongue taking a trip of three steps down the palate to tap, at three, on the teeth. Lo. Lee. Ta.'

Whoever named the grackle did not love this bird. Their tongue barely had to flex and they just picked the first and ugliest name that came to mind, a bit like my parents with Geoffrey. Instead, the Costa Rican bird-namers saved their best work for the more deserving resplendent quetzal and the magnificent frigatebird.

I enjoy a memorable morning of bird porn. I see (or rather, Biales sees and points his telescope at them for me): a turquoise-browed motmot (the centrespread of a bird book I once had as a child); a barred antshrike (which is an incredible spot by Biales as to me it looks like a shadow); a long-tailed manakin (which even Biales is excited about and he has seen a lot of bird porn); a squirrel cuckoo; two blue-gray tanagers; multiple white-throated magpie-jays; a black-headed trogon; a splendidly named elegant trogon; and of course grackles, lots of grackles. The American lady, in the meantime, topped up her suntan and told me that she was going to Las Vegas next in her friend's private jet. Some creatures don't deserve wings, or binoculars, or oxygen.

The hummingbirds are difficult to spot and even more difficult to photograph, despite feeding on the nectar of the flowers in our resort. The reason they are so photographically uncooperative is that they are only three or four inches long, which is smaller than the dragonflies and butterflies here. They resemble moonwalking insects, hovering and flying backwards. They are brilliant, iridescent and sparkle like Michael Jackson. I see a cinnamon hummingbird dancing between the flower heads on a bush by our room and I swear its song is 'shamone'. But I fail to photograph anything but blurred flowers. I am not leaving Costa Rica until I capture one in frame and in focus.

Far easier to photograph are turtles. This evening we are going on a turtle-watch. The heavy-footed American bird-scaring lady and her two daughters join us; so do three more American ladies. One of them says she is not leaving Costa Rica until she photographs a turtle. 'How shallow,' I think patronisingly.

Biales is our guide again. He seems un-delighted to see the bird-scarer again. He warns us at the outset that nature is unpredictable and that we might not see any turtles. It is, however, low tide and egg-laying season for olive ridleys, leatherbacks and hawksbills; each female will lay three times over two months, so he says we have a 50 per cent chance. Before I can fathom his mathematics, which sounds like one of those GCSE questions I could never get my head around, Biales turns on his LED flashlight and disappears up the beach, with us trailing his blue tail-light like ambulance chasers.

I once took Jackie badger-watching in West Sussex. It was one of our first dates. I am romantic like that. (At university, I took a girlfriend on holiday by bus to Auschwitz.) We sat, with a National Trust guide, at dusk and had the privilege of watching a family of badgers break cover and come out to feed. It is against the law to disturb a badger sett, which meant that we couldn't go to bed until the last badger had gone to bed. It was like a game of Whack-a-Mole. Every time seemingly the last badger went down his hole, another one popped up, only to be greeted by Jackie with: 'Jaysus, would ye feck off and go to bed, badger.'

The turtle-watch is less bountiful. We walk the length of the beach and back again, the length of the beach and back again.

There are no turtles to whack. Then Biales stops suddenly and crouches down, shining his blue torch at his feet.

'Hermit crabs,' he says. That is about as exciting as finding ants and I feel sympathy for Biales. He is losing the American women. Not physically, unfortunately; they are keeping up, although one of them did tumble down a sand bank, which was worth the admission fee alone. He is losing their interest and they start talking about Vegas again.

He is impatient with their impatience and deposits us all on a row of benches whilst he goes scouring the beach on his own. Once he has left, instead of enjoying the coastal darkness and listening to the waves rolling in from the Pacific Ocean, the iPhone torch lights come out and one of the American women lets out a scream and some wee as she realises her flip-flopped feet are surrounded by crabs.

'Are hermit crabs poisonous?' she asks stupidly.

'Only to people who live in solitude,' I reply. She either doesn't understand or doesn't find me funny, probably both, which is a shame as it is an outstanding joke. I challenge Tony Hawks (the British comedian, not the American skateboarder) to improve on such improvisation.

After ten minutes, Biales returns with a triumphant turtle-tracking grin. He has found an olive ridley, which, he apologises, is the most common type of turtle, but I can forgive him as they are not that common in Haywards Heath. He takes us to her. She is levering herself laboriously out of the ocean and up the beach. Imagine Alaskan Pam in her gossamer wetsuit, on her stomach, with flippers on both her hands and feet, and Bob dressed in armour lying on her back, and that is how arduous it is for the turtle. Except the turtle doesn't bleat and bellyache all the time. We have to keep our distance until she is higher up the beach, has found a dark and quiet spot away from the sea, and has started digging her nest.

When she is ready for us, we form a crescent around her backside and watch with fascination as her two cumbersome rear flippers become far more dexterous at digging a deep hole than my two hands with a plastic handle-snapping spade on Polzeath Beach in Cornwall. She patiently and rhythmically digs, scoops and flicks the sand until she has excavated a one-metre-deep birthing pit and then pats flat the inside of the chamber like a master potter. Biales lays his torch in the sand to cast a blue floodlight up her rear end. And the egg-laying ceremony begins.

It reminds me of a visit to a bar in Bangkok with Mike Turnbull when I was eighteen: ping-pong ball-shaped eggs are fired out of the turtle at a rapid rate, four or five at a time. The American tourists all reach for their iPhones and film the entire spectacle, which will make a bizarre video, not dissimilar to a close-up of the Patpong pros firing ping-pong balls from... the stage. As with the badgers, just as Jackie and I think there can be no more eggs up there, one more pops out. She lays a clutch of over eighty eggs; even the Bangkok vaginal gymnasts would struggle to keep up with that.

It is a much quicker process for the turtle to fill in the sand on top of the eggs and to slap the sand flat. Her underground incubation chamber will protect the eggs from surface predators (such as the toe-nibbling hermit crabs and the black vultures) and will help keep the soft, porous shells moist and at the correct temperature. Then the mother returns to the sea, but she will never return to the nest. Her hatchlings will be on their own now to survive or perish. No feeding them, no teaching them, no transporting them, no swimming lessons, no paying for their schooling and their mistakes. It is an attractive alternative parenting model which I will implement when I eventually establish my cult.

Most of my own ungrateful offspring haven't texted me for days. I regret not leaving them to fend for themselves against the black vultures when they were younger. They all have phones but they only work when they need something. Mimi needs a moan. She texted earlier tonight to tell me that her friend Ollie has been 'asked to leave' sixth form. He was caught on CCTV flicking two fingers behind a teacher's back. CCTV! Come on! That isn't equality of arms. What chance do schoolchildren have these days? If we had CCTV watching us when I was at school, most of my classmates would have been expelled: Steve Chambers for tipping itching powder down the back of Mrs Rushton's neck; Dave Gibbon for concealing a school bell in his desk and ringing it ten minutes early at the last lesson of the day; Nick Ingram for drawing obscene (but highly artistic) images on the school bags of boys he didn't like; 'Chalkie' for stealing French vocab cassettes from the languages lab to record heavy metal compilations; and so on.

My daughters are at least consistent in the company they keep: Meggie's friend was also 'asked to leave' for texting topless photographs of herself to her boyfriend. In her text, Mimi complains to me that she hates one particular teacher who has always had it in for Ollie (it was he who went to the trouble of watching the CCTV tapes). It is only the third day of the new term, so, to be fair to the teacher in question, he can't have hated Ollie for very long. Mimi is worried that Ollie will make new friends at his new school and forget about her. I tell her that on a more positive note I saw a motmot this morning, which doesn't appear to comfort or excite her, so then I offer her some sound paternal guidance, advising her that if she stays in touch with Ollie more regularly than she texts me, then he might not forget about her. I suggest that she gets drunk with him this weekend but avoids any strobe lighting.

When we return from the turtle-watch, Jackie causes much excitement back at the resort by telling the restaurant staff (we are the only guests in the bar, which I hope means the shouty American family have left or drowned) that, earlier, she saw an armadillo in the garden of our villa. It was in truth a member of the raccoon family called a white-nosed coati; they are very common (unlike armadillos), but she is too embarrassed to own up to her mistake. We go back to the villa with a few cock-tails each before anyone can cross-examine us on the armadillo, and watch *Top Gun* in Spanish.

'Siento la necesidad, la necesidad de velocidad.'

# CHAPTER THIRTY-ONE

*Explaining Brexit to a bear and a gecko – pick-up soccer*
*– let-down soccer – Romero's – armadillos*
SOUNDTRACK: FRANK TURNER – 'THE ARMADILLO'

**'G**ood morning, Mistah Red Bull,' says the beach barman with a grin stretching from ear to ear via nose and chin. It is not a nickname of which I am proud, in light of my unrealised pledge to give it up at the start of my sabbatical. But my energy levels are low this morning and my head is rattling around like Toyota parts, due to the after-effects of two dishonestly potent local cocktails, so I accept his offer of the comforting blue and silver can. It has the required invigorating effect and hope dawns on the day once more.

It is not a picturesque scene that we are overlooking from the bar – the beach and the surf are grey and indistinct – but what it lacks in aesthetics, it makes up for in drama. The sand is dark and gritty and interrupted by aggressive rocks; driftwood and body parts regurgitated from the ocean litter the shore; the sea spits a thick mist over the jungled hills; six scarlet macaws paint a stripe of colour across the stormy black sky; the waves churn and challenge anyone to step into them for one final, mortal swim. I don't rise to its challenge but instead sit at the bar, nursing my ice-cold can of Red Bull and my hangover, trying to explain to a honeymooning couple from Texas (they are not in ski gear, Larry) why democracy doesn't work.

Like Donald Trump, the new husband is built like a bear and is also in real estate; the new wife is built like a gecko and, like Melania Trump, is in trouble physically, as her husband is only going to expand. The couple fear what most of the rest of the civilised world is fearing at the moment, that a half-baked, wig-wearing, halfwit, racist misogynist might be walking the corridors of power and rebranding the White House as Trump Turf in a few months' time. Their hope is that America will learn from Britain's recent mistake caused by the 'You Kippers', so they want to understand from me how Brexit happened. I find the reasons difficult to explain, for the same reason that I find it difficult to explain why One Direction were successful, or why a gecko is attracted to a bear: because it defies all logic and reason, I struggle to objectively rationalise it.

It was the Costa Rican, Red Bull-tempting barman who brought up the subject of Brexit upon learning that I am English. It is a topic that has been raised with me regularly throughout my trip. Even the Costa Ricans, the happiest people in the world, are unhappy about the Brexit vote. Americans' reaction to Brexit has been a combination of shock and bewilderment. Everyone wants to know why it happened; I haven't met any Americans on this trip, even the Trump supporters (and there have been plenty of them), who think that Britain leaving the European Union is a good move. Pausing there, even those Americans who are going to vote for a man who can't be trusted with his own Twitter account as their Commander-in-Chief can recognise the stupidity of Britain leaving the EU. I do my best to explain to the bear and the gecko how I think Brexit came about.

An upper-class comedian called Boris used to do a stand-up routine about wanting to be Prime Minister, which we all used to find hilarious. Then for a joke he decided overnight to lead the Leave campaign. He got a campaign bus and wrote some more jokes on the side of it. His former BFF, an upper-class David, was not as funny as Boris. He was Prime Minister, so it didn't matter, because he had to take the campaign a bit more seriously, so he got support to remain from important people who were equally unamusing: the Treasury, the Bank of England, the International Monetary Fund and Barack Obama. David thought that with the support of all of his right-thinking economist friends, he couldn't lose. He didn't get a bus and he banked on telling the truth: that nothing much would change if we voted to remain; a hard sell as English people tend to like change and they certainly like jokes. The real problem is that the English public prefer pranks to politics; they prefer protest to pompous asses; and they prefer themselves to foreign people.

David forgot to tell anyone that if he lost, he would stand down.

Boris forgot to tell anyone that if he won, he would stand down.

Boris won; David lost; they both stood down.

Even a man called Nigel, who had spent the past twenty-five years leading a party who wanted to leave the European Union, stood down as soon as we had. The opposition felt left out, so they asked their man, called Jeremy, to stand down as well: he refused and was the only one who didn't resign (apart from the Lib Dems, who can't afford to have any of their remaining MPs resign).

Meanwhile, someone called Theresa, who nobody knew anything about and who hibernated through the entire referendum campaign, woke up just in time to be asked if she would like to be Prime Minister and negotiate our departure from the EU. She had nothing else to do so she said, 'Alright.' There was no referendum about that. Realising how much the British public like jokes, her first appointment was Boris as Foreign Secretary. There was no referendum about that either.

So now we have a Prime Minister whom nobody knows or voted for and who was expecting her appointment even less than the rest of us, a Foreign Secretary we would rather see on panel shows than in power, and a currency nobody in the rest of the world wants, all because the British public like jokes and dislike foreigners. That is what happens when you allow democracy to make important decisions which would have been better off left to serious people who have been elected to understand the issues. Trust me, don't trust democracy. Treat the threat of Donald Trump being elected as your next President very seriously. It could happen.

I conclude the Brexit discussion, as I have done throughout the trip whenever the topic has come up, by giving the newlywed couple the cellphone number of my neighbour, David, and suggesting that they should call or text him whenever they want, preferably late evening Eastern Standard Time, and ask him to put forward a sensible counter-argument on why it was a good idea to vote to leave. I tell them it won't cost them much in connection charges as it shouldn't be a very long call. The main argument in favour of Leave was 'We Want Our Country Back'; Donald Trump wants to 'Make America Great Again'. His jingoism, protectionism and isolationism have a worryingly familiar feel and might just prevail.

Whilst I have been lamenting the mystifying Brexit decision, symbolically it has started to rain. The rain that falls during a single shower of the rainy season in Costa Rica would submerge Southern Rail for a week without travel. Costa Ricans, on the other hand, use the time undercover to design a few new dangerous cocktails, sit back, content in their world-leading happiness, and enjoy the fresh concoctions and thunder and lightning, before carrying on as normal (albeit a bit squiffier).

It is normal on a Tuesday for there to be a football match at 5 p.m. in the local village. Anyone can play, so I am signed up. It is called 'pick-up soccer'. As the rain hammers around us in the shelter of the beach bar's wicker roof, I ask the barman, who plays each week, why it is called 'pick-up', which makes it sound more like rugby. His answer is succinct but not very illuminating.

'Because that is how the Spanish word translates into English.'

Literal translations are never a good idea. At university, my Welsh friend Lucy was dating a German. She went to stay with his parents in Bavaria. It was the first time she had met them. They cooked a meal for her; things were going well. She spoke a little German but was not yet fluent; at the end of the meal, she made a brave attempt to translate into German the common English phrase 'I am full'.

'Ich bin voll,' she declared, to express her digestive contentment.

'I am pregnant,' is what her boyfriend's parents, for that particular region of Bavaria, understood her to mean. It was a memorable first impression.

I think that in this case 'pick-up soccer' must mean 'free-for-all soccer'; that anyone can play, even 46-year-old lawyers who haven't played a competitive match for over a decade. I have, however, been in training for the game. I did half an hour on the treadmill this morning, humiliating Poppa Sloth (who it appears has neither left nor drowned) by setting my speed at twelve when he was only on ten; did some stretches that came quite close to my toes; and finished off with a granola breakfast. I am match-fit.

But when the rain and experimental cocktails stop and I return to my room, there is a message for me that the game, like a Southern train, has been cancelled due to rain. I kill the match time by, fittingly, watching Tom Cruise in Spanish *Cocktail* instead.

On the kind recommendation of the bear and the gecko, we decide to eat in the nearby village at a restaurant called Romero's. The population of the village is one hundred and fifty; the population of the restaurant is six: the couple who own it, their two young daughters, Jackie and me. I am looking forward to an intimate meal when twenty other customers join us to watch the Costa Rica *v.* Ecuador World Cup qualifier. I become suspicious. They are all wearing dirty, wet football kits. It seems that they have mistranslated the Spanish word, which in fact means 'up yours soccer'.

The restaurant owner (confusingly called Miguel rather than Romero), a handsome, stubbly, ebullient, likeable local with entrepreneurial flair and hair, is a football fan (he has no doubt just played in the village match as well, to make up the twenty-one) and is offering free shots for every goal scored by Costa Rica. Just before half-time, they take the lead. I am hoping they don't score again: the shots are Bloody Awful Marys, with red chilli and Tabasco. He proudly compares them to 'the blood of a bull'. I would prefer another Red Bull.

The food is authentically delicious Costa Rican tapas. Miguel used to work at our resort as a barman. He is a much better cook than he is cocktail mixer. He suggested to the resort owners that they should vary the menu to provide more local dishes. They didn't agree, so he set up on his own. Either that, or the owners tasted his bull's blood cocktails.

He proudly explains that he opened his restaurant less than a year ago and everyone in the village has eaten at it; importantly, more than once. But not all at once, as there are only five tables. And they don't all have chairs. I can, however, see why the locals return: it is a friendly, informal place; like visiting an open house rather than a restaurant. There is also an art gallery of paintings by his wife and, unpredictably, an Alaskan artist friend, as well as a help-yourself bar out the back. The kitchen is open-plan so that Miguel can watch and commentate on the football as he cooks. The place has the feeling of a village social club, and given that there is nowhere else to be social, other than at the Coca-Cola sign or the cliquey football pitch, I hope and believe that he will make a success of it. Costa Rica score two more goals in short succession in the second half, so we make our excuses and leave before Miguel can make any more shots.

When we get back to the resort, we discover that the turtle-watch tonight was abandoned in favour of searching for armadillos on the resort. Unsurprisingly, they didn't find any.

# CHAPTER THIRTY-TWO

*Day 40: Departure*

SOUNDTRACK: WILCO – 'HUMMINGBIRD'

I finally manage to photograph one in focus. It is a brilliant shot of a green hummingbird. I look up the species in my trusty and now well-thumbed *Birds of Costa Rica* (second edition). It is called a green-crowned brilliant hummingbird. On the With Water On Both Sides Peninsula, I have succeeded in taking a brilliant picture of a brilliant hummingbird. I feel absolutely absolute. Now I can go home.

This is Day 40 of my 41-day trip. There is nothing left on Steve's itinerary other than 'Day 41: Welcome Home'. I have mixed emotions. I will miss not being on the road and I will certainly miss America and its people, but it will be nice to see some of my family and some of my friends again. David my neighbour is not one of them; with characteristic empathy and syntactic error, he sends me a text saying, 'You should of had longer off.'

He follows this up with another irritating text, anticipating how much I must be looking forward to my commute back to work: 'The 06.29 Thameslink has new rolling stock. 12 cars open down the middle from one end to the other like the new Tube trains. Seats are close together and hard, so most suitable for people with short legs and ample backside padding, like you.'

My mother texts two sad-face, crying emojis. It worries me that she knows what an emoji is and I lose any respect remaining for her after the New York trip.

Mimi texts to say: 'Poor Daddy; seven weeks not enough?' I can't place the waspish, sarcastic side of her nature.

I have a final cocktail in the infinity pool (the irony is not lost on me) and start talking to a new arrival, a senior executive at an adhesives company in Rhode Island, a state which it has never occurred to me to visit. To be fair, he probably has no intention of visiting Haywards Heath either. His pasty, almost translucent complexion indicates to me that he is not a native American. His name confirms this: he is Seamus from Dublin. He has lived in the States for twenty years and neither lost an accent nor gained a tan. I ask him whether he will ever live back in Ireland.

'I will in my ass.' I know from Jackie that this is Irish for 'no'.

I am about to ask him why not, but I think I know. Dying in Ireland, he might well get five hundred people at his funeral, but he's here for a good time not for a long time and it's where he does his living that counts. And I am envious that where he now lives is America; one of the most diverse, dramatic, breathtaking and naturally preserved countries on the planet.

As my connecting flight takes off from Atlanta to Heathrow later that night, I pray to Charmaine's God that Seamus's new countrymen don't fuck it all up by electing a man called Donald J. Trump as their 45th President.

# CHAPTER THIRTY-THREE

*The parting of the ways – Sheikh Zayed – the difference*
*between Gallifreyans and Hartlepudlians*
SOUNDTRACK: THOMPSON TWINS – 'DOCTOR! DOCTOR!'

I have always known that travelling as the Doctor's companion could not last for ever. The Doctor has a track record of
severing all ties. He plucks his companions unexpectedly from
their ordinary routines and takes them on fantastic adventures
to distant planets. He shows them new worlds, new species and
opens their eyes to new outlooks. Their lives will never be the
same again, but eventually, inevitably, he will abandon them all
to normality (or get them killed).

It happened to Rose Tyler, when the Doctor left her standing
heartbroken on the beach of Bad Wolf Bay, unable to tell her
that he loved her.

It happened to Martha Jones, when she realised her unre-
quited love for the Doctor (who was still pining for Rose) could
never be requited. After a year of walking the earth, spreading
the Doctor's name and saving the planet from the Master, she
grew out of the Doctor and returned to her family.

It happened to the magnificent Donna Noble, when she
touched the Doctor's regenerated hand, which transferred Time

Lord DNA to her, transforming her into the Doctor Donna to defeat the Daleks and their reality bomb, but at such a cost to her sanity that she started talking in binary and the Doctor had to save her with a mind-wipe.

It happened to Amy Pond, when she allowed the Weeping Angels to send her back in time for ever so that she could be with her husband Rory, who had died… again.

Most tragically, it happened to Clara Oswald, the impossible girl, when she took a chronolock which killed the one branded with it. When it counted down to zero, the helpless Doctor didn't have a plan to save her.

And now, as inevitable as it was for each of those companions, the parting of the ways comes for the Tenth Doctor and me. After returning from the States, I have treated myself to a long weekend to visit an old friend in Abu Dhabi as a final hedonistic hurrah before becoming a solicitor again. It is at Sheikh Zayed Mosque that it happens to me, and my own bond with the Doctor is finally broken.

Neither because he is a security threat to Muslims nor because time travellers disrupt the karmic ley line of Sheikh Zayed Mosque is my plastic figurine of the Tenth Doctor denied admission. Unlike me, his knees are not showing. But instead he is impolitely categorised by the security guard as a toy. If I want to enter the mosque, I will have to hand over my figurine.

It is an agonising way to conclude my sabbatical but it's how the Doctor would have wanted to end it. Time travelling can only be in perpetuity for Gallifreyans. I am Hartlepudlian. We have voyaged across some wondrous states and scenery, the Doctor and I, but it is time to say farewell to my old friend. It feels right. I take one final photograph of him waving goodbye outside the mosque before surrendering him to the bemused security guard. My journey is coming to an end. Our parting of the ways gives me closure. The Tenth Doctor must continue his journey across the space–time continuum as a lonely warrior.

He has new worlds to save, whereas I must return to my desk at EC4 to save my old career.

# CHAPTER THIRTY-FOUR

*Favourite suit – a new hope dashed – some resolutions
– some Red Bull – Tom Hanks*
SOUNDTRACK: BOB DYLAN
– 'IT'S ALL OVER NOW, BABY BLUE'

I t is Saturday morning. I am back home in West Sussex, making preparations for when I return to work after the weekend. I check my favourite suit and it dawns on me how tragic it is to have a favourite suit. A favourite child is acceptable, but a favourite suit? It is a little dusty, but still intact apart from the inside jacket pocket, which is ripped and hanging off through excessive BlackBerry reaching. I contemplate reaching for the scissors and clipping my tie (or, more radically, my BlackBerry) for ever like Eric from LA, but I am not brave enough or cool enough to do that, man. I check the Southern Rail online timetable: it is lying to me, telling me that there is a normal service next week with no disruptions. That is an oxymoronic description for Southern Rail. If there are no disruptions, it can't be a normal service. I check the weather forecast for Monday. It is going to be sunny and windy. 'Ah yes,' I think, reminded of Kalman Kaplan's prophetic New York diary, 'but there might be agitation in the wind.'

Kalman Kaplan remains elusive. He never did reply to my email. Perhaps he is just a rude American lawyer after all. If this book is ever turned into a film, I will write him out of the script. Tom Hanks can play me, please. Charmaine will play herself, as no one does it better.

I try to persuade myself that I have got travelling out of my system for another twenty years and that I am now content to be returning to work, in a world bereft of Bowie and Prince. I look for the positives about being back. I like my house in Haywards Heath. I particularly like the new kitchen in which I am sitting as I write this, as I have recently had it designed and extended by an interior designer called James Reckless, who, overcoming the affliction of his surname, did a cautious but imaginative job. Americans would have fun with his name: surely even they couldn't think he is called Reckless James. If I could spend the rest of my career in my kitchen, listening to the birds, then I would be content.

But even the contentment of a new kitchen cannot stop the doubts from setting in that there might be more to life than the law. Despite the impact of Brexit on the property market, I convince myself that my new kitchen must have increased the value of my house. I think of Seamus in the Costa Rican pool bar. He did it: he made the break from his country of birth, moved to America and has never looked back. I do a Google search for houses for sale on Jones Street, Savannah. I find one that I like at 7 East Jones Street. The estate agent describes it as prestigious. I will be a former City of London lawyer, the former rhythm guitarist of East Kent's favourite covers band; that should set the Savannahian socialite gossips alight. Hopefully they will regard me as a prestigious new neighbour and want to bake me muffins. It is fitting that I should have a prestigious property in which to receive them and their muffins. 7 East Jones Street is white and wooden, just as an American house should be. Built in 1850, it has been meticulously restored and updated, with a veranda, original hardwood floors, stained glass windows and a carriage house. It could easily have featured in *Midnight in the Garden of Good and Evil*. Those shaded squares and that sedate pace of life could soon be mine. This is it. *Episode IV – A New Hope*. Pass me the scissors.

The new hope is dashed on Sunday when I receive the purchase price by email. It makes Blackberry Farm look like good value. I realise that I may have to stay in Haywards Heath and commute to London for another hundred years after all. I could always supplement my income, to accelerate an early retirement, by becoming a time-away inn-sitter and doing walking tours of Crawley. Crawley has untapped tourist potential as the hometown of The Cure so there might be a gap in the market for American tourists there; I could sell The Cure T-shirts. If successful, I could branch out to Haywards Heath, the hometown of Suede. I am not going to let the denial of my Savannah migration get me down. Haywards Heath is where my kids are. It is where my spare-kids are. It is where my two miniature dachshunds and their two ill-disciplined miniature bladders are. It might be a town where no one knows my name, but when they find it out they will at least know which way round it goes. 'Bury My Heart at Haywards Heath' doesn't quite have the same ring to it as Wounded Knee but I might adopt it as the alternative title to this book.

The cast of people I met in America will already have moved on to their next walk-on parts in other people's lives. Some will remain Facebook friends and will occasionally send me photographs of their dinner. Most will be preserved only in this book and would otherwise have flown like Jackie's and Jacques's transient butterflies.

They have all played their part: the population of Youghal and Knockanore for showing their respects to Ann Foley and eating her ham sandwiches; the stony-faced, stone-hearted Border Protectors (watch your backs, guys, be nice to the customs customers, the self-service fingerprint machines are coming); Joe le Taxi; Mr Benn's underground 'as if by magic' hoteliers; Kalman Kaplan and his apocryphal journal; the cameraman for *Fast & Furious 8*, who must have known that he had five extra extras in shot; Ron and Sarin, the Seattle double act; the various Jeff Stewart imposters (never did get that fireplace, Jeff); the cast and crew of the *Wilderness Adventurer* (with a special mention for Ranger Dan, who was welcomed by neither but provided so much unintentional amusement to both); Katharine Ross and the Mexican moth killers; the toothless Steinbeck strawberry vendor who is expecting me back in the spring when it is so much more 'purty'; Carmen and Jeb and his Model T pace of life; the condescending concierge from Mr C's and the plate-eating-accuser at the Cheesecake Factory; Eric and John, our trippy LA tour guide and his henchman who only came to life at the mention of kidnapping; the tour-of-duty Nashville bass player who could spontaneously burst into Wilco; Jim Carrey and Jack Black and their honky-tonk band at Robert's bar; the pretty receptionist at the Hermitage Hotel and the waitress who served my first and last ever grits; the mint-denying missionaries on the bridge; the country music-loving US marshal from Knoxville, Tennessee; Sheriff Duke and his lenient road traffic sentencing; Mike and his new hip in Savannah; country music legends Kacey Musgraves, Brandy Clark and Connie Smith; the pumpkin-headed front-row doofus (and his new, small ulcer); Biales, the bird-spotting bandy-legged footballer; Miguel and his Bloody Awful Marys; and Seamus the glue-seller from Dublin.

I tell myself that I need to draw from the people I have met, to extract their best qualities and to learn from my experiences during my work-free, care-free, time-liberated travels. I dig out my list of objectives. Like my daughter Mary in a maths test, I will have to settle for four out of ten. Photographing a hummingbird proved rather tricky and was an accomplishment in itself, but the other three were surprisingly easy. I did get to meet someone called Jedidiah; well, Jeb, but that is near enough as I have since found out that it is an abbreviation of Jebediah. I have indeed written a book. This is it. As you can probably tell, it didn't take too long and wasn't too difficult to write. But thank you for reading it; that is very sweet of you. Finally, and most importantly, I did find some nice Americans. Aside from the Border Protectors and the lawyers, most of them are nice, as it happens: happy, witty, approachable, welcoming, helpful and hospitable, regardless of their politics. I haven't quite discovered the Higgs boson; it is not the most penetrating piece of research ever conducted; but I am content with the result and have a warm feeling in my trousers about America again.

Heating my hands in my pockets, I make some important resolutions.

From now on, I will open my eyes. I will stop to listen and take in my surroundings. I don't need to always follow the paths and won't be afraid to make new trails (armed with hairspray).

I will enjoy the butterflies and look up at the trees. I may not see any flying bears, but that's not the point.

I will give up Red Bull. Seriously, I will. I might even go for a run every day before work.

I will share the enthusiasm of the American service sector. If someone thanks me for something (unlikely with American lawyers), I will emphasise my willingness to help with an 'absolutely' or an 'of course'.

I will be a more considerate, patient person. At this point in the narrative, Jackie rudely asks me if this has now turned into a work of fiction. But I am determined to celebrate people's strengths, not flaunt their flaws. And if they have flaws, I will be more forgiving of them, even if they are American lawyers. I can't promise not to lampoon them, though: that would be harder than giving up Red Bull.

I will be more Christian in my values, although I haven't made the best of starts. Charmaine kindly texts me on Sunday morning to remind me that I return to work on Monday and to ask me if I have changed. I respond with a photograph of me inside Sheikh Zayed Mosque dressed in my kandoora (a mandatory white dress lent to me by the Doctor-stealing Muslim security guard in order to cover my offensive chicken legs) and tell her that I will not be returning to work as I have converted to Islam and now have very different values, which I can no longer reconcile with being a City lawyer.

'What!!! You had better be joking?' is her unsure response.

In fact, I have not converted to Islam, but it remains to be seen whether I can reconcile my new considerate, eyes-wide-open, time-valuing self with being a City lawyer for another ten years.

It is Sunday night and Jackie is doing her best to console me before my final sleep before work. She even buys me a Red Bull and a packet of Revels (I will give up tomorrow). We view our photo slide show together. She asks what I will miss the most. In abstract terms, I will miss that sense of perfect freedom, of having no real demands on my time or what I need to do each day, of not being shackled by smart-timers to six-minute chargeable units, of not fretting about where the next big piece of litigation will come from to help me hit my billing target for the year. I will of course miss the Tenth Doctor, but I know that he will have regenerated by now and replaced me with a younger companion. But in terms of places, I surprise myself with my answer. Nashville and Savannah are the obvious candidates for their fabulous music, hospitality and architecture; Yosemite for the most breathtaking, primordial scenery I have ever seen, even if the bears let me down; visiting the scene and home of the Sundance Kid was an ambition fulfilled, even if Katharine Ross didn't let her hair down for me; watching a turtle dig her nest and lay her eggs in Costa Rica was phenomenal despite the American iPhones stuck up her backside; watching the peacocks of LA flaunt their nest eggs with their heads stuck up their own backsides was a voyeuristic pleasure; despite Jackie's assertion, the Great Smoky Mountains were far from shite; but when it comes down to it, what I will miss most is the *Wilderness Adventurer*, not for the untouched beauty and the vast wilderness of Alaska, but for the nice Americans we met, the stories they told and, simply put, the sense of belonging and community.

So here I go again. One final push to retirement. Another ten years of soliciting and Southern Rail. With a heavy heart,

I switch my BlackBerry back on and the incoming emails immediately assault me, the number counter rapidly resembling an electricity meter reading. Whoever has sent them can wait until morning and seethe all they like. I set my alarm for 5.45 a.m. I log onto Facebook before finally turning off the bedside light. My photo of the Tenth Doctor waving goodbye at the mosque has gone viral and now has a staggering twenty-three likes. I notice an outstanding friend request. It is from Pam in Durham, North Carolina. I go to ignore her. My hand hovers. I ask myself what Tom Hanks would do... and click accept.

The End (or a Fresh Start…)

# ACKNOWLEDGEMENTS

Having a grown-up book published which is not about the law is an exciting development and ambition realised for me, so in truth I am grateful to anyone who buys or even reads it, especially you (who I have always liked).

Besides you for buying it, there are others on the list.

Firstly, I would like to thank all the decent, charming, intelligent and hospitable Americans who, despite going on to elect Donald Trump, welcomed me throughout my travels and who don't deserve the hysterical treatment they are currently receiving at the hands of the international media. I am hoping that in a small way the affectionate portrayal of everyday American people contained in these pages will help redress the balance. I include within that the numerous American clients and lawyers with whom I have worked, who will, I hope, forgive me for the fun I have had at their expense in the early chapters.

I am grateful also to the partners of my firm for having the thickness of skin and the sense of humour to indulge my desire to exaggerate the internal workings of law firms in the interests of satire. That said, I will freely admit (under oath, if necessary) that the views expressed in this book are entirely my own and are in no way representative of my firm or my senior partner in particular, who has asked me to emphasise that he loves all

American corporate lawyers and doesn't find them belligerent or irritating in the slightest.

You can stop reading this page now unless you know your name appears – I would like to thank all of the following individuals for reading and sometimes enjoying the early drafts: Theo Barclay; Tony Hawks (whose *Round Ireland with a Fridge* is still for me the high-water mark); Abigail Amey; Guy Morpuss QC; Andy Millmore; Simone Potter; Steve Wilson of LateralLife (for putting together such a terrific trip for me); Clark Hood; Catherine Wolfe; Katherine Roseveare; Shelagh and David Hodkinson; Chris and Dani Williams; Matt Jones; Mike Turnbull; Jeremy and Margarita from the Wilderness Adventurer (for laughing so unexpectedly and violently); none of my kids, my mother or my sister (who were all too busy to read it and preferred to wait until it appeared in published format rather than being of any use to me); all those male friends to whom I sent a draft but who never commented or to my knowledge even read it, thereby forgoing the opportunity for their names to appear in print; and my spare-children Shauna and Jamie in recognition of their comparatively few mentions in the book but who can be main characters in the sequel instead.

All of the events described in this book actually happened and all of the people depicted are real people. I have only felt it necessary to change a few names in the book in order to protect individual privacy, so I would be obliged if everyone else featuring in it (particularly my mother) would read it with the playful spirit in which it is intended and refrain from suing me.

Finally, special thanks go to three special people without whom this book could not have happened: the wonderful

Charmaine for running my life and for quietly becoming the best supporting role of the narrative; my editor Olivia at Biteback for her enthusiasm and support and for taking a risk on a book which stubbornly refuses to fit into any particular genre; and of course Jackie, who regularly reminds me that without her I would never have the time to be able to write, paint or play my feckin' guitar. Sorry I prevented you from seeing any bears. I am thankful to you all. Now, if you will excuse me, I have a sequel to write... I am going In Search of Paradise (and there are twenty-seven places in America which claim to be just that).

# ABOUT THE AUTHOR

**G**eoff Steward has been in the legal profession for a quarter of a century. He does not wear a wig but specialises in litigation, with a focus on intellectual property, sports and competition law. He writes in his spare time and has published a legal text and a children's novel.

He spreads himself between West Sussex and north Cornwall and enjoys spending time with his guitars, his children and his spare-children. He does not want any more children, but there is always room for one more guitar in his life.